Hollywood and Whine

By Boze Hadleigh

The Films of Jane Fonda
Conversations With My Elders
Hispanic Hollywood
Leading Ladies (UK)
Hollywood Babble On
Hollywood Lesbians
Bette Davis Speaks
Hollywood Gays
The Lavender Screen (updated edition)
Sing Out! (formerly *The Vinyl Closet*)

Hollywood and Whine

The Snippy, Snotty, and Scandalous Things Stars Say About Each Other

BOZE HADLEIGH

A Birch Lane Press Book
Published by Carol Publishing Group

For Ronnie,
and in memory of Rusty—
all cats go to heaven

A Birch Lane Book
Published by Carol Publishing Group
Birch Lane Press is a registered trademark of Carol Communications, Inc.

Editorial, sales and distribution, rights and permissions inquiries should be addressed to Carol Publishing Group, 120 Enterprise Avenue, Secaucus, N.J. 07094.

In Canada: Canadian Manda Group, One Atlantic Avenue, Suite 105, Toronto, Ontario M6K 3E7

Carol Publishing Group books may be purchased in bulk at special discounts for sales promotion, fundraising, or educational purposes. Special editions can be created to specifications. For details, contact Special Sales Department, Carol Publishing Group, 120 Enterprise Avenue, Secaucus, N.J. 07094.

Manufactured in the United States of America
10 9 8 7 6 5 4 3 2 1

Library of Congress Cataloging-in-Publication Data

Hollywood and whine : the snippy, snotty, and scandalous things stars
   say about each other / [compiled by] Boze Hadleigh.
         p.   cm.
      "A Birch Lane Press book."
      ISBN 1–55972–473–0 (hardcover)
      1. Motion picture actors and actresses—Quotations.   I. Hadleigh,
   Boze.
   PN1994.9.H65   1998
   791.43'028'0922—dc21   98–19916
                                                                    CIP

Contents

Acknowledgments

Thanks are definitely due to a loyal and eagle-eyed corps of quote collectors on five continents, whether or not all the material they sent or transmitted was used here:

Linda Fresia and Michael Callen, Gillian Castlereagh, Samson DeBrier, Shige Endo, Bill Everson, Martin Greif, Ronald Haver, Jim Kepner, Ginette Lelong, Jacques Levis, Consuelo Montiel, Toshi Nishihara, James Pitula, Bob Randall, Paul Rosenfeld, Leonardo Rossi, Bob Thompson, Angela Thorne-Bardry, Yolanda Cisneros Verdugo, Wayne Warga and Rachel Fried Zimmerman. May your paths be strewn with roses, minus the thorns or pricks, as the case may be.

Preface

Celebrities have been called America's royalty. Like the "royals," they are publicized, scrutinized, and sometimes lionized. They serve as fantasy figures, icons of envy or desire, and even role models.

Nowadays there are more celebs than ever. As the general population has exploded, so has the constellation of highly paid, media-wide actors, models, types, and—occasionally—personalities. Their mythic auras and cultural reach may pale beside those of the classical Hollywood stars featured in this author's prior *Hollywood Babble On,* but if their salaries are no longer relatively modest, neither are the newer stars. Old strictures against saying too much, let alone anything controversial, are gone with the wind.

However, this book's other focus is fame itself, and its changing nature. If fame seems more attainable to more numbers and sorts of people than ever before, its pitfalls and perils are also more evident—partly because the subjects, and victims, of fame are more vocal about nearly all aspects of their public and private lives. The travails and—sometimes literally—the trials of being famous and marketable are universally apparent via gossip and media, tabloid TV, entertainment "news," and real headlines.

The fact is, today's celebrities are more vulnerable to litigation, prying, public complaints and backlashes, and intrusions by paparazzi and videorazzi, or even stalkers and potential murderers. Scandal and/or danger may lurk around the next corner or unlucky turn (something as unforeseen as a Kennedy or a showbiz Congressman fatally skiing into a tree).

Some of the rich and infamous seem to create their own problems through self-indulgence or reckless behavior: the jail-bound Christian Slaters and Robert Downey Jr.s, the violent—and too often unrepentant—

actors and athletes, the wife beaters and girlfriend batterers, ad nauseam.

Other famous figures have little if any choice in negative publicity matters: Celebrities are hounded and even goaded by videostalkers out to make *Hard Copy* and hard cash, or by lunatics intent on creating temporary headlines at anyone else's cost. Gianni Versace had a showy home on an easily accessible Miami street, but no bodyguards to protect its carefree foreign owner. Princess Diana, perhaps the classic media victim, was virtually driven to her death by the pursuing eyes of the world press and the apparent overreaction of her less media-savvy companion, who dabbled in high-profile Western women and the coveted limelight.

Thanks to news stories and candid celebrity comments, today's public is well aware that fame may be attended by misfortune as well as fortune, and that acclaim can quickly morph into automatically cynical media reaction (e.g., against Barbra Streisand, Roseanne, Demi Moore, ad femina), into contempt or amused contempt (celebs from Pee-Wee Herman to Dennis Rodman) or even, in some quarters, would-be bashing, blacklisting, and boycott (as with Ellen DeGeneres, who was uniquely brave enough to tell the truth while not on the way up or the way down).

No longer does it surprise or puzzle us that the other side of the stellar coin often entails jealousy, malice, and persecution, or that the more renowned the figure, the more suddenly vulnerable the potential victim. Such extremes are fortuantely still the exception. Yet fame and fortune's mixed blessings continue shifting in our expanding leisure culture and corporatized society wherein celebrity names, images, and tie-ins mean increased revenue, raised circulation, reflected glory, and magnetic success.

To the readers: Happy reading, and remember, true success is measured on a daily basis, not on *Daily Variety*.

★ *The Glamorous Life* ★

Goldfish Bowl

The classic movie star pattern is that the public loves you when you're on the way up, they dislike or hate you when you've reached the top, and they like or are indifferent to you while you're slipping. By which time they're busy admiring and rooting for newer stars.

—Vivien Leigh (Scarlett O'Hara in *Gone With the Wind*)

There was this, I believe, eighteenth century Talmudic scholar who said something on the line of, "If you want to live long, don't become famous."

—Woody Allen

The very first movie star was Florence Lawrence. They made money out of her until she was accidentally disfigured on the job, then Hollywood dumped her. Several years later, she killed herself by eating ant-paste.

—director Mitchell Leisen (*Lady in the Dark*)

I grieve for Princess Diana. We all do....The nature of fame has gotten more and more potentially frightening. If I were a young person starting out today, I doubt I would seek the same path.   —Angela Lansbury

The murder of Gianni Versace shows how vulnerable we all are. Those in the public glare, and people who inadvertently become involved with someone jealous or deranged. It's not a very safe world anymore.

—Madonna (Versace apparently did not know his murderer)

There are these absolutely irresponsible people who sell addresses. You can buy a magazine today—I'd like to go and shoot these people myself!—with celebrities' home addresses in it....It's a scary world.

—Sally Field (*Forrest Gump*)

There should be, and I predict there will be, laws against what can only be termed the stalker-azzi. The question is, how many famous people will have to die before we see those laws!   —videorazzi victim Alec Baldwin

★

The paparazzi, they're the worst! They literally want the worst to happen to you—they want to live off your tragedy, your accident, your suicide, your death, even.   —Joan Rivers

★

I regard [fame] with skepticism. If it were to snowball into something worse, I'd stop. Stop acting. Why would you do it? Why would you put yourself through it? Pointless. If being famous takes your life away, then stop being famous. Say no. Walk away. Simple.
          —Emma Thompson (*Howards End*), before the death of Princess Diana

★

I had a lot of problems with people following me home, literally people trying to run me off the freeway, getting into accidents. It was nuts. I...got another car with tinted windows...now I don't say what kind of car I drive.
          —Kirk Cameron

★

What's awful about being famous and being an actress and being petite is when people come up to you and touch you. That's scary, and they just seem to think it's okay to do it, like you're public property.   —Winona Ryder

★

People will say, right in front of you, "Oh, she's not as pretty as I thought. It must be makeup or something. Or the cameras." They say this as if I'm a mannequin, not a breathing human being.
          —Cheryl Tiegs, 1970s supermodel

★

My image on those [magazine] covers was retouched. They made me more perfect than I was. I feel bad about that now. The point was to have people buy the products and buy the magazines....We did an episode about that on [*Cybill*]....The show said what I really wanted to say. When I was a model, I never looked *that* good, and I don't want to keep the lie going.
          —Cybill Shepherd

★

If you're beautiful and particularly if you're blonde, men will try and redo your private life for you. But if you're also famous, then you won't have much private life, and your face and body on photographs will be a commodity everyone is trying to grab from you.

—Sharon Tate, model-turned-actress and murder victim

The British are the worst...appalling. I've been really shocked by the behavior of the British press. Richard Gere went out to dinner with Uma Thurman. They're old friends. Uma left the restaurant and she gets shoved up against a railing by journalists trying to get her photograph. She gets a cut above her eye that needed stitches. And his driver gets stabbed in the stomach trying to get them out. What's going on? For what?

—Julia Ormond

First off, the press lies. Romance sells more stories, so any time it's a guy and a girl and one of them's famous—preferably both—the photos and the stories say they're in love...and it's very convenient for gay and lesbian stars trying to pass. They don't have to try very hard; the whole media does it all for them! —Howard Rollins (*Ragtime*)

There was one night when Jim [Carrey] and I went out to dinner and [the paparazzi] followed us. Then they were trying to follow us home and take pictures of us driving in the car, and in order to do that they were driving in the opposite lane of traffic, causing other drivers to swerve off the road while they were trying to take pictures.

So what do we do at that point? Do we pull over in the car and give them their photo opportunity so that innocent people don't get killed? It's the most bizarre thing. —Lauren Holly

The videorazzi are the worst. They try to provoke you into bad behavior or even a fight, so they can sell it to *Hard Copy*. There ought to be a law....

—Tony Danza

People follow me around, especially photographers. They want to see who I'm with...like if it's another girl. Or they'll hang around a few hours, to try and see if I'm leaving with the person I arrived with!

—Drew Barrymore

Actors live in a cocoon of praise. They never meet the people who don't like them. —Sir Robert Morley

If you play bad characters, some of the moviegoers will want to insult you. But it really depends how you carry yourself. And if you're a star, then the most they'll usually do is give you a dirty look....Fortunately for me, I'm known for my versatility, so people are usually quite impressed.

—Bette Davis

To understand those days, you must consider that people believed what they saw on the screen....Audiences thought the stars were the way they saw them. Why, women kicked my photographs as they went into the theaters where my pictures were playing, and once on the streets of New York a woman called the police because her child spoke to me.

—silent-screen star and "vamp" Theda Bara

★

We are paid too much. But we're also judged too harshly and too quickly. If we make a supposedly controversial statement, next day we may have half the nation hating our guts. Which most of the time amounts to bigotry fueled by jealousy.

—card-carrying ACLU member and Oscar winner Burt Lancaster

★

In the 1950s my wife [Simone Signoret] and I were denied entry into the United States because of our [liberal] politics...and people were denied entry to work as actors for several reasons, usually politics or being homosexual, as happened to Sir John Gielgud [who was entrapped by London police]. —Yves Montand

It's a standard procedure, really, to be more guarded when speaking to the American press. They're more censorious there, so we save our franker or more provocative quotes for the papers and magazines elsewhere. Just as European releases of Hollywood pictures may contain more nudity than the American release....We tolerate more nudity than they do, but they tolerate more violence than we do.

—British actor Michael Rennie (*The Day the Earth Stood Still*)

★

The one thing I find sad when I come to Los Angeles is realizing that it is populated by millions of people who want to be actors and never will be....It's a particularly American thing, I think, to advise people to follow their dreams. You ought to be very careful about advising such things, because people have all kinds of entirely unrealistic dreams. As a result, so many people think of themselves as losers, which is the worst thing you can be called in America. If you divide society into winners and losers, 98 percent of the people will feel like losers.

—Sam Neill (*The Piano, The Horse Whisperer*)

★

Since the beginning of celebritydom, people have wanted to know gossip. Gossip was around in the Roman era. Everybody wanted to know if Julius Caesar was gay. I know sometimes I thrive on it. You hear, "Oh, Princess Di...." You hear so-and-so left his wife. "Are you kidding me?!" It's so foul, but we all want to know certain things.

—Laura Dern in the early '90s (Caesar was bisexual, as Shakespeare acknowledged)

★

Gossiping is my favorite thing—at the very least, my *second* favorite thing.

—Ivana Trump, ex-wife of Donald Trump

★

I love and adore gossip. I'd take a juicy bitch at lunch over a guy in bed anytime.

—Joan Rivers

★

I remember one time I went to an awards ceremony with a woman, and exact conversations that we had had during that evening were [later] in print. I called her up thinking she must have told somebody. They paid off the limousine drivers! So the limo drivers either recorded what we said or remembered specific quotes in the conversations.

—William Baldwin

★

What gets me is the double standard. Everyone blows off steam at times, maybe makes a bit of a scene, says a curse word or two. Other people figure you're having a bad moment, a bad day...they judge you on your usual behavior, not the outburst. Not so for the poor celebrity! That curse word or scene, after it's reported or printed or televised, becomes how millions of people perceive you from then on. You tell me, is that fair?

—frequently temperamental Dawn Steel, former president of Columbia Pictures

★

I, like many of his fans, am pulling for Pee-Wee Herman. But his fate is out of our hands.... One newspaper headline read, and this is true, "Pee-Wee's Porno Pee-Pee Controver-See!" Do you know that since the scandal, the value of a Pee-Wee Herman doll has gone up—no pun intended—from $40 to $150? But the only offer of work he's gotten since then is from Tim Burton, who's directing a sequel to *Batman*.... We laugh at how old-fashioned a "morals charge" sounds these days, but being arrested for one can still ruin your career, in show business or out of it, and that's *not* funny.

—ICM agent Eric Shepard

One thing about how the media likes to show us at our worst is, you figure why be on best behavior all the time when all it takes is one slip-up?

—Robert Downey Jr., who has slipped up often

The paparazzi make bigger bucks on unflattering photos.... The beautiful, posed stills—all coiffed and made up—those are only seen in [film publicity] press kits now. Today's photographers have flipped for reality; it's more profitable. —Mary Tyler Moore

The paparazzi follow me into the men's room. "Robin, could you hold it up? Could you make the puppet talk? Oh, you're having a movement? Oh, great! It's *Live Stools of the Rich and Famous!*" —Robin Williams

When Gianni [Versace] was shot, the English tabloids were saying, "Who's *next*, Elton John?" I was in the south of France at the time, and I got some security down there. In America, I always have a bodyguard. There are so many people who can get their hands on a gun here. That doesn't happen in Europe. There isn't such celebrity worship. It's because you don't have a royal family. —Sir Elton John

★

Of course I believe it. If [John Lennon] hadn't moved to the United States, chances are he'd certainly be alive today. —former Beatle George Harrison

★

The tragedy and irony is that Haing S. Ngor survived the killing fields of Cambodia and other horrors which he described in his memoirs. But he didn't survive the killing streets of Los Angeles. And this was the gentlest, loveliest man, devoid of malice.

—Uma Thurman, on Oscar winner Dr. Haing S. Ngor (*The Killing Fields*)

Boy George

It's not just the homophobes, you know, the fanatics and the preachers. A gay celebrity has to be wary of all kinds of gay bashers...[including] jealous pretty-boys and self-hating homosexual homophobes.
                        —Boy George, alluding to Gianni Versace's murderer

I don't like to be mean to fans, but I have to have cops around me now. The worst is when people come up and just grab you.   —Julia Roberts

★

I know some stars, like Elizabeth Taylor, don't like going where they're not recognized, if there is such a place. But not me. I don't like that fame is so permanent...and I went to an island—I won't say its name—for a vacation. They recognized me, and they kept asking me for money on the streets. When I wouldn't do it, they called me a racist! I left after two days.
                        —Inger Stevens (*The Farmer's Daughter* TV series)

★

I think if we shot more fans, the word would get out there. Shoot people. You've gotta wound people, don't kill 'em. Wound 'em. That way they'll go home with a limp saying, "Man, I'll never do that again." —Sinbad

At a [concert], early on, this rude guy, a heckler, shouted, "Are you a lesbian?" I thought, Are you the alternative? —k. d. lang

I never actually came out to them [his parents] in that TV-movie way. It's more an unspoken thing. I went out with a guy for three years and they met him, and mothers always know.... —film director Gregg Araki

★

She was venomous, vicious, a pathological liar, and quite stupid.
—Ray Milland, on Hedda Hopper

★

You had W. R. Hearst and his mistress Marion presiding at San Simeon over these large, lavish weekends. Movie stars and other notables longed for invitations...but what was peculiar or two-faced was W. R. wouldn't invite couples "living in sin." So that left out a number of prominent couples. Until they got legally married. Male–female couples....Gay or lesbian couples were sometimes guests at San Simeon. Marion Davies had several gay friends, among them the actor William Haines and his longtime partner [Jimmy Shields]. —columnist Sheilah Graham

Showbiz is about what they *show*. And it *is* a business. It's not reality, it's manufactured fantasy. Never forget that. The media doesn't—they go right along with it. Fantasy equals profits, and the truth be damned.
—screenwriter Isobel Lennart (*Funny Girl*)

In Hollywood they'll forgive you if you're two-faced. But not if you're two-chinned. —Colleen Dewhurst

I think that every religion says to love your neighbor. In Hollywood they add, "But don't get caught."
—Anita Ekberg, ex–sex symbol (*La Dolce Vita*) now living in Rome

Every actor has a natural animosity toward every other actor, present or absent, living or dead. —actor-turned-author Louise Brooks

★

Hollywood is where everyone you meet is thinking, So what can you do for me? But the Hollywood producer is the ultimate extreme. You've probably heard the one about the starlet who offers the producer oral sex in return for a bit role, and he says to her, "But what's in it for me?"

—Robert Mitchum

★

No one has a closest friend in Hollywood.   —columnist Sheilah Graham

★

Someone once said having a friend is like having a second existence. True.

—Ingrid Bergman

★

When you have fame, everyone's your friend—they *say*. . . . It's your enemies you have to watch out for—*they* never declare themselves.

—William Morris agent Stan Kamen

★

Always forgive your enemies. Just don't forget their names.

—producer David O. Selznick (*Gone With the Wind*)

★

Of course I have enemies! I'm a director and successful. How not?

—Lindsay Anderson (*If...*)

★

Friends are an actor's friends until they become critics.   —Peter Sellers

★

A critic is a man who knows the way but can't drive the car.

—critic Kenneth Tynan

★

It is possible for a critic to make an actor cry, but it ought not to be possible for any critic to make an actor wish to give up.   —Dame Flora Robson

★

They never raised a statue to a critic.   —Martha Graham

★

Critics aren't our worst enemies. Those are the people who pretend to like us, in front of our backs.   —Eva Gabor

★

My loathing of critics and gossip columnists—often the same person during the movies' purported golden age—isn't buried deep. It's right on the surface.

—Joseph Cotten, who kicked Hedda Hopper in the keister and survived

The men I knew [intimately], most of them became anything but friends....As Diane de Poitiers said, to have a good enemy, choose a man you have loved—he knows where to strike.   —Brigitte Bardot

★

Scratch a lover, and find a foe.   —Dorothy Parker

★

I make enemies deliberately. They are the *sauce piquante* to my dish of life.
                              —professional hostess Elsa Maxwell

★

When my enemies stop hissing, I shall know I'm slipping.
                                                         —Maria Callas

★

I don't have a warm personal enemy left. They've all died off. I miss them terribly because they helped define me.   —Clare Boothe Luce

★

I'm tough, ambitious, and I know exactly what I want. If that makes me a bitch, okay.   —Madonna

★

I have yet to see one completely unspoiled star, except for...Lassie.
                                          —costume designer Edith Head

★

For an actress to be a success, she must have the face of Venus, the brains of Minerva, the grace of Terpsichore, the memory of Macaulay, the figure of Juno, and the hide of a rhinoceros.   —Ethel Barrymore

★

If you have never been hated by your child, you have never been a parent.
                                                         —Bette Davis

★

If it [motherhood] doesn't interest you, don't do it. It didn't interest me, so I didn't do it. Anyway, I would have made a terrible parent. The first time my child didn't do what I wanted, I'd kill him.
                                                    —Katharine Hepburn

★

Nearly everyone wants babies. But not everyone wants children....
                                                         —Lee Remick

★

The problem with children is they are not returnable.   —Quentin Crisp

★

DREW BARRYMORE

My father said, "Hey, Drew, you want to give me an autograph too? How 'bout putting it on a check?"
—Drew Barrymore

★

Bringing up children is not a real occupation, because children come up just the same, brought or not.
—writer Germaine Greer

★

Acting is one profession where a lot of women who are heterosexual choose not to have a child. It's a showbiz thing.
—Gilda Radner

★

If you're an actor or actress and you decide to have a kid, you better raise it with kid gloves, or someday it might write a tell-all book about you!
—José Ferrer

★

One thing I'll say for Hollywood. Most of the relatively few pregnancies there are planned. Those people *want* their children. Most anywhere else, the attitude is more like sow your wild oats on Saturday night, then pray for a crop failure on Sunday morning. —Rita Hayworth

★

This is one profession where most of the lesbians get married, because of their screen image, and where a lot of the [heterosexual] women don't have kids, so they can keep looking good on screen and not interrupt their careers. In Hollywood it's all topsy-turvy.

—William Demarest (*My Three Sons*)

★

When a child abruptly quadruples her family's income, some changes may be expected. —Shirley Temple

★

There are worse C words than that.

—Brooke Shields, asked if she minds being called a "chick"

★

In the movies, if you're past forty you're practically an old crone....

—Joan Blondell, star–turned–character actress

★

I got old the way that women who aren't actresses grow old.

—Simone Signoret (*Diabolique*)

★

This business has a lot to do with sex and sex appeal. People tend to think of sexuality as the main ingredient young people have to offer. I beg to differ. I think older people exude bundles of sexuality. It's just that older men and women tend not to run around like cats and dogs in heat.

—fifty-something Jacqueline Bisset

★

I want to go beyond the limitations of gender....I want to get to the point where I can age gracefully. I've heard that in your seventies, men aren't threatened by your sexuality anymore. I guess I'm curious about that. I want to get beyond what I'm allowed as a woman, which only happens with age. It will happen if we keep pushing, but right now everything puts limits on women. —Susan Sarandon

★

To be somebody, you must last. —late bloomer Ruth Gordon

★

I'll be eighty this month. Age, if nothing else, entitles me to set the record straight before I dissolve. I've given my memoirs far more thought than any of my marriages. You can't divorce a book.   —Gloria Swanson

When I was young, I was terribly concerned with what people thought of me. But now I'm more concerned with what I think of *them*.

—Bette Davis

Now that I'm over sixty, I'm veering toward respectability.

—Shelley Winters

★

The secret of staying young is to live honestly, eat slowly, and lie about your age.   —Lucille Ball

★

A woman needs a little selfishness, or a lot. Same as men do. Because much of the first half of your life is smudged up by your parents, and much of the second half by your kids. You know what I mean....

—Dame Peggy Ashcroft

★

The reason some men fear older women is they fear their own mortality.
—magazine editor Frances Lear, ex-wife of producer Norman Lear

There are three ages of actresses: youth, middle age, and "You look fabulous, darling."   —Gypsy Rose Lee

★

To the young, sex is what grownups do. To the elderly, sex is what the young do.   —musician Ned Rorem

★

Old age is not so terrible when you consider the alternative.

—Maurice Chevalier

★

If at first you don't succeed, try again. Then give up. No use being a damn fool about it.   —W. C. Fields

★

I've been poor and I've been rich. Rich is better.   —Sophie Tucker

★

A successful man is one who makes more money than his wife can spend. A successful woman is one who can find such a man.   —Lana Turner

Show me someone who never gossips, and I'll show you someone who isn't interested in people. —Barbara Walters

★

Gossip is the art of saying nothing in a way that leaves practically nothing unsaid. —Walter Winchell

★

A gossip is someone who talks to you about others, a bore is one who talks to you about himself, and a brilliant conversationalist is one who talks to you about yourself. —singer Lisa Kirk

★

Probably the biggest topics of gossip are who's gay, who's getting divorced, and who's had plastic surgery? —Gilda Radner

★

If I want to put my tits on my back, that's *my* business. —Cher

★

I had [breast] implants. But so has every single person in Los Angeles. These are things that people don't realize. —Pamela Anderson Lee

★

In her seventies my mother decided to have her breasts lifted. I tried to dissuade her....Then the doctor told her she could die on the operating table. She said, "Don't worry about that. If the worst happens, you'll bury me topless." —George Hamilton

★

[Plastic surgery] sucks....Every chick's got a chest full of styrofoam, and we all encourage each other to do it...so [I did] it too. I'm sorry I gave in to that shit. —facelifted Robert Blake

★

Some guys look at themselves in the mirror for twenty years, then decide to get a nose job or an ear lift or something. I don't know. I just couldn't see myself getting my knees stretched. —Danny DeVito

★

It's pretty sad when a person has to lose weight to play Babe Ruth. —John Goodman, who did

★

I wish I had a dime for every time I've been called "diminutive." I'm not. I'm just damn short. —Michael J. Fox

★

Just because one is small does not mean one should play only small roles.
　　　　　　　—dwarf actor Hervé Villechaize, who took his own life
★

I'm magnificent! I'm 5′11″ and I weigh 135 pounds and I look like a racehorse.　　　　　　　　　　　　　　　　　　—Julie Newmar
★

I look fabulous for my age.　　　　　　　　　　　　　—Jane Fonda
★

Outside every thin woman is a fat man trying to get in.
　　　　　　　　　　　—nonthin standup comic Totie Fields
★

You do have the fattest people on earth—the jumbo, all-American circus-size. *Beyond* the normal fat one finds everywhere. And one reads in American periodicals about people who have to "contend" with being fat. As if it were thrust upon them! If they make themselves that big, of *course* they have to contend with it. You seem to be a nation that likes to shift the blame.　　　　　　　　　　　　　　　　　　—Benny Hill
★

In Hollywood it's not how you play the game, it's how you place the blame.
　　　　　　—producer Don Simpson (who blamed his fatal drug habit
　　　　　　　　　　　　　　　　　on "the industry")
★

I think fur coats should have a label on them saying how they became fur coats. People don't know the indignity, the horror, that animals go through.
　　　　　　　　　　　—Bea Arthur (*The Golden Girls*)
★

I learned a magical thing long ago, and now my daughters have learned it: there are no wrinkles on the heart.　　—Jolie Gabor, well-known mother
★

News is supposed to be impartial. Here's an example: CNN reported the highly anti-Hillary (Rodham Clinton) results of a poll. ...What they didn't say—I *read* it later—was *where* the poll was taken: in the cafeteria in Washington, D.C., of some Republican group!
　　　　　　　　　　　—writer-producer Paul Jarrico (*Salt of the Earth*)
★

Royalties are nice and all, but shaking the beads brings in money quicker.
　　　　　　　　　　　—stripper and author Gypsy Rose Lee
★

There ain't nothin' that breaks up homes, country, and nations like somebody publishing their memoirs. —Will Rogers

★

Autobiography is a wonderful way to tell the truth about other people.
—Will Geer (*The Waltons*)

★

In show business, the most respectable form of lying is called autobiography. —Thelma Ritter (*All About Eve*)

★

If you want a place in the sun you have to expect a few blisters.
—Loretta Young

★

Fame has sent a number of celebrities off the deep end, and in the case of Michael Jackson, to the kiddie pool. —Bill Maher

★

Nothing risqué, nothing gained! —Jayne Mansfield

★

The casting couch is the name of the game in Hollywood. I know there are stars, especially women, who have made a career from sexual favors.
—Phyllis Diller, who didn't

★

The best way to attract a man immediately is to have a magnificent bosom and a half-size brain and let both of them show. —Zsa Zsa Gabor

★

Hollywood, then: an actress took off her clothes before she got the job. Hollywood, now: an actress takes off her clothes after she gets the job....And if she's a big star, they can exploit some unknown actress to be her nude body double. —director Fred Zinneman (*The Nun's Story, Julia*)

★

By the way, never loan an ex-husband any money...he will only use it on other women. And what can hurt more than knowing that your ex-husband is off in Rome with a girl who looks like Sophia Loren's daughter—on *your* money? —Zsa Zsa Gabor

★

Up with the birds, and to bed with anything.
—Red Skelton's mock advice on how to succeed in motion pictures

★

In Hollywood, a starlet is known by the company which keeps her.

—British blonde bombshell Diana Dors

★

Most models do not make the transition to actress. Most serve as a pool of potential dates, mistresses, and wives for successful actors, singers, and closet gays. The good thing about a model is she's decorative and usually not too bright or too ambitious....She isn't competition, the way most actresses are.   —Hollywood reporter Ruth Batchelor

★

Fame is like being a pretty girl: people turn and look at you. But that's about all I've gotten out of it. I have found that it doesn't get you laid, and you don't get as much free stuff as you'd think.   —Anthony Edwards

★

I don't get pissed off about the bad stuff, but I milk it for everything it's worth because you have to have some balance in your life. If there are free seats to the baseball game, you bet I'm there.   —Mel Gibson, movie star

★

I'm nowhere near as sexy as I come off on camera. Film just loves me.

—David Caruso

★

I say that alimony is the biggest killer of romance there is.

—nonhousewife Zsa Zsa Gabor

★

Darling, I'm a marvelous housekeeper: every time I divorce a man, I keep the house!   —Zsa Zsa Gabor

★

I enjoy being sexy...and it's harmless, like a stock in trade. But sometimes boyfriends have trouble with it, and a husband unquestionably does.

—sixties sexpot Elsa Martinelli

★

A bad thing about jealousy is the element of pornography in it: the stimulation of visualizing one's darling in someone else's arms.

—Colette

★

There was an upside to playing a nymphomaniac on TV. I'm not married anymore.   —Téa Leoni

★

CESAR ROMERO

With some men, the older they get, the campier they get. Take Vincent
Price. He was perfect for horror films—he hadn't worked out as a leading
man: too fey and florid. But as a horror star....He once told an interviewer,
"I have the heart of a boy, you know. I keep it in my laboratory."

—Cesar Romero

★

I'd give up fame first. Then money. Then sex. Fame is not important to me,
but ask me after *Melrose Place* is over....Money provides me with a lot of
freedom, but having sex I connect with love...and that's the most
important thing in my life.   —Courtney Thorne-Smith

★

You can try and hold on to most of the money you make as a success in this
business. If you don't, you have yourself to blame. But fame? Try holding on
to *that*...luck and trends have more to do with it than your own talent,

looks, or charisma. Because the fans are fickle…like a husband or beau whose attention can always be taken by a prettier or newer face.

—Kay Kendall (*Les Girls*)

I find people in the porn world are very lively and animated. So what if they [screw] for a living? I like a lot of them better than the actors in Hollywood—who are the real whores, to be perfectly honest with you.

—Sandra Bernhard

Any woman who can't say a four-letter word sometimes is deceitful.

—Fanny Brice

You get an image…you get pigeonholed, and that's that. It's how producers and casting directors see you. It reduces what's available to you as an actor, an artist. It's as if you were a painter, but you were only given two colors to use on your canvas: red and blue. For the rest of your life.

—Bonnie Bedelia (*Heart Like a Wheel*)

Nobody would be in this business if he were normal.   —Vincent Price

I don't care how anyone identifies me as long as I can do my work.

—Lily Tomlin, on her reaction to "being identified as a lesbian"

Television is more of an image creator than movies, as it's so close up…and it's in your living room or bedroom, each week. So once you'd done a role in a series, that's how the public will think of you, for years.…It took a long time for people to realize that I really am not gay.

—Billy Crystal, who played gay on *Soap*

I'm not a straight man, but I play one on television.

—Dan Butler (*Frasier*)

Do you know what's the longest word in the English language? "And now, a word from our sponsor.…"   —*Jeopardy!* host Art Fleming

I'm delighted with [television], because it used to be that films were the lowest form of art. Now we've got something to look down on.

—director Billy Wilder (*Some Like It Hot*)

I hate television. I hate it as much as peanuts. But I can't stop eating peanuts.   —Orson Welles

[Television:] A device that permits people who haven't anything to do to watch people who can't do anything.   —radio star Fred Allen

[Television:] A medium of entertainment which permits millions of people to listen to the same joke at the same time and yet remain lonesome.

—T. S. Eliot

I must say I find television very educational. The minute somebody turns it on, I go to the library and read a good book.   —Groucho Marx

They call TV chewing gum for the eyes. Now, with some of the new, sexier cable channels, it's chewing gum for the groin too.

—Robert Reed (*The Brady Bunch*)

I'll tell you how I feel about porn channels. They don't educate us, they don't enlighten us, and they don't come in clearly enough where I live.

—Bill Maher

If it wasn't for masturbation, most men wouldn't know that anything could happen.   —Jerry Seinfeld

I'd rather be serving time in a women's jail where there's at least sex, than being in the closet in Hollywood.   —comedian and actress Marga Gomez

★

Yeah, I'm a dyke. So what? Big deal!

—screen comedian Patsy Kelly (*The Gorilla, Rosemary's Baby*)

★

Interviewers ask me how people feel about my being gay, and I'm like, "Take a sedative—it's not my job to make you comfortable with my being gay. How do I feel about you being straight?"   —director Tom Kalin

★

I think that if we had spent half as much time dealing with the government as we've spent yelling at each other, we would have had our rights twenty years ago.   —lesbian comedian Lea DeLaria

★

And another thing—we have *lives,* not "lifestyles."

—Lance Browne

★

This sweet little blonde girl (from *The Sonny and Cher Show*) turned out to be [gay]. There's something wonderful about that, because that's life.

—Chastity Bono, activist and ex-singer

★

Addressing a national meeting of P-FLAG (Parents & Friends of Lesbians and Gays): I'm the mother, and I could have made it so much easier for her....   —Cher, on knowing her daughter was lesbian
                                  but not wanting to have to deal with it

★

The family that you acquire once you leave your own family is sometimes even more special because you really choose these people.   —RuPaul

★

When you're younger, you think one way must be right. But I don't feel that way anymore....When I was with men, I didn't feel buffered from every storm because I was with them. You can't get that from somebody else. I did not buy the fantasy of Prince Charming and all that garbage....Any kind of love is acceptable, and you don't have to do it in the usual way.

—Diane Keaton

★

Who's to distinguish between love and love? Love is love, period. And I don't think we have so much love in the world today that we should let governments and hate groups go around trying to diminish or disenfranchise some of it.   —Viveca Lindfors

★

I got filmed going out of a restaurant by *Hard Copy.* They said, "Here Antonio is, getting into this car with his new girlfriend." It was my sister! I went out with my sister to dinner.   —Antonio Sabato Jr.

★

That's just a total lie. I don't even know who that person is. There's not one ounce of truth in that. I don't know who the person is, and I never sent flowers to that person.

—Matt Dillon, on published rumors that he sent
a Scandinavian model 300 roses

★

It's appalling, but celebrities have no secrets....My life in and 3,000 miles from Hollywood would have been considerably easier if I'd been homosexual, inasmuch as my private relationships would then have remained private. —Rex Harrison

We all [in show business] share a profession lent to us by businessmen and audiences who can leave us in a day. —Joan Rivers

★

Certainly if anyone was worried about doing it, then that would call their sexuality into question more than if they did it. It's like, what are you scared of? That you might like it? So what if you do?
—British actor David Thewlis, queried by *Premiere* if he had any "qualms" about "homosexual love scenes" opposite Leonardo DiCaprio in *Total Eclipse*

★

I heard CAA freaked out when they read Leonardo [DiCaprio] was going to be in [the gay-themed] *Frisk* with me and supposedly pulled him out of it....Soon they'll try to marry him off...basically the way it works now is that only the gay people get married in L.A. Straight people don't bother anymore. —Craig Chester in 1994

★

The class clown often becomes a comic, especially if he's gay or a minority. Most of my roles are comedic, though I wasn't a class clown or a minority.... —Richard Deacon (*The Dick Van Dyke Show*)

★

I'm a supporter of gay rights. And not a closet supporter either.
—Paul Newman

★

No, I'm *not* gay. —Liberace

★

No romantic leading man will ever work, in my opinion, if he says that he is gay. You don't see any of them doing it, do you? —columnist Liz Smith

★

I have the same feelings as anyone else. It just happens that I like my career so much that I'd like people to remember my music and not my personality....What's the big deal about my sexuality? Anything as controversial as homosexuality is boring!
—openly gay non-actor Johnny Mathis

★

ROCK HUDSON

I know lots of gays in Hollywood, and most of them are nice guys. Some have tried it on with me, but I've said, "Come on, now. You've got the wrong guy."   —performer Rock Hudson

★

I almost worked with Ross Hunter once. He was the biggest movie producer of his day, in the '50s and '60s. Hit after hit...then one spectacular miss (*Lost Horizon*): end of his movie career....After he died, I read all the obits I could find on him. Finally, in an English paper—the Manchester *Guardian*—I saw the only mention of Jacques Mapes, the set decorator who was his professional and personal partner for over fifty years....
                                          —William Hickey (*Prizzi's Honor*)

★

I am not sorry. I will tell anybody that, and it is the truth. I lived the way I wanted and never did what people said I should do or advised me to do. And I want my children to do the same. Let the world know you as you are, not as you think you should be, because sooner or later, if you are posing, you will forget the pose, and then where are you?   —Fanny Brice

★

Hollywood kids have different values. It's a different world. The best illustration is the famous story of a movie star whose child had to write an essay for school about a poor family. It started, "Once upon a time there was a poor family. The parents were poor, the children were poor, the butler and maid were poor, and the cook and the gardener and the pool man were also poor."   —Bill Bixby (*My Favorite Martian*)

★

My older sister and I both started out in musical theater. She has a great voice and she had more of a chance of making it than I did. But she couldn't take the rejection. You have to get up there and say, "You like me?" And if they say, "No," it's like, "Up yours! Next? How about you? Do *you* like me? Or you? Or you?" Eventually somebody will say "Yes."
                                          —Jennifer Lopez (*Selena*)

★

In Hollywood, every man you meet, his attitude is, "What can you do for me?"   —Betty Field (*Picnic*)

★

I favor sex over violence any day. Or night....Bruce Willis is a hypocrite. He's announced that he doesn't want his kids to watch his upcoming movie (*The Jackal*) until they're teenagers, because it has too much violence.

What about everyone else's kids? For them it's okay, because he gets millions for making such stomach-turning movies in the first place?

—novelist Harold Robbins

I don't know what that mystery ingredient is that makes some of us make it, and some of us cross the line and never come back. I think of all the times I wanted to kill myself, I think of all the times I tried to kill other people, and I don't know why I'm here.   —Robert Blake (*Baretta*)

No more bare bodies [in her film scenes] for me. For my children's sake, I must stop. The other kids at school keep throwing it up to my children, and they are not kind.   —Ellen Barkin

Beautiful young people are random accidents of nature. But beautiful old people are deliberate works of art.

—Butterfly McQueen (*Gone With the Wind*)

A young leading lady is lovely but self-centered. An older leading lady, if she still is a leading lady, is bound to be manufactured and monstrously egotistical.   —mogul Jack L. Warner

The public is quick to get a crush on you, and quickly fickle. But they can dislike you for years. My press agent says, "They love you in haste but detest you at leisure."   —Ava Gardner

Some of the greatest love affairs I've known have involved one actor—unassisted.   —Wilson Mizner

I've known some actors who were intelligent, but the better the actor, the more stupid he is.   —Truman Capote

The most important thing in acting is honesty. If you can fake that, you've got it made.   —George Burns

The public sees you playing someone sweet or innocent or unsophisticated. Then when they find out you are different from that, many of them become upset! But after all, you have been playing a role....   —Ingrid Bergman

JOHN SCHLESINGER

I know somebody who is Jewish and homosexual. His parents told him, "We *know*.... But you must marry. After that, you can carry on whatever way you want." I consider that the most awful piece of family advice I've ever heard. Of course, they're an American family, and Americans seem to have more hangups about these things than the Europeans do.

—openly gay British and Jewish director
John Schlesinger (*Midnight Cowboy*)

★

Photographers want to catch you at your worst.... The posed, beautiful photos don't sell for as much as one of a star looking old or disheveled—look at that photo of Rita Hayworth when she got off the plane all mussed and confused and [suffering from] Alzheimer's.   —columnist Joyce Haber

★

Can you guess which female celebrity, caught topless, would ensure a million-dollar fee? It's sixty-five-year-old Elizabeth Taylor!

—columnist Liz Smith

★

You can see through celluloid, and it is brittle. Neither of those things is true about me.

—Elizabeth Taylor

Lest I ever take myself too seriously, I have framed on my bathroom wall a review of my young self in the picture *Dodsworth* [1935]. It says that I'm Samuel Goldwyn's latest discovery and that I'm "tall, dark and not the slightest bit handsome."

—David Niven

The name is so important for an actor, a foremost part of one's image. I like my name...but as an actor, it has often been a detriment. I have been mistakenly billed as Peter Dull, and under my correctly spelled name I've been reviewed as having delivered a performance which was "pure Bull."

—British actor Peter Bull

As an actor, you work with what you've got. Talent can transcend appearance but not erase it. A critic once wrote that I had a face to launch a thousand dredgers....What was most difficult for me was to *pretend*—to act when my mother was in the audience. That shattered the atmosphere of illusion for me. It could make me feel like a child again, playing pretend with her mother looking on. An adult actor does not completely lose such feelings.

—two-time Oscar winner Glenda Jackson, now a Member of Parliament

You have to be smart to play a dumb blonde over and over and keep the audience's attention without extraordinary physical equipment.

—Judy Holliday

An actress must be very pretty or very talented. In the short run, being pretty is more important....

—actor-director Ida Lupino

I think of my body as a temple. Just fine as it is! I don't want to build any unwanted additions.

—child-free Jean Arthur

Most actors don't like blemishes on their characters. But blemishes on their skin or clothes? Heaven forbid!

—director Robert Moore (*Murder by Death*)

NOEL COWARD

It was my mother who helped push me into the business, having recognized my budding genius at an early age....She took me to a children's audition at a theater where I did my little act and got hired immediately. The stage manager then took me back to my mother and said to her, "Shall we say three pounds a week?" and my mother replied, "I'm sorry, but we couldn't possibly afford to pay that much."

—Sir Noel Coward

★

I once asked a famous movie queen if she was really as narcissistic as everyone said, and she vehemently denied it. Then she excused herself to get up and check her hair in the mirror.   —Sheilah Graham

★

It got reported that I argued with my director (of *Bent*) about my wardrobe. Not true. We did spend time on it, though. I'm playing a drag queen, and my legs do look better in short dresses. I'm as vain as the next guy....

—Mick Jagger

★

It took me several years to realize I didn't have too much talent for acting, not true acting. But by then I couldn't give it up, because I had become too famous.   —Fernando Lamas, Latin sex symbol

★

I may not be a great actress, but I've become the greatest at screen orgasms. Ten seconds of heavy breathing, roll your head from side to side, simulate a slight asthma attack, and die a little.   —Candice Bergen, pre-TV

★

Clint developed his way of talking [on the screen] by studying the breathy speech pattern of Marilyn Monroe.

—Sondra Locke, Eastwood's ex–co-star and ex-paramour

★

If I lived there, I'd *move*.   —Clint Eastwood, on Los Angeles

★

The movies are the only business where you can go out front and applaud yourself.   —Will Rogers (honorary mayor of Beverly Hills)

★

In Hollywood it's okay to be subtle, so long as you make it obvious.

—Alfred Hitchcock

★

A big hard-boiled city with no more personality than a paper cup.

—Raymond Chandler, on L.A.

★

Isn't it wonderful that people who prefer New York City to Los Angeles live there?   —Charlotte Greenwood (*Oklahoma!*)

★

Hollywood is like being nowhere and talking to nobody about nothing.

—director Michelangelo Antonioni

★

There are two million interesting people in New York and only seventy-eight in Los Angeles.   —Neil Simon

★

New York now leads the world's great cities in the number of people around whom you shouldn't make a sudden move.   —David Letterman
★

It's all relative, after all. A cowchip is paradise to a fly....And I like an atmosphere and a set that's far from tranquil. Without friction in the oyster, you can't produce a pearl.
—director James Bridges (*The China Syndrome*)
★

To survive [in Hollywood] you need the ambition of a Latin American revolutionary, the ego of a grand opera tenor, and the physical stamina of a cow pony.   —Billie Burke (Glinda the Good Witch), in her memoirs
With a Feather on My Nose
★

A pretty good sign that somebody has had it with showbiz or is retiring is when they move to Palm Springs. Its nickname is Death's Waiting Room.
—Sonny Bono (mayor of Palm Springs)
★

[In the 1970s] I lived in Beverly Hills, and I'd go jogging. Then one time the cops stopped me, frisked me even though I proved I lived there. They said I looked like someone who'd done a robbery there....I soon moved away, went home.

—Pam Grier
★

There was a time, when I was working in Hollywood, when I seriously considered getting circumcised so I could fit in better and be more popular.
—Omar Sharif
★

They once announced on U.S. television that I was dead. When they rang to tell my daughter, she said I couldn't be, that she was talking to me twelve minutes ago in Australia. They said, "No, he's dead. It's just the time difference."   —Patrick Macnee (*The Avengers*)
★

Without question it's a tough business on relationships. You really have to think seriously about what it means to be a "husband." You have to go the extra mile. It's not so much just that temptation is all around you, because as far as I'm concerned, that's not an issue. It's *absence*. Absence is difficult.   —Australian-based actor Sam Neill (*Jurassic Park*)
★

I don't think the average family in Cleveland would be very happy if their block knew about their daughter's bulimia or abortion or broken marriage. However, they're very happy to hear about it about their favorite star who they go to see twice a year in a movie. I find that very strange and unfortunate.   —Jason Patric (*Speed 2*)

I like to work in Hollywood, but I don't like local habits like fans and tabloid people going through your trash cans. People who live there often have to take their name off their mailboxes and front door buzzers, for privacy or even safety. Some can't have mail delivered to their homes because fan magazines or books list their addresses—so they have to get their mail elsewhere via a private mailbox. People living in Hollywood also have to stay home if they're in a foul mood; anything outside the home is potential publicity.

As I say, I like working there, but not to live there.

—Jeremy Brett (*My Fair Lady*)

I like Hollywood, I like Los Angeles. But I like most everywhere. Because I like people....But when you are thought of as a celebrity and people recognize you, they treat you in a way which is not really their fault but it can make you uncomfortable. And the way writers write about you, it can be uncomfortable too—as if you are a symbol of a place or an idea.

—Haing S. Ngor

I came into the industry in 1961. I stopped reading reviews in 1962.

—Ann-Margret

I dislike the flashbulbs so much....What I have learned is, the best way to cope with all the fuss and maintain one's dignity is to remain quiet. Smile now and then, but stay quiet....And you should not care *too* much what people will think or say about you; you cannot control it anyway.

—Ingrid Bergman

★

As you become famous, it sometimes happens, for some public figures, that they begin to hate the public that made them famous. That's sad...but it's very natural to start hating the press, which is so negative. If you give an interview and say ten nice things and five negative things, it typically runs with you saying one or two nice things and four or five not-nice ones.

Because rudeness and shock value sell better. —Dean Paul Martin

★

The more successful you are, the less you have to worry about money. But the more about everything *else*...like, Will the public tire of me very soon, particularly if I go on TV? And, What if I go out and everyone wants my autograph? Or, What if I go out and *no* one wants my autograph? You're a winner, but you can't win. —Toni Collette (*Muriel's Wedding*)

★

I stopped signing autographs after I was asked to sign one while standing at a urinal in a restaurant...I was already quite cool about the idea after being asked for about the thousandth time, "Can you remove your sunglasses so we can see your blue eyes?" I started saying, "I'm so sorry, but if I take off my glasses, my pants fall down." Which doesn't deter some of them....
—Paul Newman

★

Movie actors get more respect from the public. There's more distance, less familiarity than with TV actors. Anything can happen. ...A guy once bribed me to kiss his wife, who was no beauty. I refused the bribe and kissed her on the cheek. He wasn't happy...or the time I initialed my name on a guy's dick. That only occurred because my autograph wouldn't fit. He wasn't happy either. —Rick Nelson (*Ozzie and Harriet*)

★

Twice I've gotten into loud quarrels with alleged fans who said I *owed* them an autograph. Never again. You can't reason with such dumbbells....If, in return for my salary, I go to work, do my job and then also perform mandated publicity, how am I left owing anybody anything? By what logic?
—Lex "Tarzan" Barker

★

I've heard stories where people have actually paid other people to call newspapers and say they've seen screenings of movies that were bad—just because they wanted to sabotage the movie. That happens all the time.
—Danny DeVito

★

In direct proportion to how successful one is, that's how much the need is to chop him or her down. —Michael Douglas

★

Prying eyes make unhappy subjects.
—Sarah Ferguson, the Duchess of York

Some of the press are like leeches, particularly the photographers. They
never, never get enough. They stop acting human, they want to suck you
dry.   —Barbra Streisand

I do...I try to be a responsible rich citizen.
    —Robin Williams, whose film contracts prohibit commercial tie-ins to soft
          drinks, junk food, tobacco, alcohol, toys of violence, and weapons

Sorry, Rush [Limbaugh], Newt [Gingrich], and Jesse [Helms], but the artist
as citizen is here to stay.

                                              —Barbra Streisand

Sometimes journalists aren't sensitive enough to actors. As for example
during a press conference for a new movie. I nod to a journalist who
prefaces his question with the remark that he "hated" my movie. I try and
smile, and I'm supposed to go on from there....

                                              —Jane Fonda, former movie star

They'll make up entire stories, especially the tabloids. The public doesn't
know because they don't have the facts. Your friends and relatives only have
half the facts, so there's always explaining to do....I remember one story—
they claimed I even wrote it! It was a tabloid, and among the minor details
that were absolutely wrong was the word "wacky." I haven't used that word
since kindergarten or something!   —John Goodman

I only know the rear entrances of the hotels I stay in. I always have to climb
over garbage cans and hampers full of dirty linen and sneak up to my room
on foot or in the service elevator.

                            —Greta Garbo, on a legend's unglamorous life

Why can't we avoid being followed and examined? It is cruel to bother
people who want to be left in peace. This kills beauty for me.

                                              —Greta Garbo, in 1938
                              ★
Our town worships success, the bitch goddess whose smile hides a taste for
blood.   —Hedda Hopper
                              ★
Hollywood isn't dog eat dog, it's man eat man.   —Wilson Mizner

Nobody is allowed to fail within a two-mile radius of the Beverly Hills Hotel.

—Gore Vidal

★

Most stars' *reel* lives have little, if anything, to do with their *real* lives.

—Anita Loos

★

When you're famous, people feel free to stare. No matter where or what the situation. And they stare as if you can't see them staring at you. Or as if it doesn't matter!   —John Travolta

★

The minute you leave your mansion, you're doing public relations.

—Paul "Pee-Wee Herman" Reubens

★

Are you sick of hearing about me? *I'm* sick of hearing about me.

—Ellen DeGeneres, on the media blitz surrounding her coming out

★

When you're out in public with anyone but your husband, people stare at whoever you're with. Or rather, whoever's with you. Which isn't fair to my friends.   —Demi Moore

★

The first time my girlfriend and I were followed by street photographers, she wanted to bash them. But I said no, then you would be the lesbian Sean Penn. Just grin and bear it.

—Chastity Bono, daughter of Sonny and Cher

★

The public pushes right in, does not see anybody but you. This is difficult for men. Some are furious at the intrusion, and I never see them again. Others join in too much and clown with the fans. Either way, I am embarrassed.   —Joan Rivers

★

We're absolutely stupid to be embarked in a business where our face is connected with our accomplishments. When you get it from morning to night, it's no longer wonderful. No dear public ever did anything for me, and a few people in our industry have the courage to say, "Oh, my dear public, I'd kick 'em if I could."   —Cary Grant

★

Politics is for people who are too ugly to get into show business.

—President Bill Clinton

An artist does not stop being an artist after a certain age. The industry may think it, but the public doesn't. I think that's why *First Wives Club* did so well....I don't believe that men age better than women.   —Diane Keaton

★

I've had some plastic surgery. Anybody can look at me and tell. But people can have too much. The trouble is, you don't look better. So you're damned if you do and damned if you don't. That's the bottom line.

—Angie Dickinson

★

All they talked about was my tits for the next four years [after *The Deep*]. God, if I was going to do a picture like that, I'd have done it a lot sexier. That looked like two fried eggs on a platter.   —Jacqueline Bisset

★

My problem is my bum. I'm not going to show you my wiggle, but I can tell you, it's like having live ferrets jumping around in a bag.

—Sarah Ferguson, Duchess of York

★

When you are called a character actress, it's because you're too ugly to be called a leading lady.

—Kathy Burke, Best Actress winner at the 1997 Cannes Film Festival

★

Sooner or later a public figure becomes a public bore or a public joke.

—Richard Burton

★

I think I have seven years left, which is the average career in Hollywood. I look at my aunt, Rosemary Clooney, who has been very successful and then not. She didn't get less talent along the way, she just got less successful. Three years from now I could be saying, "Paper or plastic?"

—George Clooney

★

Between pictures, there *is no* Lon Chaney.

—silent-screen star Lon Chaney

★

Nothing is so emboldening as a mask.   —Colette

★

People used to say I told the truth. I still do. But now my detractors say I'm being cynical. It's the same thing.   —Lillian Hellman

★

Once you become famous, you have to watch every word. Anything can be quoted, forever more, and used against you.   —producer Ross Hunter

★

The more famous you are, the more there'll be some people who hate you. Hopefully not most of them.... There's no way to make everyone love you, but hundreds of ways to make people hate you, and inadvertently.

—Ella Raines

★

The paparazzi have gotten out of hand. If they could sell them, they would take pictures of one micturating [urinating].   —Richard Burton

★

Everyone seems to want a piece of you. It's just take, take, take, take, take.

—Whoopi Goldberg

★

Any activity one does outside the house, now one has to give everything a second thought.... It's all grist for the endless publicity mill and the voyeurs' goldfish bowl.   —Hugh Grant

★

Publicity used to be something you did on purpose. Today it's all-encompassing, it's from the time you close the front door behind you.

—Elizabeth Taylor

★

I don't care about the publicity. I like the money much better.

—Macaulay Culkin

★

You can be a celebrity and not get too noticed. Unless you're out with a publicity hog like Madonna.   —Sandra Bernhard

★

Publicity can be terrible. But only if you don't have any.

—Jayne Mansfield

★

Show me a great actor, and I'll show you a lousy husband; show me a great actress, and you've seen the devil.   —W. C. Fields

★

To be an actor it is essential to be an egomaniac. Otherwise it doesn't work.

—David Niven

★

The chief thing for any actor to remember is that it wasn't his brains that got him to stardom, it was only his acting.   —Lon Chaney

First I thought it was my [last] name that made me famous, and I resented it. Then I thought it was being pretty, and I resented that for a while. Now I don't care about why, just so people keep noticing me.

—Drew Barrymore

At some point, I noticed people staring at me from behind. Close up. I became rather paranoid about it. Until I realized they were looking for plastic surgery scars.   —Joan Collins

★

Actors get it from all sides, talented or not. Whether you imitate or innovate, half the audience and most of the critics will hate what you do.

—Robert Mitchum

★

K. D. LANG

People can be so rude. If I'm in public with someone, everyone wonders if she's my girlfriend. Or they'll say something out loud like, "I thought she'd have a cuter girlfriend that *that*." —k. d. lang

★

Scratch an actor and you'll find an actress. —Dorothy Parker

★

A happy childhood is poor preparation for human contacts. —Colette

★

Becoming an actor can be embarrassing. Having to cry in front of the world, or be seen naked on screen.... It's also a virtual confession that you had a rotten childhood or are some kind of emotional cripple.

—Henry Fonda

★

Every time I get close to Hollywood I get excited. —Newt Gingrich

★

I'm not naturally paranoid, but you gotta watch your every move. That, or the public does. Ever since I got arrested and jailed for smoking pot, I get all sorts of people, and actors sometimes, looking at me funny when I light up a cigarette.... Hell, I like to shock people, so I'm not about to quit.

—Robert Mitchum

★

When I wake up and look in the mirror I realize one of the reasons I don't own a handgun: I would have shot my thighs off years ago.

—Oprah Winfrey

★

I think the things that are necessary in my profession are these: taste, talent, and tenacity. I think I have had a little of all three. —Lillian Gish

★

Every critic is a would-be celebrity, hence the jealousy and bitterness. To last, and happily, you must try and not let them get to you.

—Guy (*Lost in Space*) Williams

★

A bad review is like baking a cake with all the best ingredients and having someone sit on it. —writer Danielle Steel

★

The important thing in acting is to be able to laugh and cry. If I have to cry, I think of my sex life. If I have to laugh, I think of my sex life.

—actor-turned-politician Glenda Jackson

Once you're a star, you must never look back. Except in interviews, which are comprised of your past and your future, and possibly a few lies about your present....Because if you look back, you're apt to see that others are gaining on you.   —Ava Gardner

★

When you perform...you are out of yourself—larger and more potent, more beautiful. You are for minutes heroic. This is power. This is glory on earth. And it is yours, nightly.   —dancer-choreographer Agnes De Mille

★

My voice had a long, nonstop career. It deserves to be put to bed with quiet and dignity, not yanked out every once in a while to see if it can still do what it used to do. It can't.   —diva Beverly Sills

★

Acting is standing up naked and turning around very slowly.

—Rosalind Russell

★

Five stages in the life of an actor....(1) Who's Mary Astor? (2) Get me Mary Astor. (3) Get me a Mary Astor type. (4) Get me a young Mary Astor. (5) Who's Mary Astor?   —Mary Astor

★

We were worse name droppers than people who dropped our names. Another actor was a "best friend," "know him very well," "died in my arms."   —Mary Astor

★

A celebrity is a person who works hard all his life to become known, then wears dark glasses to avoid being recognized.   —comedian Fred Allen

★

I think it was Schopenhauer who said an individual can only be himself when he is alone. That goes double for an actor—in public, they're always acting.   —Raul Julia

★

Once upon a time there was a six-toed cousin. Mine. When I first saw him, I knew I was in show business. Kids in the neighborhood couldn't afford pennies, but I made them pay five pins every time they got a look at him.
—actor–turned–gossip columnist Hedda Hopper

★

When life became intolerable at home, I ran away to New York [from Pennsylvania] and went on the stage....Inasmuch as I left home to escape the heritage of being a butcher's daughter, it seems ironical that I was to spend the rest of my life dealing in ham. —Hedda Hopper

I would willingly give up my whole career if I could have just one normal child. —Beverly Sills, mother of two

You cannot have it all. —Katharine Hepburn

If a woman wants to have it all, she should expect eventually to wind up alone....I always knew I would end up alone. —Bette Davis

I stopped believing in Santa Claus at an early age. Mother took me to see him in a department store and he asked me for my autograph.

—Shirley Temple

Elizabeth Bowen said that no one speaks the truth when there's something they crave or must have, a sentiment especially true about actors and the movie factory. —director Fred Zinneman

There is a Jewish saying that a half-truth is a whole lie. Yet in the film business, a whole lie is half the truth. At least. —Lilli Palmer

What you see is usually all the public *gets*....In the case of actresses, the public, producers and critics usually don't try to probe beneath the skin-deep level.... —Lee Remick

If a beautiful actress doesn't acquire talent or personality along the way, in due time she'll possess nothing but memories.

—Yugoslavian sex symbol Sylvia Koscina

Being a sex symbol is a heavy load to carry, especially when one is tired, hurt, and bewildered. —Clara Bow

The more "up" we go, the more is expected of us and the harder we must work....Right now I have only one hope: that I will not be a disappointment. —diva Maria Callas

★

They love to build you up. Then they pause a bit. And then they love to tear you down—or *try* and tear you down.... —Ingrid Bergman

★

Once you've made one film, you've handed yourself over to posterity. But you may have a little birdshit on your shoulder. Actors shouldn't get too intense about what happens to us, or doesn't happen. —Jack Lemmon

★

Being a star is so complex. And so negative, once your stardom starts to slip....You know, star spelled backwards is *rats*. —Valerie Perrine

★

If people know your name, you're famous. If they only know your face, it doesn't count. It's the *name*. One reason I became *Zero* was so if I accomplished only a middle level of fame, I still wouldn't be a zero. If you know my name, how can I be a zero? Smart, huh? —Zero Mostel

★

I've always been this acting fool. "Hire me!" And it doesn't happen all the time. You don't get hired all the time like you did when you were young.

—Brenda Vaccaro

★

I went to a plastic surgeon for a facelift after a friend said it would be a good idea. The surgeon suggested I change my friend, not my face.

—Sally Burton, Richard's widow

★

Success—big success or sudden success—can be very disorienting. If it stays, you become spoiled. If it leaves, you become suicidal.

—Broadway star Larry Kert

★

Now that I'm here, where am I? —Janis Joplin

★

Is is possible to succeed without any act of betrayal?

—director Jean Renoir

★

I agree with Abraham Lincoln. He said, "When I do good, I feel good. When I do bad, I feel bad. And that's my religion." Exact quote.

—Henry Fonda

★

Many people here believe Hollywood is *it*. The epitome. They don't question....I love what [the Mahatma] Gandhi said when he arrived in

England from India and a pompous journalist asked him, "What do you think about western civilization?" He replied, "I think it would be an excellent idea." —Richard Burton

★

What the Roman emperor Marcus Aurelius said...is true today, for actors and everyday people, for women and for men: "A man's life is what his thoughts make of it." —Simone Signoret

★

I never really felt at home in England. When I first set foot on American soil as a very young man, it came to me like a flash: This is what I like. Here I'd like to stay. And when I married an American, I hoped we would live in America. But as fate would have it, my wife hates America and only wants to live in France. That's the way it goes. —the Duke of Windsor, former king

★

When you start out, you do want to be famous...but then it gets to the point where you can't control it. When Anne [Heche] and I travel, these guys are in the airport with video cameras. They'll say anything to get you mad—they'd bring up stuff about my sexuality. I never thought about getting violent, but.... —Ellen DeGeneres

★

Those who know the joys and miseries of celebrity...know it is a sort of octopus with innumerable tentacles. It throws out its clammy arms...and gathers...all the gossip and slander and praise afloat to spit out again.... —stage legend Sarah Bernhardt

★

The sad truth is, outside of Hollywood, 95 percent of the things told to you in confidence you couldn't get anyone else to listen to. In Hollywood the percentage is maybe 50 percent, but it's very juicy. And of course there are the taboos that we're not allowed to print, only to imply, and even then. —columnist Joyce Haber

★

I have no interest in confirming or denying [rumors that he's gay] at *all*. ...I'm a public figure, so you can say what you want about me; you can *speculate*....But when you start lying [that he starred in a porno movie], when you start spreading *factual* untruths, you're going to have to see me in court. You're going to have to face *me*. You're going to have to look at *me*. —Kevin Spacey, suing for libel on the Internet

★

Most actors are like the very young. They long to rebel and conform at the same time. Now they do this by defying the public and copying each other.

—Lorne Greene (*Bonanza*)

If you are unhappy before fame, you will probably be unhappy during fame.

—Haing S. Ngor

I think those celebs who are universally reputed to be difficult or impossible to get along with were that way before they achieved fame and fortune. Those sorts of people, who make everything tough on themselves and others, they exist in every walk of life. As any office worker knows.

—Rudy Vallee (*How to Succeed in Business Without Really Trying*)

Shaw said it best: An actor can have only one great love—himself.

—Peter O'Toole

It's one thing to be in love with oneself; most actors are. The unsettling and miserable thing that happens to actors who are in it for the love of money and renown rather than the love of acting is that they become bitter and extremely envious of all competitors....I once knew an actress who sat for her portrait, and was furious when the painter depicted her the way he saw her. She said, "But I don't *look* like that—aged and soured." He assured her, "Just wait—you will." —Sir John Gielgud

As a longtime painter, I carry around snapshots of my favorite paintings the way other old geezers my age carry around pictures of their grandkids. Grandchildren are wonderful, but a good painting can help support you in your old age. —Red Skelton

My grandmother keeps pressuring me. The other day she asked me, "Rita, when am I going to be a great-grandmother?" and I said, "I guess when you do something really *special.*" —Rita Rudner

I left L.A. because of the rat race. But it's true of everywhere now: the more people there are, the worse they behave toward one another. Just like lab rats. —Audrey Meadows (*The Honeymooners*)

LORNE GREENE with Michael Landon and Dan Blocker

My countryman Henrik Ibsen said that a person's friends are dangerous not so much for what they make us do as for what they keep us from doing....I think it's wiser to cherish one's friends than to blindly follow them. More so yet when you are famous, when friendships are like the temporary reflection of others' reaction to and envy of your fame.

—Norwegian actor Liv Ullmann

Princess Diana didn't copy other members of royalty...but Princess Grace [of Monaco] did. Both won the goal that millions of girls dream of: marrying a prince. Alas, both had problems. Diana had an unfaithful husband, the eating problems, and low self-esteem. Grace Kelly had two semi-scandalous daughters and was an alcoholic....Each died prematurely, in a car crash.   —writer Anthony Burgess

I remember after I was first on television and I became famous overnight and my pictures were on every magazine cover. George [Sanders] and I, we walked on the street one night in Hollywood, and some teenagers came up to us and said, "Zsa Zsa, Zsa Zsa, can we have your autograph?" And one young girl said to George, "You are so familiar. What is your name?" When I saw his face, I knew that was the end of my marriage.   —Zsa Zsa Gabor

An ugly trend has emerged of late, with husbands and wives airing their dirty linen in public. Frequently in restaurants. It's the lack of self-control I object to, and the tawdriness...a general lack of maturity....Jim Carrey and his [soon to be divorced] wife [Lauren Holly] got together for dinner...with the version I read saying it became a screaming match after she began to cry and got up to leave. Then he runs after her. See, such episodes did *not* take place in times past, flawed though they were. Stars wouldn't behave that way in public. They *cared* enough not to.

—Kirk Douglas

The public fancies that we all know each other very well, that we're dear friends and closely connected socially. The truth is, most of my fellow picture stars I only know well enough to sneer at.

—Constance Bennett (*What Price Hollywood?*)

I've been on a calendar, but never on time.   —Marilyn Monroe

★

[To interviewer:] I'm telling you the truth here. I'm too old [eighty-six] to remember the lies. —Marc Lawrence (*The Asphalt Jungle*)

★

In Europe the pace and outlook are more forgiving to human beings....An actor can grow into acclaim gradually. Here, if you aren't a big star by thirty, you are in the supporting parts the rest of your career. And Europe accepts the aging process a little more realistically. Here, you don't see a forty-year-old model on a [magazine] cover. It's a tradition here I dislike, both because Lancôme sales didn't go down due to my age, and because the population is aging and yet the advertising tradition is not responding accordingly. —Isabella Rossellini

★

My advice to new actors is the best there is; I often follow it myself: Be happy now. You may or may not make it big...it's a crapshoot. Don't defer happiness. Make yourself happy, and be aware of it. For the saddest thing would be, later, to look back and see that you were happy without realizing it. —Geraldine Page (*Sweet Bird of Youth*)

★

This is it. Life is not a dress rehearsal. —Mr. Blackwell

★

The purpose of life is the expansion of happiness.
—the Beatles' guru, Maharishi Mahesh Yogi

★

It is a pity, for their sake, that most of the celebrities seem more to resent the occasional misfortunes...than to value their usual good fortunes....Look at most people in any country in the world, even the developed countries—the celebrities are so very, very blessed.
—Dr. Haing S. Ngor

★

Most stars look on box office and riches as their just desserts. The arrogance becomes in-built, once you experience stardom long enough....Mostly, they fear the death of their fame...and most would rather be infamous than go back to anonymity....The worst thing you could possibly say to a star would be, "Didn't you used to be famous?"
—Truman Capote

★

IAN MCKELLEN as Tsar Nicholas II with the royal family

I've always worked very hard, and when I started acting, it wasn't easy for me and I wasn't good at it. I taught myself, and I lived in a part of the world where I could get a lot of practice. I just got better at it. It was good being part of a generation that didn't expect to reach fulfillment till middle age. So many young people are encouraged to think they must have an immediate success. If they don't, they think something's gone wrong, and nothing's gone wrong. People develop in different stages. I see a long future for me in my business, and I don't feel I've ever been acting as well as I am now.   —Sir Ian McKellen

CONAN O'BRIEN

You wonder if they ignore them, or if their mothers even taught some of the current celebrities certain basic manners. Like David Duchovny: Don't throw coffee at photographers! Or Raquel Welch: Don't throw mirrors at hairdressers! Christian Slater: Don't hit your girlfriend and don't bite the stomach of a guy who tries to help her! and for goodness' sake, Mike Tyson: Don't box with your mouth full!   —Conan O'Brien

★

It was the most public flip-out in human history. A friend of mine heard about it watching TV in Beijing.

    —Margot Kidder, proudly, about her April 1996 manic-depressive
        episode, which ended in police taking her to a psychiatric ward

★

The studios urged us, gleefully, to spend extravagantly and publicly. The reasons were twofold. Our homes, automobiles, and clothes were indirect advertisements for the films we starred in. In that era, audiences were very devoted to their screen favorites and would see all our pictures. Part of our allure was how we lived, which was publicized in the many fan magazines which the studios more or less controlled.

Secondly, the more we spent, the more we owed. Therefore the more we relied on the studio, which had the power to suspend us without pay if we hesitated or refused to do a particular film or got out of hand in any way, real or imagined....Actors really were studio properties, and we could also be coerced by negative and cautionary publicity in the gossip columns—and not just Hedda [Hopper] and Louella [Parsons].   —Cary Grant

★

In the '70s and '80s, celebrities started behaving badly...sometimes going ballistic. In the '90s we're seeing that misbehavior of tantrums and violent outbursts spreading to publicists, gossip columnists, and photographers, etc. In other words, the handmaidens of celebrity now feel entitled to behave like celebrities, and in their minds that means *badly*....That New York columnist who punched out a cab driver after he didn't stop when the alleged scribe tried to flag him down...and that cranky butch photographer who jumped out of her cab and screamed at a crippled old man because he was momentarily slowing her down! New York, New York: rude, rude, rude!   —former news correspondent Nancy Dickerson

★

Let me pose to you a modern version of an ancient Greek piece of logic. My colleague says that all actors are liars. But my colleague is an actor. So he is lying, yes? So therefore actors are not liars. Therefore he speaks the truth, and therefore actors are liars, so therefore he lies, and so on, and so on....Wonderful! As an actress, I understand this completely.

—actor-politician Melina Mercouri

★

I heard on the news last night that they shot two innocent people in Hollywood. You know, that's surprising. I didn't know there were two innocent people in Hollywood.   —Chris Farley

★

I always have a quotation for everything—it saves original thinking.

—Dorothy L. Sayers

★

I love [quotations], because it is a joy to find thoughts one might have, beautifully expressed with much authority by someone recognizedly wiser than oneself.   —Marlene Dietrich

★

Words, once they're printed, have a life of their own.   —Carol Burnett

We must be careful what we say. No bird resumes its egg.

—Emily Dickinson

Material World

I never intended to buy a whole town, but sometimes you start out shopping and wind up investing. It's nice when you can mix the two.

—Kim Basinger

I don't have a lot of needs. I drive the old pickup I used in *Bridges of Madison County*. If I find something I like, I keep it usually. I have a helicopter.   —Clint Eastwood

President Clinton is a seafood man. He sees food, and he eats it.

—Jay Leno

I don't necessarily consider McDonald's [food] junk food. You know, they have chicken sandwiches, they have salads.   —President Bill Clinton

You get all the french fries the president can't get to.

—Al Gore, on one of the perks of being vice president

I'm always happy to see [President Clinton] enjoying his food. I think it's terribly important. There is so much fear of food around, and people are not enjoying it enough.   —chef Julia Child

It turns out that back in 1980, Hillary Clinton invested in sugar, hogs, and cattle. She got the idea from watching her husband eat breakfast.

—Conan O'Brien

I love, love, love apricot baby food. My closet in the kitchen is filled with jars of it. I love Lucky Charms and Cocoa Pebbles cereal. I love my purple couch and I love dancing. I used to have the best stuffed animals, but my dog Samson ate them.   —Alicia Silverstone

Michael Jackson is such a doll...and he gave me a doll of himself for a gift.
It was unforgettable.   —Elizabeth Taylor (the gift was life-sized)

★

Cosmetic surgery.

—Bill Paxton, replying when asked his favorite tax deduction

★

Everyone knows I adore Barbra Streisand...one of my proudest purchases
was a thirty-inch doll of Barbra, custom-made and just perfect, right down
to her little Fu Manchu fingernails....What I *don't* spend much on is
food—what a waste! It's here today and gone to flab tomorrow.

—exercise maven Richard Simmons

★

They have wonderful cooks here [at the White House]. As Chelsea could tell
you, there is a whole little kitchen where they don't do anything but make
pastry and sweet things.

—President Bill Clinton, addressing children on TV

★

Chili concocted outside of Texas is usually a weak, apologetic imitation of
the real thing. One of the first things I do when I get home to Texas is have
a bowl of red. There is simply nothing better.   —Lyndon Johnson

★

Food doesn't have to be gourmet to taste good. A cheese ring is always very
pleasing.   —Jimmy Carter

★

Never invest in anything that eats or needs repairing.

—showman Billy Rose

★

Part of the loot went for gambling and part for women. The rest I spent
foolishly.   —George Raft, on how he lost his fortune

★

We have a place in Montana, but we really live in Los Angeles. Montana is
nine months of winter and three months of house guests.

—Dennis Quaid

★

The main thing you learn about living in a big family is that the first one up
in the morning is the best-dressed.   —author Kitty Kelley

★

"My relatives don't know how to handle my fame...."I need a new roof for my house." They assume I'm rich. They'll say things like that because they don't know what else to say. I don't even go to family reunions anymore.

—James Earl Jones

In posh places, you get to like avocado and spinach and other way-out foods. So you have them every time. You learn about wine, and that's the scene for a while. When you've done all that, then you can go back. You realize that the waiter's just there to ask you what you want, not what anyone expects you to want. So if you feel like cornflakes for lunch, you ask for them, without feeling like a northern comedian. —Paul McCartney

I'm getting to the point where my stomach rebels, and this does not help my relations with foreign powers. I bit two of them today.

—President Franklin D. Roosevelt, complaining to wife
Eleanor about White House food

I do not pretend not to dislike peas. I cannot stand them.

—Henry Kissinger

Lots of kids don't like broccoli, but I doubt very many adults like it either.

—George Bush

I've learned to love delivery food.

—Luke Perry (*Beverly Hills 90210*), after becoming famous

For me a kitchen is like science fiction. I only go there to open the refrigerator and take something out. —Ann-Margret

Why do Hollywood divorces cost so much? Because they're worth it.

—Johnny Carson

Why the courts don't tell a husband who has been living off his wife to go out and get a job is beyond my comprehension. —Joan Lunden

★

I don't even have a mantel to put this [Academy Award] on. I'll have to buy a new home. —Brenda Fricker (*My Left Foot*)

★

ADAM SANDLER

I was in New Hampshire with my family at a pizza place. The kid working there goes, "Hey, you look like Adam Sandler." I said, "Yeah, I know." He goes, "What's your name?" I go, "Adam Sandler." And he goes, "Whoa, that's a coincidence!"   —Adam Sandler

★

Living well *isn't* the best revenge. Not unless people *know* about it. Publicity's damned important.   —Tom Arnold

★

The only reason to have money is to tell any SOB in the world to go to hell.
                                    —Humphrey Bogart

★

Money does buy happiness. And I'm healthy already.   —Mel Brooks

★

My mother always told me never to accept candy from strange men. Get real estate instead.   —Eva Gabor

★

Our mother used to tell us, "She who marries for money earns it. The hard way." She believes you should fall in love with a rich man first, *then* marry him. —Magda Gabor

★

I once read that people who think money can do anything can usually be suspected of doing anything for money.... —Peter Finch

★

Money does buy happiness. But happiness isn't everything.

—Jean Seberg

★

Whether you're a movie actress or a drag queen, money—lots of money—is heaven-sent, because you can buy all the clothes you need and want. And for me, clothes unmake the man. —Divine

★

If I went onstage in a business suit, they would think I was crazy. It's like putting Marlene Dietrich in a housedress. —Liberace

★

It's a good thing that I was born a woman, or I'd have been a drag queen.

—Dolly Parton

★

I'm a drag addict. Not a drug addict. —Boy George

★

Fashion is made to become unfashionable. —Gabrielle "Coco" Chanel

★

The Duchess of Windsor was a perfect example of a woman who had no natural beauty, but she spent a lifetime slim and exquisitely attired, and thus simulated beauty and elegance....In the end, she was more to be admired than the natural beauties who gain weight, lose their looks, and put on those atrocious caftans. —Lilli Palmer

★

Nature gives you the face you have when you are twenty. Life shapes the face you have at thirty. But it is up to you to earn the face you have at fifty.

—"Coco" Chanel

★

Shopping is like temporary therapy for those who are rich and shallow, insecure, or clutter-happy. —Natalie Wood

★

Food is the most primitive form of comfort. —columnist Sheilah Graham

You'd be surprised how much it costs to look this cheap.   —Dolly Parton
★

If we had more women scientists, I am sure by now they'd have invented edible makeup.   —Gilda Radner
★

I don't have the time every day to put on makeup. I need that time to clean my rifle.   —Henriette Mantel (*The Brady Bunch Movie*)
★

If women were all that attractive to men, we wouldn't have to wear fancy outfits and unnatural shoes and paint these masks on our faces to get men in the mood to procreate with us.   —Roseanne
★

I was rejected by a ballet school for not being bulimic....I'm just a person trapped inside a woman's body.   —Elayne Boosler
★

There are no ugly women, only lazy ones.
          —Helena Rubinstein, who got rich via makeup for the millions
★

My weakness is wearing too much leopard print.   —Jackie Collins
★

I did not have 3,000 pairs of shoes—I had 1,060.   —Imelda Marcos
★

I never go out unless I look like Joan Crawford the movie star. If you want to see the girl next door, go next door.   —Joan Crawford
★

Dear, never forget one little point: It's my business. You just work here.
          —cosmetics magnate Elizabeth Arden to an employee
★

The biggest reason a celebrity loses his old friends is that unless they become celebrities too, they can't compete with you, spending-wise. Even the few who wish to try.   —Ginger Rogers
★

If you want to say it with flowers, remember that a single rose screams in your face: "I'm cheap!"   —Delta Burke
★

Where large sums of money are concerned, it is advisable to trust nobody.
          —Agatha Christie
★

Money makes you beautiful. —Madonna

★

I'm basically a homosexual man. I love clothes. I love good, fine fabrics. I work out. I'm concerned about my looks. I'm vain.

—Sarah Jessica Parker

★

Careful grooming may take twenty years off a woman's age, but you can't fool a long flight of stairs. —Marlene Dietrich

★

Another reason I like going out with gay men to escort me is how well they dress. You don't have to be apprehensive about being embarrassed by a guy who dresses way down or too loud. —Virginia Mayo

★

It's no wonder we know how to dress—we've spent centuries in closets.

—Isaac Mizrahi, openly gay fashion designer

★

As regards shopping, dahling: I'm too impatient to do it often. But I have the simplest tastes—I'm satisfied only by the best. —Tallulah Bankhead

★

I love to smoke alone. But I hate to shop alone.

—Joan Hackett, who preferred cigars

★

Brevity is the soul of lingerie. —Dorothy Parker

★

I choose my outerwear, but my husband accompanies me when I shop for underwear. —Heather Locklear

★

You *can* fall in love with a house—its appearance, its looks and lines and beauty. *I* did. —Madonna, on her Florida house

★

A white Cadillac is fine for me. I don't go for cars in wild colors, and that includes no pastels!

—Hattie McDaniel (*Gone With the Wind*), possibly alluding to Stepin
Fetchit's pink Rolls-Royce or Francis X. Bushman's lavender one

★

It's weird how you get used to things that you never thought of doing before. You have to travel in a private jet. You get used to that, to having your own bed and your own stuff on this jet. I can't sleep on planes, never could, but I could sleep on that one. You suddenly have to have that. How else are you going to travel? There's no other way, you think. It just gets real scary about what you have, and what you are going to need, just to be okay.

—Tom Arnold

Tinted car windows are one of the first things a celebrity buys once they become a celebrity. They're an absolute must.   —Whoopi Goldberg

My favorite thing to buy, or have people buy for me, is cookies. I love cookies, period, but since becoming famous, I'm very picky about which cookies I'll eat. And I can't pig out as often as I used to.   —Tom Arnold

That was the best ice cream soda I ever tasted.

—the reported last words of Lou Costello (1906–59) of Abbott & Costello

JOHN WATERS

I don't dislike animals, but I don't have a problem if they test medicines or even cosmetics on them. Eyeliner has been important in my life. If ten chickens have to die to make one drag queen happy, so be it.

—director John Waters

When you get to be famous, you have to decide about two items...that's guard dogs and someone to answer all the fan mail. The first is practically a necessity. The second is optional, because no star has time to read that mail, plus some of it's nasty or depressing, and it's very expensive to deal with it, even if it's pleasant and even if they aren't writing to you to ask for photos or advice and all that.   —Janet Margolin

Actors should pay more attention to their work and less to their fan mail.

—silent-screen star Lon Chaney

When I was a girl, I always wanted to be a veterinarian. That was my dream. Acting was a detour for me...not a career I really planned. I was never into becoming a star, because it had taken me away from my privacy. Fame destroyed my anonymity. But now [post-Hollywood], I'm free.

—rich animal lover Kim Novak

I love horses, and one saying I do resent is "fat as a horse." When did you ever see a fat horse? Unlike humans, they only eat on an empty stomach.

—Barbara Stanwyck

I eat, therefore I ham.

—Chris Farley, another overweight comedian who died young

Women should try to increase their size rather than decrease it. Because I believe the bigger we are, the more space we'll take up, and the more we'll have to be reckoned with. I think every woman should be fat like me.

—Roseanne

Performing's what I do, and food tends to be my hobby. I freely admit I do overeat.   —John Candy (see Chris Farley)

★

I had my jaws wired shut [to lose weight], but it didn't work. Where there's a will, there's a pliers.   —producer Allan Carr

I went on an ice cream diet...I gained fourteen pounds....Where do you go to get some of this anorexia? I'd really like to know!   —Shelley Winters

I used to know Vera-Ellen, one of Hollywood's best dancers but not a big self-promoter. Unlike, say, Annie Miller....Vera-Ellen had a complex about her weight. It went from bad to worse, even after she'd become svelte and sophisticated....She'd weigh herself religiously. She once told me that— and this is how obsessive she had become—whenever she weighed herself, which she always did nude, she made sure she wasn't wearing her contact lenses.   —Hollywood columnist Lee Graham

Once during Prohibition, I was forced to live for days on nothing but food and water.   —W. C. Fields

Daddy always warned me about men and alcohol, but he never said a thing about women and cocaine!   —Tallulah Bankhead

Dahling, of *course* cocaine isn't habit-forming, and I should know: I've been using it for twenty years!   —Tallulah Bankhead

I've been smoking shit for about forty years, but it never got to be a habit with me.   —Robert Mitchum

When you have this much money, you buy everything you want. Then you do the stupid thing and buy drugs, because you've already bought everything else, too much of it, and it's not exciting anymore.

—Boy George

★

The cost of living has gone up another dollar a quart.   —W. C. Fields

★

Drugs...but don't act like it's totally new or alien to Hollywood. Half the stars of the golden era were actual alcoholics.   —Larry Blyden

★

Prohibition is better than no liquor at all....   —Will Rogers

★

Everyone says I have a drinking problem. I don't have any drinking problem, for gosh sakes. I have a problem *not* drinking.   —Dean Martin

★

Prohibition was a very American concept—dictating people's morals, telling them they legally could not drink. For the entire 1920s! Of course, it was good for one group of people: the police. It actually gave them something to do, because Prohibition was responsible for the rise of organized crime in America. Once again, the so-called do-gooders did more harm than good.

—Ray Milland, Oscar winner for the alcoholic-themed *Lost Weekend*

★

I'm not exactly a shopaholic. But I like to spend a lot, go on occasional sprees. Probably because my childhood wasn't the best time of my life, just the most lasting. —Michael Landon

★

My money has never brought me happiness. Not happiness that lasts...and the older I get, the more I realize it can't buy love, either. Men find money glamorous, but eventually it doesn't make them any kinder or more devoted. —Woolworth heiress Barbara Hutton

★

I made $500 a week playing *Maverick* the first year, $600 a week the second year, and $1,250 the last year. As a matter of fact, I made $92,000, I figured once, when I was under contract to Warner Bros. for about four years—and I paid $100,000 to my lawyers to get out of it. So I lost $8,000 during that period. —James Garner

★

The screenwriter may be low man on the Tinseltown totem pole, but he earns more than the guy who writes books. He's also safer, in a way; you know what they say to new authors: If you steal from another author, that's plagiarism. But if you steal from many, that's research.

—Steve Tesich, Oscar-winning writer (*Breaking Away*)

★

I was twenty-one and *Platoon* had just won Best Picture and grossed $100 million. Suddenly you're not paying for meals or drinks. You don't drive anymore. You get success. The more money you make, the less people want you to spend. It's very bizarre. —Charlie Sheen

★

When people say they want to be rich and famous, just try rich and see if that doesn't get most of it for you. —Bill Murray

★

Sad to say, but once you're rich and your face is nationally known, you find you have relatives and long-lost friends you never knew you had. Your fame, the smell of your success, draws them like bugs…and behind them cockroach smiles they all got one thought: gimme, gimme, gimme.

—Howard Rollins

You never realize how short a month is until you pay alimony.

—John Barrymore

Being married to a beautiful girl is expensive. Because you also have to hire a cook.   —Sammy Davis Jr.

The fact that husbands don't live as long as wives can be seen as nature trying to make up for the inequality of sexism. For, some widows are bereaved, but many are simply relieved.   —Rachel Roberts

Burgess [Meredith] and I had a lot in common when we got married. I loved him and he loved him.   —Paulette Goddard

Hollywood tells us to trust in romance. To marry the romantic stranger. Hollywood is wrong.   —screenwriter Eleanor Perry

No government has the right to tell its citizens when or whom to love. The only queer people are those who don't love anybody.

—screenwriter Rita Mae Brown

Do we really know anybody? Who does not wear one face to hide another?

—screenwriter Frances Marion

My husband loves to shop, but if I go with him he always manages to lose me and go off on his own. He doesn't like [my] picking out his clothes. But he likes to pick out *mine*.   —Carolyn Bessette Kennedy, on JFK Jr.

The only thing I like more than my wife is my money. And I'm not about to lose that to her and her lawyers, that's for damn sure. And you can quote me on that.   —rocker-actor Jon Bon Jovi

★

Years ago, I saved up a million bucks from acting—a lot of money back then—and I spent it all on a ranch outside Tucson. Now when I go down there, I look at the place and I realize my whole acting career adds up to a million bucks' worth of horseshit.   —Robert Mitchum

★

Michael Jackson offered a million bucks to some hospital in England to buy up the bones of the Elephant Man. Is that sick, or what? At least they said no, they weren't for sale. But it makes sense, though—one freak trying to buy the remains of another freak.   —comic Sam Kinison

★

When I was growing up, a self-supporting woman was a contradiction in terms. Motion pictures have done the most to change that, at least on a widely visible level. I have mixed feelings.... I don't approve of the growing tendency to discuss one's salary or wealth in public. Information may leak out, but I *never* discuss my earnings publicly.

—Mary Pickford, silent-screen superstar and producer

★

There are three things I've yet to do: opera, rodeo, and porno.

—Bea Arthur

★

I'm at an age where my back goes out more than I do.   —Phyllis Diller

★

Whenever I date a guy, I think, Is this the man I want my children to spend their weekends with?   —Rita Rudner

★

I think, therefore I'm single.   —Cesar Romero

★

A girl can wait for the right man to come along, but in the meantime that still doesn't mean she can't have a wonderful time with all the wrong ones.

—Cher

★

Any intelligent woman who reads the marriage contract and then goes into it deserves all the consequences.   —Isadora Duncan

★

If you want to sacrifice the admiration of many men for the criticism of one, go ahead, get married.

—suffragist Katharine Houghton Hepburn, to daughter Kate

★

When a man of forty falls in love with a girl of twenty, it isn't her youth he is seeking, but his own. —screenwriter Lenore Coffee

★

Men often marry their mothers. —novelist Edna Ferber (*Giant*)

★

Marriage sometimes turns a man's wife into someone more like his mother or sister. So he then looks outside the family circle for a very sexy, sexual mistress. —Donald Pleasence (*Halloween*)

★

The only time a woman really succeeds in changing a man is when he's a baby. —Natalie Wood

★

I nevah found a man strong enough to stay married to Bette Davis.
—double Oscar winner Bette Davis

★

I leave before being left. *I* decide. —Brigitte Bardot, on relationships

★

Any woman who lets a man walk over her is a dumb idiot and deserves no better. —chanteuse Edith Piaf

★

Bette Davis has said you cannot have both [career and family]. But I think you can. But not at the same time....But it is easier for an actress. I think it is more difficult for a woman to work in an office every day and raise her children...and actresses do not work every day, especially those who make films. Theater actresses work at night.... —Catherine Deneuve

★

I have help with my kids. Money does help a lot for hiring the best-quality people. —Demi Moore

★

If you're gonna have kids or a kid, it's better if the father's willing to be a parent too. Not just a sperm donor. —Brad Davis

★

You mean apart from my own?
—Zsa Zsa Gabor, when asked how many husbands she'd had

★

Marry an outdoors woman. Then if you throw her out into the yard for the night, she can still survive. —W. C. Fields

★

I dedicate this book to myself, for the many years of loving service and kindness I willingly gave him.

—Carlotta Monti, Fields's longtime companion and author of *W. C. Fields and Me*

Personally I know nothing about sex, because I've always been married.

—Zsa Zsa Gabor

It was so cold the other day, I almost got married.   —Shelley Winters

We are not planning to need [a prenuptial agreement] because of our unique compatibility which will keep us together.

—Shawn Southwick, Larry King's latest wife (in 1997)

My dream man, because I am a stickler for good grammar, is one who can put a sentence together. I don't like the "dees, dose, and dems" guys.

—singer Mariah Carey

I don't think anyone really marries beneath himself. Or herself. I think when people get married, they get just what they deserve.   —Eva Gabor

Yeah, I did marry beneath me. Doesn't every woman?

—Roseanne, on divorcing Tom Arnold

★

Sex without marriage being involved is like having a wonderful meal without later having to clear away the dishes and wash them up, stack them, and wonder if it's time to replace them and where are you going to get some that're reasonably priced and halfway attractive.

—director Richard Brooks

★

Sex is emotion in motion.   —Mae West

★

If I had a son and he was watching some guy making music on TV, and he came downstairs with makeup on and his mother's shoes and said, "I want to be like so-and-so," I'd beat the shit out of him....

—Eddie Murphy, prior to the 1997 publicity about him and a transvestite prostitute

Hypocrisy, thy name is Eddie Murphy.

—Karen Dior, transvestite star who claims close friendship with Murphy

★

Marry in haste, repent in Reno. —Hedda Hopper

★

Marry in haste, but repent among the leisure classes. In other words, marry *rich*. —Anita Loos, author of *Gentlemen Prefer Blondes*

★

I go for jerks some of the time, but I do have standards....I try and learn from others' mistakes. Long ago I had a girlfriend. Her boyfriend, a louse if there ever was one, got her pregnant. I couldn't convince her to leave him—eventually he dumped her. She defended him. She said, "He's so gallant. He says he'll marry me if it's a boy...." —Ava Gardner

★

I married my first husband [barber Frank White] because he smelled so good. My second [gambler Nick Arnstein] because he looked so good. And my third [producer Billy Rose] because he *thought* so good—mostly about the shows he was starring me in. —Fanny Brice

★

It looks as if Hollywood brides keep the bouquets and throw away the grooms. —Groucho Marx

★

With men it's like I'm trying every color in the jellybean jar to see what's going to taste good. —Raquel Welch

★

I don't sleep with married men, but what I mean is that I don't sleep with happily married men. —Britt Ekland

★

The main problem in marriage is that for a man sex is a hunger, like eating. If he can't get to a fancy restaurant, he'll make for the hot dog stand.

—Joan Fontaine

★

Well, everything.

—Hillary Rodham Clinton, when asked to identify
her husband's favorite food

★

The difference between us is sex. I can take it or leave it. But my kid brother...well, now, he enjoys his reputation. Sex is the most important thing in his life. It's his hobby, you could say.
—Shirley MacLaine, on Warren Beatty
★

There should be more women in power. They have great compassion for humanity. The men don't give a shit...only kidding.
—Bette Midler, to a *mixed* industry audience
★

I have a reputation, you know. Something to try and live up to. Heaven help me if I ever did!   —Frank Sinatra
★

Someone once asked me why women don't gamble as much as men do, and I gave the reply that we don't have as much money. That was a true but incomplete answer. In fact, women's total instinct for gambling is satisfied by marriage.   —Gloria Steinem
★

Children are, let's face it, a vital accessory for most actresses past the age of thirty.   —Paulette Goddard, who didn't have one
★

...an entirely humiliating, embarrassing, and degrading experience.
—Joan Fontaine, on giving birth to her only child
★

When a man has a son, it's like admitting he can't make a name for himself on his own.   —Colleen Dewhurst
★

You know the problem with men? After the birth, we're irrelevant.
—Dustin Hoffman
★

Marry me—or you can't see your baby!
—Debbie Rowe, impregnated by or via Michael Jackson (wags have dubbed the possible future divorce *Rowe vs. Weird*)
★

Macho does not prove mucho.   —Zsa Zsa Gabor
★

Plain women know more about men than beautiful ones do.
—Katharine Hepburn

SUSAN SARANDON

In Hollywood there are women who spend every afternoon shopping for wrinkle-free dresses to go with their wrinkle-free faces.

—Susan Sarandon

A woman is as old as she looks before breakfast.

—columnist Cholly Knickerbocker

A woman is as old as she feels. Except in Hollywood.

—Oscar winner Lila Kedrova (*Zorba the Greek*)

Money can buy you fabulous clothes. It can't buy you a fabulous face.

—Joan Collins

I don't diet. I just don't eat as much as I'd like to.

—supermodel Linda Evangelista

You figure as you get older you don't have to diet as much. You can let go a little. *Wrong!* A thin older actress is mostly unwanted; an overweight older actress is completely unwanted.

—Alexis Smith

Just recently I got asked to do a film where the guy was exactly the same age as me and they go, "No, she's too old." —Daryl Hannah

★

For an actress, the important thing is not to *look* married. You can *be* married, but if you look it, there goes half your star value.

—Alexis Smith

★

Husbands: a necessary, very obtainable, but very costly accessory for the actress at or near the top. —columnist Sheilah Graham

★

One of my favorite movie lines—one of *my* movie lines—is "The thing that separates us from the animals is our ability to accessorize." I believe that, I endorse it. Among actresses overall, there's too much time and money spent on clothes, and replacing clothes, and keeping up with the next actress's clothes. If you accessorize well, you can save your time and money for more important things—like everything *else*.

—Olympia Dukakis

★

Wealthy women are fascinating to be with and study, to write about. They make an art of spending money. —Truman Capote

★

Truman never wrote that many books. He wrote well, but it didn't come easily to him. He said as much, often....His downfall as a writer and a person was when he cut down on his writing and instead became socially promiscuous. A good writer shouldn't see too much of people, whether they're rich or not. Truman traded in his talent for hobnobbing...and after he *wrote* about those fancy do-nothing wives, they dropped him and he was left with neither friends nor career nor any impetus to continue.

—writer-director Colin Higgins

★

A car is a car is a phallic substitute. —Peter Sellers

★

I once drove with friends from Cannes to Nice. It took about an hour, and we dieted all the way. —hostess with the mostess Elsa Maxwell

★

Conrad Hilton said his motto was "Your guest is as good as mine."

—George Sanders (who, like Hilton, was married to Zsa Zsa Gabor)

★

TIM ALLEN

I'm not buying a Gulfstream jet just because Arnold Schwarzenegger has one. That would be silly. I'm not that competitive or materialistic. But I bet my jet will have more special features than his....   —Tim Allen

It's a famous story, probably apocryphal. About an aspiring actor who was hired to announce the arrivals at the Oscar ceremonies at Grauman's Chinese Theatre. Mr. Grauman tells the nervous actor to be sure and pronounce the names right, because it's on national radio. Grauman says, "Deborah Kerr pronounces her last name *car* but John Kerr pronounces his last name *cur,* so don't make a mistake or you'll never work in this town again!" So the stars start arriving, and the announcer says, "Deborah *Car's* car has just pulled up...and now there's John *Cur* getting out of his *car,* oh, and here comes Alfred Hitch*car's cock*!"   —José Ferrer

★

I rather like children. But not until they're twenty or twenty-five and are easier to entertain.   —Hugh Grant

★

I'm not child-less, dahling. I am child-free.   —Tallulah Bankhead

★

I was visiting Hollywood, and I was at a party where Shirley MacLaine was expected any minute. The hostess put on some rather exotic, slow music. A guest remarked, "I can just hear Shirley now. She walks in, hears the music and says, 'May I have the next trance?'"   —Diana Dors

★

I'm Jewish, yet people always ask me, "What are you doing for Christmas?" I tell them, "What is Christmas doing for me?"   —Sophie Tucker

★

Nostalgia isn't what it used to be.   —Simone Signoret

★

I don't care to remember when. It's all I can do to remember *now*.
          —Estelle Winwood, who lived to 101

★

Tallulah [Bankhead] told me that one time she was relaxing with a lady friend, listening to a waltz or some old-fashioned music like that. And her friend sighed, "Oh, Tallulah, do you remember the minuet?" And Tallulah said, "Dahling, I can't even remember the men I *slept* with."
          —Patsy Kelly

★

Elizabeth [Taylor] is an expert, and she says fame is the best deodorant....I say that hunger is the best sauce.   —Richard Burton

★

Whenever I was picky at the table, my mother would remind me, "Oatmeal is better than no meal."   —Jack Albertson

★

Fred MacMurray held on to a buck like each one was an endangered species.
          —director Mitchell Leisen

★

Tell a woman anything she wants. What does it cost you? But never put it in writing....   —Orson Welles

★

The word "gratitude" is not part of the Hollywood dictionary.
          —Columbia mogul Harry Cohn

★

Everyone is born naked and after that, everything is drag.   —RuPaul

★

Harry Cohn once said to my face that he didn't like my looks. I recovered my composure enough to say, "That's all right. I'm not selling them."

—Judy Holliday

★

Jennifer Grey of *Dirty Dancing* had her nose done, and it almost ruined her career. Times *have* changed....

—Jed Johnson, member of Andy Warhol's "Factory"

★

The hideous Howard Stern has boasted about not having had his nose fixed. Why didn't he have his taste fixed? You could look up "bad taste" and "deliberately bigoted misinformation" in the dictionary, and Howard's ugly puss would be in there, illustrating the definition.   —Jed Johnson

★

Barry Manilow said if he'd had a nose job, he'd have ruined his voice. Yet as he grows older, the nose keeps growing but the voice isn't getting any better.   —director Emile Ardolino

★

The people who like going online best are people who can't sustain a relationship for more than five minutes.   —Madonna

★

Peanut butter is pâté for children.   —Brigitte Bardot

★

Fashion is what you think you should be. Style is who you are—if you *are* someone.   —Simone Signoret

★

For *Deconstructing Harry,* Woody Allen wanted me to look like a Jewish psychiatrist. I didn't even know what that look was....In a movie I just finished with Tim Allen, I have to move in with the Amish. I'm not that vain, but this look was a nightmare. Kelly McGillis looked good playing Amish in *Witness* when she was about eighteen, but a forty-year-old should not wear Amish shit, that's my viewpoint.   —Kirstie Alley

★

A friend, perhaps mine, once stated that perhaps the dress I was wearing was a little "young" for me. "Do you really think so, dear?" I replied. "Yours suits you perfectly. It always has."   —Dorothy Parker

★

Back when Charlton Heston had hair, they say that he supposedly went to a barbershop in Hollywood where the barber asked how he'd like his hair cut.

Charlton reportedly answered, "In complete silence."

—Edward G. Robinson

I think being into yourself is wonderful, because then you can give so much to other people....One of my goals is to someday have my own billboard. People would see it and be a little happier.　　　　—Jayne Mansfield

Hey, I'm so in this world of my own that I even have my own religion: Judyism.　　　　—Judy Gold, comedian and joke writer for Rosie O'Donnell

Being an actress is more competitive than being an actor, because we usually don't last as long. But it's true, we're all sisters under the mink.

—Joan Bennett

I attempted to make a reservation [at the Ritz Hotel in the late 1950s] while in Madrid. I didn't see why all actors should suffer as the result of one boorish one. So I requested a reservation "as soon as possible." The reception clerk was very polite and rather icy. He said, "I'm sorry, we are completely booked. We won't have a room available for you until January 1973." I stared back at him and I demanded, "Book it for me."

—George Sanders

Personal upkeep, once you pass a certain age, is the worst. But what choice do you have? My body is my instrument.　　　　—Bette Midler

[Hollywood publicist] Lee Solters used to represent singers like Streisand and Sinatra. But in 1997 he signed another singer and changed the guy's name to El Niño, to cash in on the publicity from the weather....Gimmicks can't replace singing talent, and Solters's previous clients didn't need to change their names to get noticed.　　　　—actor-coach Bobby Lewis

★

Wagner's music is better than it sounds...like the acting of several of the better-looking actors and actresses. A second hearing or a second viewing reveals more than you thought was there the first time.

—lyricist Hal David

★

Tinseltown funerals call for conscious couture...something depressed but not down-and-out, something chic and not too *everyday* black....A friend once bought a mourning suit in a color called "light black" but better known as licorice.

—Pamela Mason

I hate funerals. They aren't for the one who's dead, but for the ones who are left and enjoy mourning.　　　　　　　　　—Humphrey Bogart

Now, I know I dress like a freak—I think I enjoy it....Pants are comfortable. In front of the camera, I get paid to be uncomfortable. But not in my own, my private life....Because my God, that trip, until you go down the drain, is very short.　　　　　　　—Katharine Hepburn

I don't think Katie ever wore a skirt but once, to a funeral. I insisted. Said I wouldn't go with her unless she wore a skirt.

—George Cukor, Hepburn's close friend and ten-time director

My most annoying expenditure is, um, you know, coloring my hair.

—Madonna

Jewelry is usually a better investment than a rich husband. Unless he's very, very rich, like Jane Fonda has, and I don't think she even *likes* jewels!

—Zsa Zsa Gabor

★

Jewelry isn't necessarily so beautiful in and of itself. But it's important because it makes your *mood* beautiful.　　　　　　—Winona Ryder

One of the most important lessons I learned at [MGM] was from my acting teachers: wearing expensive clothes can improve one's personality. At least that's true for a star....These days [the 1960s], actresses must no longer believe that. Or perhaps they don't believe they have a personality to improve....　　　　　　　　　　　　　　　—Joan Crawford

★

I have an Egyptian scarab that's a treasured possession of mine. I do believe it brings me luck. You know, the Egyptians believed in all that for 3,000 years, and none of our religions are that old yet, so who am I to scoff?

—Karen Black

★

I wanted to buy the Batmobile or, better yet, have them give it to me....No deal. I did get to drive it off the set though.

—Chris O'Donnell (*Batman Forever*)

★

California has, like, half the swimming pools in the whole USA. After you're an actor and making real money, you can't *not* have a pool. Here, a house without a pool is like a neck with no diamond necklace...a swimming pool is like jewelry for your house. You owe it to yourself, and to your house.

—Drew Barrymore

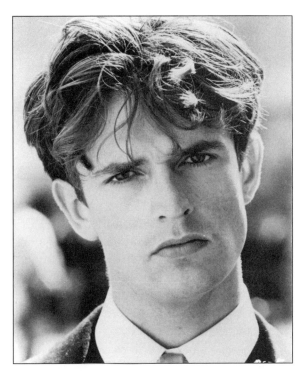

RUPERT EVERETT

Yes, I do own some red leather pants. They're from an Italian outfit called Trussardi. They're just for fun—unlike most clothes.   —Rupert Everett

★

It seems embarrassing to admit to some purchases, but the newspapers seem to have spies in a lot of the stores....I did buy a custom-made S. T. Dupont lighter with my family crest on it.   —George Hamilton

★

I love Los Angeles, I really do! And I would like to live there. But I am afraid of the—how you say?—hurt-quakes...because then, all your possessions get broken.   —Gianni Versace

★

I like how it looks, like a pirate...it's sexy. But when a man wears two earrings (one on each ear), what does *that* mean? He is bisexual? Or is he not saying which?   —Ursula Andress

★

At least comediennes aren't so hassled about looking their best or staying thin. But it's funny how it's got to a place where every female in showbiz now feels she has to have a baby or adopt one...even the more stereotypically gay ones. There's a new joke about it: What do you call homosexuals with kids?...*Lesbians.*   —novelist David Feinberg

★

We were bought and used, and when our usefulness was over, we were dismissed. I was sent to boarding school at ten and never lived at home again. I never had a family, nothing that could remotely be called normal.
          —Christina Crawford, one of Joan's four adopted children

★

I have five dogs. I rescued all of them. I think all animals should be rescued, from all bad situations....I'm trying to encourage people to follow their hearts and be true to...love, honesty, and friendship. That's what I have with animals, and that's what I want from friends.   —Alicia Silverstone

★

[Women] live longer for several reasons....We can cry whenever we wish...and we don't have to be soldiers or play dangerous games [sports] or worry about things like paternity and impotence and alimony....I also think women are generally more sensible.
          —British actress Athene Seyler (1889–1990)

★

Shakespeare asked what's in a name, but Shakespeare didn't live in an age of brand names. Or famous names. Or image....A rose by some ugly name might smell just as sweet, but if it was called a *smegma,* say, who'd bother to stop and smell the roses?   —Danny Kaye

Chanel No. 5.
          —Marilyn Monroe's answer to "What do you wear to bed at night?"

★

JULIUS "GROUCHO" MARX

I ought to—I married one.
  —Groucho Marx, when asked if he knew the definition of an extravagance

★

True story. Clergyman walks up to me, shakes my hand, and says, "I want to thank you for all the enjoyment you've given the world." I shook his hand back and said, "And I want to thank you for all the enjoyment you've taken out of the world."   —Groucho Marx

★

Oh, no. I had the radio on.
          —Marilyn Monroe, when asked, "Did you really have nothing
                              on when you posed for those photos?"

★

California is a fine place to live in, if you happen to be an orange.
                                          —Fred Allen, radio star

★

"Italy" will be sufficient.
              —composer Giuseppe Verdi, when asked by a journalist
                              for his full postal address

Don't lend your friends money, or they won't stay your friends. Unhappily, we don't choose our relatives. So don't lend your relatives money—they'll still be your relatives....And if you're a celebrity, your friends *and* relatives will interpret the word "loan" to mean "give."   —actor Leon Ames

★

One day an actor friend I'd lent money and been trying to avoid caught up with me. Says to me, "Please, if you'll just lend me your ear." I stopped and said, "All right—but nothing else."   —Ed Wynn

★

I don't know, I've never tried.
            —George Burns's reply when asked if he (like pal Jack Benny)
                                              could play the violin

★

I prefer the city. You can't get orchestras, opera, theater, and major art in the countryside....Nature's nice, in limited doses. And don't forget, nature also means blazing heat, freezing cold, blizzards, earthquakes, hurricanes! No, I'd say I'm at two with Mother Nature. In her womb, I don't want to be.
                            —Gloria Grahame (*The Big Heat*)

Ties...I hate places where you need one just to get in the door.
                                              —Gianni Versace

★

Girls—never wear a dress that makes you look as if you're about to sing.
      —Edith Head (who inspired the graffito "Edith Head gives good costume")

★

In some old movie, the man tells the actress, "That's quite a dress you almost have on." I do think in the States they favor open-toed shoes and open-chested dresses too much.   —British actress Celia Johnson

★

Tennis is very big in Hollywood. It's also the only chance an actress gets to wear white.   —Jerry Colonna, comedian

Women want men, careers, money, children, friends, luxury, comfort, independence, freedom, respect, love, and a three-dollar pantyhose that won't run.   —Phyllis Diller

★

Matrimony or matriphony? Half the marriages in Hollywood, well, they're like tennis—where love means nothing.   —Jerry Colonna

Golf can be frustrating at times, even masochistic. It's also *flog* spelled backwards. —Jerry Colonna

★

Why are O. J. Simpson and Heidi Fleiss bad golfers? Because he's a slicer and she's a hooker. —Robert Mitchum, among others

★

Like the bug said to the windshield: "Yeah, that's me all over!"
—Ish Kabibble, comedian and member of Kay Kyser's band

★

Some guys drink to drown their problems. I'm more moderate. I just irrigate my problems....

—Forrest Tucker (*F Troop*)

★

Last night Sammy [Davis Jr.] asked me what I'd like to drink to. I said, "About four in the morning." —Dean Martin

★

Thanksgiving's the best holiday of the year: food and drink, all you can celebrate. At my house, before we drink we say *bon appétit* and then we toast our creditors—Long may they waive!

—John Barrymore (a.k.a. Drew's grandfather)

★

There is no love sincerer than the love of food. —George Bernard Shaw

★

I'm worse than broke, dahling. I'm *shattered.* —Tallulah Bankhead

★

Not me, brother. A [psychiatrist] is a fellow who finds you cracked and leaves you broke. —Humphrey Bogart

★

When you work in a beauty parlor, you can't talk back to the customers. But with dead folks, you can tell them how you really feel about them. I'd say, "I'm glad you're gone. You were a creep."

—Whoopi Goldberg, who was a beautician in a mortuary

★

Alimony...it's the high cost of loving. —Johnny Carson

★

Alimony is proof that you pay for past mistakes. And pay....

—Peter O'Toole

★

God is love, but get it in writing.   —Gypsy Rose Lee

★

I have never hated a man enough to give his diamonds back.

—Zsa Zsa Gabor

★

Diamonds last longer, but I've always liked men too. Especially athletes—they don't smoke, they don't drink, and they keep their bodies in top working condition. Yeah, a hard man is good to find.   —Mae West

★

Her husband says that Jackie Onassis suffers from chronic affluenza.

—columnist Joyce Haber

★

Success is the degree to which other people envy you...and want what you have.   —Peter Sellers

★

You've got two choices: you can live the life you like, or you can like the life you live. Some people don't even do the second.   —Liberace

★

The more money you have, the less satisfaction you get.

—Barbara Hutton, heiress

★

I buy art, mostly paintings. I believe in enjoying the beauty of what you purchase. It also happens that my paintings appreciate in value every year.

—Edward G. Robinson

★

Quality's nice, but quantity's impressive.

—tycoon Helena Rubinstein, about her painting collection

★

Some in this town buy things or collect things. Others try to live very well. Still others try to buy or influence people. Tell me what you buy, and I'll tell you what you are. It's more true than with food; you *are* what you buy.

—columnist Joyce Haber

★

The rich get richer, and the poor have children. You can't guarantee you'll get rich, but you can guarantee your own and your loved ones' poverty by having a large family on a poor man's wages. ...It's ironic that in Hollywood, where wages are so high, families come in smaller sizes, if at all.   —novelist Harold Robbins

★

Your value as a performer is both what you are paid and what you *receive*. ...I was under contract to [David O.] Selznick, who loaned me out to [Twentieth Century–Fox] to do *Frenchman's Creek*. The studio paid Selznick $2,500 a week for me, of which I received $1,200 from Selznick. ...I informed the director in a very civil way that I would be giving him $1,200 worth of work a week, and no more.   —Joan Fontaine

★

It's a funny thing, because everything in my life that I ever wanted, if I tried for it, I can say that I got it. But with men, the harder I tried, the harder I flopped.   —Fanny Brice

★

★*All About Me*★

Pretentious, Moi?

We French found it and called it *joie de vivre*—the joy of living.
> —Renée Repond, French actress (1888–1965)

I can throw a fit, I'm a master at it.
> —Madonna

If I was just normally intelligent, I could probably get away with it, but I'm fiercely intelligent, and that's threatening.
> —Sharon Stone

★

I felt a special relationship to Elvis Presley because he was from Mississippi—he was a poor white kid...he sang with a lot of soul.
> —Bill Clinton

★

I don't mean to be a diva, but some days you wake up and you're Barbra Streisand.
> —Courtney Love, after showing up hours late for a photo shoot

★

I think a man can have two, maybe three affairs while he is married. Three is the absolute maximum. After that, you are cheating.   —Yves Montand

★

Oprah Winfrey issued a statement saying that even though she appeared on the *Ellen* coming-out episode, she's not gay. Meanwhile, Ellen DeGeneres issued a statement saying even though she appeared on *Oprah,* she's not black.
> —Conan O'Brien

There is nothing wrong with playing a serious mom once, but it gets boring.
> —Christine Lahti, on why she turned to TV

★

The only two things I ever demand of anyone is that they never hit me and they never lie to me. The relationship is over the second that happens.
> —James Woods, on his engagement to a much younger woman in 1997 (a former wife accused him of wife beating)

Being a star, aw shucks....As a bartender, I was the *only* star. I was the only superstar bartender. You wouldn't believe how popular I was.
—Bruce Willis

★

One of the preview cards at the Coronet screening had scribbled on it, "Francis, you can't win 'em all." But whoever wrote that was wrong. I can.
—director Francis Ford Coppola

★

I'm thankful at Thanksgiving time for having the guts to have always been myself and never moved one inch, right or left, and I'm still here to tell about it. —designer-critic Mr. Blackwell

★

It sounds vain, but I could probably make a difference for almost everyone I ever met if I chose to involve myself with them either professionally or personally. —Kevin Costner

★

If I don't get sexually aroused onstage, then there's something wrong.
—Michael Hutchence of INXS

★

Enemies are so stimulating. —Katharine Hepburn

★

To have stardom on a Julia Roberts level...would be so detrimental to my family and me. I don't know how she does it. —Kyra Sedgwick

★

If you have too much fame, you become a prisoner of your own success. What fun is that? I can't imagine being Michael Jackson or Madonna. To me, that would be the biggest curse in the world.
—singer Belinda Carlisle

★

I don't think I'd want Madonna's fame. You have no time, you have no opportunity, to be yourself. It's next to impossible, and I think it really limits your ability to be creative. —Sandra Bernhard

★

If you go to a restaurant and you have to tell them who you are...you're not famous. —Gregory Peck

★

Do I trust the safety of my country to women? Well, yes. I know that they're quite capable, quite mean, quite everything. And I feel the same way about gay men or gay women—the meanest fuckers in the world. I feel wholly secure with them guarding the country. Seriously. They've had the best parades.   —Tom Arnold (*The Stupids*)

★

There are certain people that are marked for death already. I have my little list of journalists that have treated me unfairly. Like, I was totally happy, totally confident with my work in *Selena*, but out of the 700 reviews—and I read every single one—I can quote the [bad] one....I definitely have my list of people that are going to get their justice.   —Jennifer Lopez

★

It was God who made me so beautiful. If I weren't, then I'd be a teacher.
—supermodel Linda Evangelista

★

I agree with the gay Englishman [Irishman Oscar Wilde] who said you should either look like a work of art or, if you can't, wear one. Sometimes I do both!   —Julie Newmar

★

Of course, *the Magnificent Seven* would have been nothing without me.
—Yul Brynner

★

Just to be nominated makes me feel like a real actress.
—Sissy Spacek, at the Oscars (she won—and became a real actress)

★

New Jersey?
—Tori Spelling's reply when asked to name the capital of New York

★

Every city I go to is an opportunity to paint, whether it's Omaha or Hawaii.
—Tony Bennett

★

I really resent it when people say actors are dumb. We're very well educated, especially in life and the real things.
—high school dropout John Travolta

★

Actors are not stupid, but most actors can't be intellectuals—there isn't time. You either read books or you go out and entertain.
—British blonde bombshell Diana Dors

★

In America sex is an obsession; in the rest of the world it is a fact.

—Marlene Dietrich

The difference between acting-directing-producing-writing and just acting is the difference between masturbation and making love. It's a lot more fun if you're not alone. —multi-hyphenate Warren Beatty

I don't think that I'm the greatest entertainer who ever lived, like a few other people think....I never thought that in my worst egomaniacal days. I thought that I was damn good, a superstar, you know. But the greatest? Get outta here. —Sammy Davis Jr.

To get my resources, I have to hang. I have to know and be in touch with and keep the pulse of every walk of life, man. —Matthew McConaughey

If my film makes one more person miserable, I'll feel I've done my job.

—Woody Allen

There are three kinds of pianists: Jewish pianists, homosexual pianists, and bad pianists. —Vladimir Horowitz (who fit two of these categories)

You don't [get over a broken heart]. It...never gets any easier. I understand, however, that playing one of my albums can help.

—Frank Sinatra

★

Every time a friend succeeds, I die a little. —Gore Vidal

★

I've been naked in a number of films....A friend of mine once joked that Richard Gere, who I think was the first name actor to do frontal nudity, was "stiff competition" for me. I had to reply, "Not from what I've seen." ...I've done it in *Trainspotting* and *Brassed Off*...but when *The Pillow Book* opened in Scotland, where my parents live, I warned my dad he might not want to go see it. But they did, and my dad sent me a fax, said it was a great film and he added, "I'm glad to see you've inherited one of my major assets." —Ewan McGregor

I'm too busy to count sheep. If I have insomnia, I count elephants. That way I don't have to count so many. —Jackie Gleason

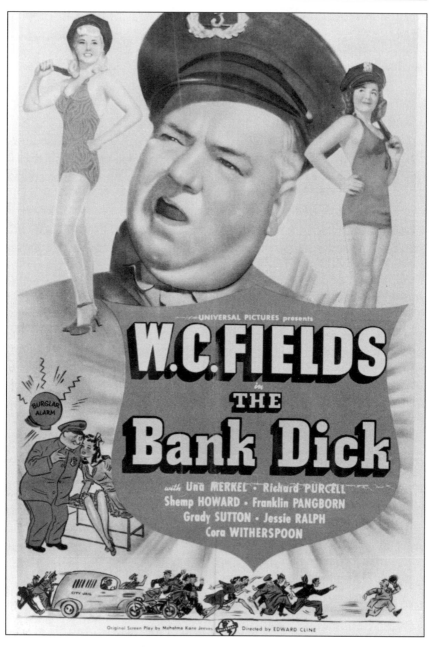

W. C. FIELDS on a poster for *The Bank Dick*.

In the wrong.   —W. C. Fields, when asked "Where is a woman's place?"

I never vote for anyone. I always vote against.   —W. C. Fields
★

With women, I've got a long bamboo pole with a leather loop on the end of it. I slip the loop around their necks so they can't get away or come too close. Like catching snakes.   —Marlon Brando
★

You buy a bad car, it breaks down, what are you going to do?
          —Charlie Sheen, explaining why he was separating
          from his wife of five months
★

Making love in the morning got me through morning sickness. I found I could be happy and throw up at the same time.
          —Pamela Anderson Lee, speaking of her pregnancy
★

The actor is not quite a human being—but then, who is?
          —George Sanders
★

Actors are crap.   —director John Ford
★

Actors should be treated like cattle.   —Alfred Hitchcock
★

Disney, of course, has the best casting. If he doesn't like an actor, he just tears him up.   —Alfred Hitchcock
★

You can pick out actors by the glazed look that comes into their eyes when the conversation wanders away from themselves.
          —Michael Wilding (also the second Mr. Elizabeth Taylor)
★

I never travel for pleasure, dear. I've traveled for work....You know, I don't travel to see places. When I do choose to, I travel to be seen.
          —Mae West
★

Dahling, I have enemies I've never even met. *That's* fame!
          —Tallulah Bankhead
★

There are people in Bel Air and Beverly Hills, who when they aren't invited to an A-list party, turn out all their lights so their neighbors won't know they're not at that party.   —columnist Joyce Haber

Eva Gabor with Merv Griffin.

If you don't already know who someone is, why on earth would you want to meet him?
                                                          —Eva Gabor
                              ★
I never speak of them [her ex-husbands], except under hypnosis.
                                                          —Joan Collins
                              ★
I dress *down* so people will know I'm *not* trying to look my best....Just showing up at an event is a real effort on my part.   —Brad Pitt
                              ★
If you stay in Beverly Hills too long, you become a Mercedes.
                                                          —Robert Redford
                              ★
I once heard a producer at RKO say about Howard Hughes, "He's entitled to his own opinion—and as many others as money can buy."
                                                          —Robert Mitchum
                              ★

In my opinion, the sound of clapping seriously overstimulates a child's nervous system. Sometimes permanently.

—Adolphe Menjou, older actor who supported Shirley Temple onscreen

★

Most males don't mature; they just grow taller. —Mary Astor

★

I don't think you can label emotions or assign them. But now they keep telling everyone to get in touch with their "feminine side." Fine, okay. But that's all? Why don't women get in touch with their "masculine side"? It couldn't hurt the gals I know. —Lee Van Cleef (*How the West Was Won*)

★

American women expect to find in their husbands the perfection that Englishwomen only hope to find in their butlers.

—writer W. Somerset Maugham (*The Letter*)

★

I do charities—but not for charity. You have to spend money to make money. —worst-dressed "expert" Mr. Blackwell

★

[In Hollywood] even the air is dishonest. —Uma Thurman

★

No Leica. —Walter Kerr's review of the film *I Am a Camera*

★

One of my favorite expressions is "golly." Now I know why: I found out it used to mean "God love me." —Betty Grable

★

I think Hollywood can teach Washington [D.C.] a few things about morality. I do. —Congressman Sonny Bono

★

You see an awful lot of smart guys with dumb women, but you hardly ever see a smart woman with a dumb guy. —writer Erica Jong

★

You never see a man walking down the street with a woman who has a little pot belly and a bald spot. —Elayne Boosler

★

Girls got balls. They're just a little higher up, that's all.

—singer Joan Jett

★

A bachelor is a man who never made the same mistake once.

—Ed Wynn, who was Jewish and married an anti-Semitic woman

These types of movies—they're so pervasive—they're everywhere now. I'm not going to change them....[The question was], am I ever going to make one of these [action] movies? And the answer was, "Yeah, probably." So if I'm ever going to *try* to make one—even just as some challenge or exercise—I want to make it when I'm still young [thirty-one] and with the best people possible. And...there was something about the ocean.

—Jason Patric, explaining why he agreed to star in *Speed 2*

Being an actor is always a struggle....Acting is the greatest profession because you're dealing with yourself all the time. It supports the self-discovery process.

—Kyle MacLachlan

I was never a dangerous woman because I like women and it's always been that women like me, but they like me more now today. And when I say less dangerous, what I mean is that I'm not the prissy blonde woman that could take your husband away, even if I don't intend to.   —Catherine Deneuve

I'm too *good* to play that role.

—Sophia Loren, explaining why she declined the role of Alexis on *Dynasty*

I don't feel old, and I'm not. I have an aunt who is 130, and I will someday reach that age. I believe it.

—Gina Lollobrigida, on turning seventy in 1997

I look for a good story. Why just do *Rambo*? I feel cheated when I see things like that. I feel like a fool....What kept me going between *Bad Boys* and *La Bamba*? I could have taken a lot of work and been on a TV series, but I don't want to sell soap or cars.   —Esai Morales

★

I don't think I'm macho *or* the sensitive type. I think I'm *very* aware of people, and I think I'm very protective in that way, whether it's a woman or a guy....There's something about nobility and chivalry that I try and find in all my characters.

—Jason Patric

★

The great thing about a director is to admire an actor enough and tell him so enough, so that the actor feels free. —Katharine Hepburn

★

I never claimed to have invented the motion picture, but I did do more than my share, yes. —Mary Pickford

★

Don't you *know* who I am?!

—Denzel Washington at an L.A. eatery, before yelling at a maitre 'd who stated he didn't have a free table

★

I really like Warren Beatty and I'd like to hang out with Warren Beatty, but the bottom line is I'm busy. —Quentin Tarantino

★

Most people don't go to the movies, and most people love me even if I don't have a hit movie. —Goldie Hawn

★

Michelle Pfeiffer's roles are a lot less sexy than mine are. —Sharon Stone

★

People think I look so fantastic. It's like practically everyone has a crush on me. —Brad Pitt

★

Personally, I don't believe I'm the most attractive girl in the world. —Heather Locklear

★

I did dedicate my memoirs to my mother. Without her I might have been somebody else. —Mae West

★

Some people did say I made cross-dressing too popular.... That was quite a burden to have on my shoulder pads. —Boy George

★

Cold sober, I find myself absolutely fascinating! —Katharine Hepburn

★

I'm bringing a woman's point of view to novels, which is rather revolutionary. —Joan Collins

★

I'm proving that a woman can be succcessful as a singer. Really, totally successful. It's a whole new concept. —Madonna

★

I know I'm capable of creating true art through my talent and natural artistry. But Hollywood only wants me to show off my bust.

—Jayne Mansfield

I'm trying to bring classiness and an international spirit to music, and to have a good time at the same time.   —David Bowie

The reason I'm doing Shakespeare is to see if today's audiences can still relate to that....I'm not old or English, or anything, so this'll prove it once and for all.   —Keanu Reeves, on performing *Hamlet* in Canada

No, I never do commercials. Except in Japan, where it doesn't count.

—Woody Allen

It really, really bugs me, to the point that if there is a wounded bird on the sidewalk, I look at it and I go, I think I'll just kick it.

—Jodie Foster, discussing weakness

I write things down. I have a get-even list. I don't seek anyone out, but if they should cross my path when I am doing a picture, there is no work for them.   —Joe Pesci

It's so demeaning for a writer to have to deal with a Hollywood movie producer...a low-grade [individual] with the morals of a goat, the artistic integrity of a slot machine, and the manners of a floorwalker with delusions of grandeur.   —Raymond Chandler

★

Marlene Dietrich's legs may be longer, but I have seven grandchildren.

—Gloria Swanson

★

I don't care if my pictures don't make a dime, so long as everyone comes to see them.   —producer Samuel Goldwyn

★

I used to earn a living as a metal worker. I was a very butch metal worker. Not all of them are, you know....As an actor, some critics and some segments of the audience have resented how masculine I am, but that's how I am; I don't apologize or try to change.   —Nicol Williamson

★

I keep my Oscars right next to the bathtub, so I can take a bath and look at them. What else are you going to do with them?   —Jodie Foster

★

In spite of everything, I have continued to be a person first and an actress second. Acting is a profession; it isn't my life. I've always wanted to be a person first.   —Brenda Vaccaro

★

I'm not a bimbo.   —Anna Nicole Smith

★

I'm a multifaceted, talented, wealthy, internationally famous genius.

—Jerry Lewis

★

The difference between film and theater is the difference between masturbation and making love. Given the choice, I think most actors would prefer theater.   —Susan Sarandon, at the 1997 Tony awards

★

I'm a highly, highly, highly creative human being.   —Kim Basinger

★

No one else can do what I can do. In any medium. That's what I call talent.

—Jackie Gleason

★

As a world-class singer, people didn't often give me enough credit as an actress.   —Diana Ross

★

My only regret in the theater is that I could never sit out front and watch me.   —John Barrymore

★

Making use of what nature endowed you with is a talent in itself.

—supermodel Christy Turlington

★

I can honestly say, hand on heart, that I have dated nineteen guys in my life. And of those nineteen I have slept with fifteen.

—Pamela Anderson Lee

★

She's got talent and personality. Give me two years and I'll make her an overnight star.

—Columbia mogul Harry Cohn, on a starlet

★

Don't say yes [until] I finish talking.   —Fox mogul Darryl F. Zanuck

The Academy of Motion Picture Arts and Sciences? What art? What science?

—pioneering film director D. W. Griffith

A place where they shoot too many pictures and not enough actors.

—columnist Walter Winchell, on Hollywood

I have done it all. I've played everything but a harp.

—actor Lionel Barrymore

Actors are quite brilliant people, for the most part. Brilliant at improvisation...nothing fazes us, and being English, we're marvelous at flying into a great calm. A friend of mine was in a play. He was supposed to get shot by his opponent with a gun. When the moment came, the actor found that he had no gun, thanks to the erratic property manager. So the actor had to do *something,* and finally *kicked* my friend, who was inspired to fall to the floor and gasp, "The boot...was poisoned!"

—comedic actor Kenneth Williams

I really want to be a serious actress.   —Anna Nicole Smith

I tend to get bad reviews and I don't know exactly why. It would be fair to say that what I do isn't easy, and maybe it looks easy....Maybe it's fair to say that many of my movies are not particularly quality pictures. I can understand that point of view. I don't happen to agree. I think the world of my pictures.   —Chevy Chase

For a time, I was a singing waiter. I don't sing anymore. I got used to singing only when I got paid for it....For whatever reason, nobody in Hollywood wants my talent in a musical.   —Burt Lancaster

Am I a better singer or actor? Why do people ask me that? I'm a wonderful singer! As an actor, well, judge for yourself—just don't tell me about it if you don't think I'm very good.   —Dean Martin

★

I paint. I don't have enough creative outlets, so I paint. I happen to own an outstanding art collection which includes Monet and Rodin....I enjoy painting. I also enjoy the thought that someday some of my works may be in other people's collections....A subject I'm really into is painting the theme of how fame can annihilate or destroy big stars.

—Sylvester Stallone

Don't do something. Just stand there.

—Clint Eastwood, on his "acting" method

When I'm working well, I like to think I'm doing God's work.

—Faye Dunaway

I hired, fired, cast, produced, directed, wrote, acted, hyped [*Baretta*] in the media. I spent all my time trying to bring lousy scripts to life, trying to bring mannequins with suits on to life. —Robert Blake

I was always independent, even when I had partners.

—Samuel Goldwyn

You can't buy a knighthood, you know. You can't lobby for it. It's given by the queen on behalf of the nation. That's the theory. I think it's a very appealing idea, that the nation should say thank you, choosing to say thank you to me. —Sir Ian McKellen

I think I'd be a part-owner now if I played football, the kind of money that Deion Sanders is making now, and he couldn't carry my jockstrap.

—actor and ex-player Fred Williamson

The [actor] I was reading with got lost because he was so busy watching me. —Samuel L. Jackson, re one of his auditions

The only agent I need, baby, is God. I know what I want to say. I know what I want to do....I don't need nobody to feed it to me.

—Martin Lawrence, who in 1996 ran into a busy traffic intersection,
shouting at cars and carrying a gun

★

Firewalking is part of my process. Rebirthing is part of my process. I follow the medicine path and I attend sweat lodges, an ancient Native American ceremony of purification. —LeVar Burton

I don't think I was born beautiful. I just think I was born me.

—Naomi Campbell

I believe that mink are raised for being turned into fur coats and if we didn't wear fur coats those little animals would never have been born. So is it better not to have been born or to have lived for a year or two to have been turned into a fur coat? I don't know.

—Barbi Benton, former *Playboy* Playmate

I'm not naïve about finances. Once when my mother mentioned an amount and I realized I didn't understand, she had to explain: "That's like three Mercedes." Then I understood.   —Brooke Shields

Smoking kills. If you're killed, you've lost a very important part of your life.

—Brooke Shields, who married Andre Agassi

I built my body to carry my brain around.   —Sylvester Stallone

Why do people treat me with fun [make fun of him] just because I am the biggest, strongest, and most beautiful man in the world?

—Arnold Schwarzenegger

Yeah, I've made stupid movies. But I like my work in every film I've done.

—Bruce Willis

I've made some great ones. *Risky Business* still stands up. It's timeless. They study that film in film school.   —Rebecca DeMornay

★

It's a spiritual message. And forgive me, but I think it's almost a deeply religious message on a very personal level.

—Elizabeth Berkley, on the universally reviled *Showgirls* script

★

I think reviews are terribly, terribly unfair, and I can explain that. Reviews are terrible because they hurt actors, and reviews are also terrible because trees have to die to make that paper. You see?   —Jayne Mansfield

★

Money doesn't mean anything to me except as an affirmation of the music.

—John Tesh

I'm astounded by people who take eighteen years to write something. That's how long it took that guy [Gustave Flaubert] to write *Madame Bovary,* and was that ever on the bestseller list?

—sometime screenwriter Sylvester Stallone

Histrionics are against him.

—NBC's word-challenged John Tesh, assessing a male gymnast's chances for an Olympic medal

I actually don't need a raise. It would be nice, but it's not going to sway me.

—Jerry Seinfeld, on whether he would sign on for a ninth season (already earning $1 million per episode)

We've all had hypothermia at times on *Baywatch....*But it's easier for me to endure the cold because I'm an owner of the show and I'm the highest-paid guy.

—David Hasselhoff

I was [in Hollywood] with no money and all these people saying they wanted to do this and that for me. People wanted to marry me. People wanted to put me in the movies.

—Pamela Anderson Lee

People think modeling's mindless, that you just stand there and pose, but...I like to have a lot of input. I know how to wear a dress, whether it should be shot with me standing up or sitting. And I'm not scared to say what I think.

—Linda Evangelista

[Some movie producers] wanted me to take a drug test. I was very insulted and I didn't do it. I'd done like thirty-one movies up until that point and a lot of lead roles, and here I am showing up for a week and three scenes and they want a friggin' drug test. I was like, "Read my shoulder, pal." I've got a new tattoo. It says *EMA.* It stands for Eat My Ass.

—Charlie Sheen

★

I perpetrate reports that I'm hard to work with. I'm very proud of those. I work on them. I cultivate them. I don't mind any of that. It makes my life a lot easier. I have enough Christmas cards. It's really okay if I don't get any more. I don't make films to make friends.

—Debra Winger

★

I don't have any desire to be popular. It's humiliating, I think...and confusing.
                                                    —John Malkovich

★

I don't make these movies for you, for critics, for studio executives. I really make a movie like this [*The Postman,* which he directed] not even for a specific audience. I make a movie like this for myself.
                                    —sometime auteur Kevin Costner

I tend not to like ugly, dumb, hostile women. I find them less attractive, frankly.
                                                    —Jerry Seinfeld

ELIZABETH BERKLEY

It's not like it's just "Here's another breast scene." At its heart, it's about moral choices. What you give up for love. How far would you go to get what you want? What would you give up for your dream? These are the questions [the character] is faced with along the way. I just hope that people really care about my character and go on that journey with her.

—Elizabeth Berkley, on *Showgirls*

★

United Artists asked me what the story was, and I told them it was about this homosexual who married a nymphomaniac, and they said, "Great, go ahead!"

—director Ken Russell, re his Tchaikovsky biopic, *The Music Lovers*

★

I am free of all prejudice. I hate everyone equally.   —W. C. Fields.

★

Now [post-trial] it's a lot easier [to get dates]. It's this bad-boy mentality. Why girls like rockers.   —O. J. Simpson, bad boy and ladykiller

★

The chicks still dig me.   —aged rocker Keith Richards

★

I'm a very shy woman, very sensitive, very emotional, very volatile, with quite a sense of humor.   —Joan Collins

★

Deep inside I'm so...I mean, I'm so sensitive.

—Jean-Claude Van Damme

★

I'm old. I'm young. I'm intelligent. I'm stupid.   —Warren Beatty

★

I'm just a hair away from being a serial killer.   —Dennis Hopper

★

I'm no alcoholic. I'm a drunkard. The difference is, drunkards don't go to meetings.   —Jackie Gleason

★

So I'm not the world's greatest actress.   —Madonna

★

I am not a slut.   —Vanessa Williams

★

I don't know, people say I'm a sex symbol, but I think I'm an actress.

—Pia Zadora

I'm not perky.   —Kathie Lee Gifford

I'm no actor, and I have sixty-four pictures to prove it.   —Victor Mature

I'm an actor, not a star. Stars are people who live in Hollywood and have heart-shaped swimming pools.   —Al Pacino

I'm an instant star. Just add water and stir.   —David Bowie

I am known in parts of the world where people have never heard of Jesus Christ.   —Charlie Chaplin

When the Beatles said they were more popular than Jesus, they weren't necessarily trying to shock....Most of the world is not Christian and never will be. And mass communications being what they are, there are in fact parts of the world where a particular star or stars may be more popular than the Buddha or Christ, Mohammed, Confucius, and so on.

                              —Buddhist actor Peter Finch

I made a solemn decision...to not perform my older songs again after 1990. As an artist, I think it's important to make radical decisions for oneself to prevent complacency building.   —David Bowie

I wasn't afraid for my safety. I'd rather take a bullet in the head than not make a movie.

          —Lara Flynn Boyle, about going on location in East Los Angeles

★

Do you know what I am? I'm successful [in 1973]. Destroy me, and you destroy your British film industry. Keep me going, and I'm the biggest star you've got. I'm Mr. England.   —Oliver Reed

★

You're acting! Don't act! I don't act, that's why I'm a star.

                              —Errol Flynn, to a more talented actor

★

I specifically negotiate that I don't *have* to do *any* press. I only do it when I think it's going to make me extra money.   —Jack Nicholson

★

JODIE FOSTER

Most people who...work in the entertainment business spend 70 percent of their time selling products. "Please buy this washing machine."
                        —Jodie Foster, who began selling Coppertone sun-tanning lotion
                                    ★
The physical labors actors have to do wouldn't tax an embryo.
                                                    —writer Neil Simon
                            ★
Thinner actors are often jealous of me. Because of my oversized aura on the big screen and the little screen.   —John Belushi
                            ★
If you live through the initial stages of fame and get past it...then you have a hope of maybe learning how to spell the word "artist."
                                                    —Patrick Swayze
                            ★

What you make of your life is what you make of the random moments in your life.

—Geraldo Rivera

★

I happen to dig being able to use whatever mystique I have to further the idea of peace.   —Garrett Morris, former *Saturday Night Live* star

★

I never think about what I want. It's about what you want to give to other people.   —Oprah Winfrey

★

I want to encourage others not to be ashamed to have a human condition called pain.   —Rod Steiger

★

If I've made it a little easier for artists...to work in violence, great, I've accomplished something.   —Quentin Tarantino, graphic director

★

When a man hits a woman, one of two things happens. Either she hauls ass in the opposite direction, or she becomes yours.   —Richard Pryor

★

Four hundred years ago I was burned at the stake as a witch....I am glad that my kind of sorcery goes by a different name today. Perhaps this time it can do me more good than the last memory I have of it.

—French singer-actor Juliette Greco

★

I was doing like half an ounce of cocaine every three days. I was drinking half a gallon of rum a day with twenty-eight beers. I never had a problem. It was other people, crawling around on the floor, blithering idiots, who had the problem.   —Dennis Hopper

★

I didn't want it, because I really didn't want the responsibility that year.

—Jon Voight, after not winning the Oscar (he did later)

★

I hope my earrings don't fall off. That's the only thing I'm nervous about.

—Sigourney Weaver, at the Oscars

★

[My parents] live in Dartmoor, and I visit them whenever I can. I particularly love that area because there's a lot of quartz in the ground, and it's very energizing.   —English actor Stephanie Beacham

★

Tragedy can strike in an instant, but film is immortal. Vic lives forever. Just before the last take, Vic took me aside to thank me for the opportunity to play this role.

—director John Landis, in whose film *The Twilight Zone* Vic Morrow and
two children were killed in an accident because of negligence
★

I learned to act on the big screen. I was never a spear carrier. I was always the star. Always.   —Rob Lowe
★

Lew Wasserman was my agent. When I started in pictures in 1948 he said, "Tony, it's going to take you ten hard, heavy years to become internationally known." So I put my head down and for ten years I made pictures, three a year. I didn't stop. I never thought about it....After ten years, Lew was right. Every country in the world knew me.   —Tony Curtis
★

I've gotten succcess enough to have my own stereotype. That's really climbing right up there to the top.   —Alan Alda
★

I don't like having to explain myself. I resent having to make it comfortable for other people to understand. My job is not being in the public eye. My job is acting.   —thespian Julia Roberts
★

Nothing would disgust me more, morally, than receiving an Oscar. I wouldn't have it in my home.   —director Luis Buñuel
★

How they could not give it to me was a bit of stupidity.
—Kirk Douglas, on not receiving an Oscar
★

Academy Awards are like orgasms...only a few of us know the feeling of having had multiple ones.   —John Huston
★

I think nothing diminishes a work of art more than criticism.
—Kevin Spacey
★

Of course we who are so successful as singers can live in the best houses and drive the best cars, travel to the most exciting places in the world. But none of that is what we're trying to achieve. What we real artists are trying to achieve is honesty in our work and music.   —Maria Callas

Once, I was walking down the street and dogs were barking at me. I said, "Ah, I must have made it. Even the animals recognize me!"

—Jon Lovitz

★

Anyone I've ever wanted to be with, I've had.   —Calvin Klein

★

My clothes aren't just fashion. They are art.   —Christian Dior

★

If everyone wore my clothes, I don't think there would be wars, truly. Of course, then I would be the richest man in the world and most people would become bankrupt. My clothes are expensive. So maybe [having] wars is better.   —Yves Saint Laurent

MICHAEL JACKSON

I was sent to this earth to bring happiness and inspiration to people, especially children. —Michael Jackson

★

Sometimes I design for the Oscars...mostly I design for the ages.
—Halston

★

I've been planted here to be a vessel for acting, you know what I mean?
—Leonardo DiCaprio

★

I may not be quite as talented as some older actresses, but people keep saying how happy they are to watch me because I'm so pretty, and that's a talent in itself. —Brooke Shields

★

My honor is my work. There is none greater. —William Hurt

★

If my film becomes a cult movie, that's fine with me. Because after all, *culture* begins with *cult*.... —Pamela Anderson Lee

★

I was a very good hairdresser [known as Mr. Danny], but not as good as I am an actor. —Danny DeVito

★

[As an unknown actor] I'd walk out of offices with my fingers in my ears so I wouldn't hear someone who didn't know as much as I did telling me what to do. —Kevin Costner

★

I'm so extremely intelligent that it's actually harmed my career as an actor. Actors are supposed to be cattle. —James Woods

★

Some people hate me 'cause I'm so ahead of my time. But I don't think I was born too soon. I think the backward people were born too late.
—Roseanne

★

I can turn on the sex appeal when I wish. I *have* it, up there [on the screen]. When I turn it on, there isn't any man that can resist me.
—Kathleen Turner

★

I'm so pretentious, I love it! —Julie Delpy

What I do, only I can do. I've come to that conclusion. I don't underrate myself now....I'm deeply sensitive, but people don't give me credit for that.
—Sylvester Stallone
★
I like young girls. Their stories are shorter.
—screenwriter Thomas McGuane (*The Missouri Breaks*)
★
I did sort of think I deserved an Academy Award nomination for Catwoman [in *Batman Returns*]. But I was fully aware that people don't ever get nominated for *Batman* movies....I got nominated for something else that year.   —Michelle Pfeiffer
★
You've personal charm. So have I. But I have talent too. I am very clever indeed. I have this God-given talent, but I don't abuse my talent ever. I work hard at it.   —Noel Coward, to actor Michael Rennie
★
Why don't you write your next script on Kleenex? That way when you hand it in, we'll have some use for it!
—Brett Butler, to one of her *Grace Under Fire* scriptwriters during a production meeting
★
I'm not difficult. Never difficult. I'm talented, I *am* demanding, I give my best, I expect the same from others. I'm deeply serious about my work.
—Faye Dunaway
★
Everyone's entitled to my opinion.   —Madonna, to her staff and crew
★
Art is the only thing that matters. In comparison with art, wealth and rank and power are not worth a row of pins. We are the people who count. We give the world significance. You are only our raw material.
—W. Somerset Maugham (*The Razor's Edge*)
★
If I ever start talking to you about "my craft" or "my instrument," you have permission to shoot me point-blank.   —Drew Barrymore
★
I'm everything.   —Madonna
★

Poor Me

I've been outed and I'm not even in.   —Jerry Seinfeld

I don't happen to be gay, but in a movie love scene I'd rather kiss a woman [as in *Bound*]. With a man, it can be really painful, all because of beard burn!   —Gina Gershon

It's not enough money.

    —O. J. Simpson, who complained to the press that his reported
        $30,000-a-month pension means he can't afford to fix his teeth

Marriage in Hollywood is like a nice hot bath. It's just not that hot anymore. It cools off after a short while.   —Jack Nicholson

The reason I drink is because when I'm sober I think I'm Eddie Fisher.

                               —Dean Martin

With every smell, I smell food. With every sight, I see food. I can almost *hear* food. I want to spade the whole lot through my mouth at Mach 2. *Basta!*   —Sarah Ferguson, the Duchess of York

Whenever I meet one of those Britishers I feel as if I have a papoose on my back.   —Dorothy Parker

I dig my father. I wish he could open his eyes and dig me. —Peter Fonda

I have this mouth that speaks the truth, and that's not so good.

                              —Robin Givens

It came out in the newspapers that I mugged some people. For a living. I had to. But I don't like to talk about it now that I have found something I do so much better.   —French screen star Gerard Depardieu

I wasn't comfortable with being the son of famous people [Barbra Streisand and Elliott Gould]. That's why I'm pursuing an acting career. It's a way of

overcoming my shyness and getting to know myself better and facing my worst fears: being judged and compared.   —Jason Gould

★

I'd hit a dry spell in my career in the mid-1980s. I come from a family of health care professionals, but I was too old for med school, so I thought about enrolling in the MacAlister School of Embalming ... for $5,000 I could have been an undertaker.   —actor Michael Jeter (*Evening Shade*)

★

The worst job I had in L.A. was driving strippers to private parties. I was in charge of collecting the money, getting their clothes at the end of the evening, and making sure that they got out safely.   —Brad Pitt

★

First I was too busy supporting myself [in Hollywood] and then auditioning. Then when stardom hits, every daytime hour is spent making movies, and too many nighttime hours are spent socializing, usually needlessly...and nothing bores like a bad party—Barbara Stanwyck calls them *fêtes* worse than death.   —Veronica Lake

★

Hollywood parties are pretty ritzy, all right. Everything's very pretty, you know, and the conversation can be pretty stimulating. There's usually a lot of food for thought. But not that much food.   —Red Skelton

★

It's true, you can be lonely in the middle of a crowded set. And your nights can be lonely when everyone thinks you're always busy and so no one ever calls to ask you out.   —Rita Hayworth

★

People automatically think that if you're a star your social calendar must be filled weeks in advance. Not so. I remember years ago when I was going through a depression, I phoned Joan Crawford and said to her, "Joan, you've been waiting for the phone to ring too, haven't you?" And she said, "Yes." So I said, "Let's go and have a meal." She was delighted to do so. And that was the great and glamorous Joan Crawford.   —Rod Steiger

★

Ginger Rogers was in a wheelchair for about ten years and grew fat. Then she started walking on her own and lost some weight. She was ready and willing to go back to work in mother and grandma roles. Until she was interviewed by a young agent at CAA who asked her what pictures she had done....Ginger walked out of the meeting.

—Irving Fein, celebrity manager

I'm sixty-five and I made the film (*Mother,* her big-screen comeback) when I was sixty-four. There are very few great roles for women my age that are fun and warm and have a good chance to be a successful film....I took three months off from Las Vegas, which was hard, but my fans thought it was great. —Debbie Reynolds

Every director bites the hand that lays the golden egg.

—producer Samuel Goldwyn

I think the biggest dilemma I'm going to have is figuring out whether the O.C. is lower-case.

—k. d. lang, upon being invested in 1997 as an Officer of the Order of Canada, signifying national merit and achievement

I want a man who's kind and understanding. Is that too much to ask of a millionaire? —Zsa Zsa Gabor

Men are beasts, and even beasts don't behave as they do.

—Brigitte Bardot

I had to get out of Beverly Hills! I sold my home there because I do like to drink a bit, but my neighbors were far too health conscious. Most of them hypocrites....We moved to Miami, where parties and drinking socially are a way of life. In California, people drink secretly, behind closed doors.

—Michael Caine

★

For so many years, I'd dreamed of going to Africa. I wanted to see where my ancestors came from....When I did go, it was rather interesting. But I found I had so little in common with them. They were foreigners. I was, I am, an American. —writer James Baldwin

★

Did you know, I just got back from a pleasure trip? I drove my mother-in-law to the airport. —Henny Youngman

★

ELTON JOHN

The press exaggerates so! I do love flowers. They're a luxury perhaps, but also a necessity....I read in the paper that I employ five gardeners and two florists to keep my two homes stocked with flowers. I only have *four* gardeners....   —Elton John

★

I'd always wanted to play T. E. Lawrence [of Arabia]....I found little in my research to indicate a significant sense of humor....But once, in Egypt, he was forced to attend a cocktail party. The socially ambitious hostess was delighted to have a celebrity guest, and wouldn't leave him alone, despite his lack of conversation. Being a good Englishwoman, she enthusiastically tried the weather: "Ninety-two today, Colonel Lawrence. Just think of it! Ninety-two." He bowed stiffly and said, "Many happy returns, madam."

—Sir Alec Guinness

I hate aging, but at least in France people are wiser about it. They say that forty is the old age of youth, and fifty is the youth of old age.

—Brigitte Bardot

Strange word...and it starts out like "monotony." Ends up the same way too....I was on an English "chat show." The host asked my opinion of monogamy. "Oh, I've only heard good things about it. I've heard it makes the best coffee tables." —Lee Van Cleef (*The Good, the Bad and the Ugly*)

My sister was wailing and moping around after her first divorce. I finally says to her, "Honey, husbands ain't copyrighted. There's plenty more where he came from." —Mae West

Before I met Nicoletta, I was not in a good time. I had a smiling face, but inside I was not happy. I was surrounded by people, but I was lonely, and the worst loneliness of all is in the crowd.

—Luciano Pavarotti, sixty-two, after leaving his wife of thirty-five years (mother of their three children) for his twenty-eight-year-old assistant

I try to conduct my life with a certain amount of dignity and discretion. But marriage is a hard, hard gig.

—Kevin Costner, divorced after his "childhood sweetheart" wife found out he'd been intimately involved with models, actresses, a publicist, a hatcheck girl, and a hula dancer

For the first year of marriage I had a basically bad attitude. I tended to place my wife underneath a pedestal. —Woody Allen

Women tolerate sex in order to have men in their lives. And men tolerate women in order to have sex in theirs. —Dame Sybil Thorndike

[Publicist] Chuck Jones was sentenced to four years in prison for having sex with Marla Maples's shoes. But the joke is on the judge, because he sent Chuck to boot camp. —Bill Maher

There's no such thing as a hard woman—only soft men.   —Raquel Welch

★

The only really happy folk are married women and single men.

—H. L. Mencken

★

Happiness is not something you experience, it's something you remember.

—Oscar Levant

★

Marriage is the last proposal a man is allowed to make, unchallenged.

—actor Larry Blyden (*On a Clear Day You Can See Forever*)

★

The first few years of marriage are a time of much promise—broken promises....   —musician Cab Calloway

★

With a second marriage, you keep your fingers crossed and you act optimistic.... Somebody did say that a second marriage is a victory of hope over experience.

—Natalie Wood, on remarrying Robert Wagner (her third marriage)

★

After being alive, the next hardest work is sex.... Some people *get* energy from sex, and some people *lose* energy from sex. I have found that it's too much work. But if you have the time for it, and if you need the exercise, then you should do it.   —Andy Warhol

★

Sex: for something that takes so little time, it can lead to the most monumental headaches and consequences.   —Merle Oberon

★

A woman drove me to drink, and I never even had the courtesy to thank her.

—W. C. Fields

★

As far as I'm concerned, being any gender is a drag.   —Patti Smith

★

My life is a drag—thank goodness! But the one role I've always wanted to play and never been offered is a Mother Superior; I always wanted to be Nun of the Above.   —cross-dressing actor Divine

★

I do want to get rich, but I never want to do what there is to do to get rich.

—Gertrude Stein

How come if a woman comes to work in a tailored men's suit, that's considered stylish—but if I show up around here in a simple floor-length gown, I'm weird? —*Politically Incorrect* host Bill Maher

★

Drag is more complicated than you can possibly imagine. I was fitted for a bra that was filled with birdseed—to simulate the real thing, er, things. Then I was informed I shouldn't go to the beach and swim with it on. Like that would even enter my head, right? I said, "Why not?" Because of seagulls? They said, no, because birdseed swells up in water....At least it's one way not to drown! —Robin Williams

★

I'm not sure how qualified some psychiatrists are. My brother's psychiatrist once said to him, "Maybe life isn't for everyone." —Andrea Martin (*SCTV*)

★

Childhood can be so difficult. Especially beause children haven't yet developed the gift, or weapon, of wit. Though there are exceptions....A friend told me about a little neighbor boy. She was being given a tour of their home, and when they got to the boy's room, she asked him, "Why are you playing with your sister's doll?" and he said, "Because my parents are too cheap to buy me one of my own!" —Liberace

★

I did everything I could, so that after she died I had not one instant of guilt. Zero. I still don't. Now I feel quite neutral toward her, though it's taken fifty years to get there.

—Christina Crawford, fifty-eight, about her adoptive mother

★

After we made our first [Marx Brothers] picture, I bought a house in Great Neck...and I inquired into joining a local swimming club. The club's manager said they wouldn't be able to accept me as a member because I'm Jewish. "Well, then," I asked, "how about my little son? He's *half*-Jewish. Can he go in the water up to his waist?" —Groucho Marx

★

When I got back from [doing] *Apocalypse Now,* I was seventeen. Everyone said, "Larry, you'll work all the time." If I had been a white boy, I'd be making more than Charlie Sheen, based on talent alone. That really [screwed] me up for a while, but I go with it. At least I'm working.

—Laurence Fishburne

★

The two worst things about making movies are the schedule—it's day in, day out...for months. And it's mentally exhausting!

—Jason Patric (*Speed 2*)

★

I'd love to do a movie where the girl kisses me voluntarily.   —Ray Liotta

★

I think no woman should go outside of her home without a machine gun.

—Roseanne

★

The longer I'm around a man, the more likely he is to try something funny. Like they always say, familiarity breeds attempt.   —Jayne Mansfield

★

You know you're asking essentially bullshit questions. I'm giving you bullshit answers, but I'm doing it because there's a movie opening and the studio expects me to do it.   —Richard Gere, to the press

★

When I'm on [stage], the audiences have a wonderful time, and it looks like I'm having a wonderful time too....But I'm working. I'm an illusionist, and my illusion is to make everything seem like one big good time.

—comedian Robert Klein

★

I don't drink. I don't like it. It makes me feel good.   —Oscar Levant

★

Wives are people who feel they don't dance enough.   —Groucho Marx

★

I don't want the Beverly Hills circuit. I haven't got time for people who ask you how your grandchild is and don't listen to your answer.

—Jerry Lewis

★

That depends on the liver.

—W. C. Fields's reply, when asked if life was worth living

★

After thirty, your body has a mind of its own.   —Bette Midler

★

This strange beating together of hands has no meaning. To me it is very disturbing. We try to make sounds like music, and then in between comes this strange sound you make.

—conductor Leopold Stokowski, to an audience in 1929

BETTE MIDLER

Oh, hecklers...but also people who insist on talking loud while you're doing your act. Fortunately when you're up on that stage, you have a temporary brassiness that you don't have in everyday life....One time, I had to ad lib to a woman in the audience—fortunately the audience loved it—"Shut your hole, honey. Mine's makin' money."   —Bette Midler

The scenery was beautiful, but the actors kept getting in front of it.

—critic Alexander Woollcott, reviewing a play

★

Your manuscript is both good and original. But the part that is good is not original, and the part that is original is not good.

—Dr. Samuel Johnson, to a would-be author

★

I liked your opera. I think I will set it to music.

—Ludwig van Beethoven, to a fellow composer

★

I did find that my [lack of] height wasn't an impediment, as an actor. So I was lucky there. But they say that as we grow older, as human beings, we shrink. If you're me, you don't want to think about that. —Danny DeVito

★

Well, we live and learn, said a fellow actor to John Barrymore. To which the Great Profile replied, "Yes. And then we die and forget it all."

—Spencer Tracy

★

Virtue is not photogenic. What is it to be a nice guy? To be nothing, that's what. A big fat zero with a smile for everybody.   —Kirk Douglas

★

[A] director feels that if he signs Burt Reynolds he's selling out because he's signing the most commercial actor in town. If he wants to be known as an auteur...he'll instead hire one of the darlings—Robert De Niro, Al Pacino, or Dustin Hoffman. A lot of directors in this town don't realize that the hardest thing to do in movies is to make chicken salad out of chickenshit, and I've done that a lot.

—Burt Reynolds, now no longer burdened with being so commercial

★

Every time I bring out a new movie, nobody bothers to review it....They don't review my work, they review me.   —filmmaker Orson Welles

★

Oh, acting. I was somewhat pressured into it. I'm not sure I'd choose it, if I had it to do over again. The rewards are great, for the talented or the merely photogenic. But the staring...people always *staring*!   —Laurence Harvey

★

I'm not sure I would have been an actress. It's not in my nature to be looked at, the center of attention. But my sister [the late Françoise Dorléac] dragged me into it. Françoise was very open, and I was shy.

—Catherine Deneuve (who was a.k.a. "the most beautiful woman in the world")

★

Fame always brings loneliness. Success is as ice cold and lonely as the North Pole.   —writer Vicky Baum (*Grand Hotel*)

★

Some of the more snobbish critics at first criticized me because I didn't speak the king's English or even the president's English.

—Tony Curtis ("Yondah lies da castle of my foddah")

★

When a woman behaves like a man, why doesn't she behave like a *nice* man?   —Dame Edith Evans

★

They are afraid of spontaneity [on David Letterman's show]. They tell you the questions and they literally tell you the answers and of course all they really wanted to talk about was my father.

—actress Alison Eastwood (daughter of Clint)

It wasn't easy growing up, having a famous grandfather [architect Frank Lloyd Wright]....For the longest time, I got asked about him...I'd get asked *his* opinions on things....One newspaper headlined my interview: "Anne Baxter Proud of Her Grandfather's Erections."   —Anne Baxter

Acting can be quite demoralizing.

—Marlon Brando, explaining why he has his lines fed to him through an earpiece rather than memorizing them

I am enacting a Conservative Prime Minister [Harold Macmillan] who in point of fact was bisexual....Some visiting Americans who see the play then begin to wonder if I am bisexual myself.   —Edward Fox

It's not an altogether comfortable feeling [visiting the United States]. Somewhere over three-quarters of the world's serial killers are there [in the United States], quite apart from the ordinary, run-of-the-mill murderers.

—director David Lean

I heard O. J. Simpson and the sports announcer who likes ladies *and* their dresses [Marv Albert] were so sad and so angry to be dropped out of the American sports hall of fame [sic]. But: were they surprised? Could they be *so* surprised?   —soccer star Pele

It drives me crazy when your parents try to read your mind. It's even worse when they try and read your mail.   —ex–child star Macaulay Culkin

I was so scared that I actually wet myself the first time I went out on stage, literally pissed myself.   —Tim Roth

I spent twenty years reaching out for a glass or pill to make me feel good. Having a different woman all the time was part of the same dream. If a woman wasn't available, drugs eliminated the need for one.

—Tony Curtis

We are so busy talking about sexual harassment in corporate America, but in Hollywood it's so rampant. I have experienced sexual harassment from a woman. It didn't have anything to do with the fact that she was attracted to me. It was a power trip.　　　—Martha Plimpton, on harassment, period

★

Being bisexual, you're very much looked down upon by the uppity members of gay lib....If you swing both ways, you are swinging. I just figure, you know, double your pleasure.　　　　　　　—Joan Baez

★

I can't stand nobody touching my toes. I have a real phobia about it.

—Roseanne

★

Everyone has pet peeves or even worse, phobias. I don't like clowns...or little tiny babies with their little rolling heads.　　　—Johnny Depp

★

For years I've admitted my fear of policemen. What I can't do is explain it. I haven't really *done* anything, yet I always feel very guilty when near a policeman. So perhaps I have done something....　　　—Alfred Hitchcock

★

It's hard to enjoy it without a Valium.　　　—Dustin Hoffman, at the Oscars

★

I've overdosed on tranquilizers, so I think I'm all right.

—Emma Thompson, at the Oscars

★

I figure I made history. I'm the only nominee who's lost twice in one night.

—Sigourney Weaver, after the Oscars

★

I still ride the subway and no one recognizes me.

—F. Murray Abraham, Oscar winner (Best Actor for *Amadeus*)

★

My mother never was one for paying any compliments....She died in 1989 and I found all these cuttings [press clippings] she'd kept. I never thought she kept anything like that. She never showed any interest.

—Julie Walters

★

The finances ain't easy. You gotta live and hire like a star. In my office I got a sign to remind me. It says, "A dollar saved is a quarter earned."

—Alan King

It's like I blot my lipstick with the paychecks I get. It's like, Should I floss my teeth with this or blow my nose on it? And I'm not just being a little bitchy actress [saying], Life is so hard, I'm not getting paid anything. I'm *not* getting paid anything. —Parker Posey

★

I don't want to be super-famous, man. That would be awful.

—Keanu Reeves

★

Acting has destroyed my ego. I have very little self-respect now. I don't particularly admire actors, and so to be one is something I don't particularly admire. —Hugh Grant

★

The problem is not that you can't get a job. The problem is that the jobs that are out there aren't that interesting. —Paul Newman

★

I've done time in [prison] and at Betty Ford. Big deal. You could write a book now about stars who've done time. In either place. What I can't stand is the whole pity-me attitude of today's newcomers. If you're rich and famous and you do time, don't ask anyone to pity you. It's the least you can do, to *seem* decent. —Robert Mitchum

★

I don't think anybody allowed me to grow up. They didn't say, "You know, this girl got on the show when she was eighteen and a half, let's cut her a break." Instead, it was like this fleet of piranhas attacking me and putting me out there for a feeding frenzy. —Shannen Doherty

★

I cannot walk out of my house without expecting someone to call me Diane [her name on *Cheers*]. That's *still* going on.... —Shelley Long

★

If half the public loves what I do as a performer, that's fine and dandy. But I'm also aware there's a significant percentage that hates what I do, hates me and wishes me ill. —comedian Totie Fields

★

Some people like me, some don't, many don't care. But I think for every one person that loves me, there's probably one that can't stand me.

—Jerry Seinfeld

It almost works in inverse proportion. The more accolades you get, the more Emmys you get, the more everything you get, the scareder you get. Because you know it's an accident, you know it may not happen again next week, that you've been getting away with murder. That's the way it has been with me. I just recently, about a week ago, stopped drinking. I find it was the best thing I've ever done.   —Harvey Korman

★

I would be so embarrassed to have one of those [psychic hotline] numbers appear on my phone bill. I don't know how I would explain it to my business manager. It would almost be like saying, Okay, I'm white trash.

—Jennifer Tilly

★

My biggest embarrassment was when I fell flat on my face. The guy had just won a brand-new car in a bonus round. I was clapping so hard, I was so excited for him, I missed the last step and fell right on my face. It was terrible. I was so embarrassed.   —quiz show assistant Vanna White

★

It's very difficult to measure trust. You either trust somebody or you don't. I've mistakenly trusted and been screwed more times than a hooker.

—Sean Connery

★

Marriage is wild. I thought it was this perfect land of happiness and joy. Wrong! After you say you do, you *don't* for a long time.

—John Leguizamo

★

[Movie sex scenes are] never romantic, and you're never swept off your feet. It's always very technical....I'm counting the beats: Okay, we're supposed to kiss for two beats, then I say my line, then they want another kiss for four beats. I'm going, One Mississippi, two Mississippi, three and break. It's like choreography. Sometimes you have actors who feel that it's their job to get as far down into your throat as possible. You're like, Excuse me, I like you, but not that much.   —Sandra Bullock

★

I never needed to be famous. I still don't. It's annoying. It's the last thing that I looked for.   —Jodie Foster

★

Ellen DeGeneres on the cover of *Lesbians on the Loose*

Kissing girls is more natural to me, but as a performer I've only kissed guys for the camera. So, so far I'm more comfortable with that, and when I do kiss a girl for the camera [on *Ellen*], they're gonna make such a big deal about it.... —Ellen DeGeneres

★

I did a pilot for a TV series last March which did not get picked up, thank goodness. I only say thank goodness because those people I know who've gotten into that game say that it's really the golden handcuffs. You can get very rich and be in this gilded cage for years. It can be very frustrating and very confining. —film actor Keith Carradine

★

I asked [daughter Laura Dern] not to be an actress. I said, For God's sake, do not be an actress! This business is extremely tough on men. It burns up their manhood....But if you think it's hard on men, it's manure on women.

—Diane Ladd

You've got to find a way to keep a certain amount left to yourself, otherwise you just feel like you've been invaded. I could walk away from all these interviews just feeling like I've been raped for hours. There are times when you feel like that. —Rob Lowe

I wish people would ask me interesting questions. I wish people would get beyond the same ten things I get asked all the time. —Bruce Willis

I'm stuck with this celebrity name which I hate. I'd rather have my married one, but now I'm stuck with *Hemingway*. —Mariel Hemingway

Being famous has little to do with happiness. —Barbara Walters

I look at my honesty as a virtue, but I really do have to pay a high price for it. —Sean Young

When you make a sexy movie like *The Big Easy*, even before you have kids you say, My mother's going to see this. It's either your mother or your kids....You've got to be an orphan without children to do it without guilt.

—Dennis Quaid

I feel very nervous when they treat me like a star, because I like to be with other people, I like to mingle with them. But when I feel that they treat me like somebody else, very exceptional, I suffer very much. I really do.

—Sophia Loren

People are always wanting me to smoke with them or drink beers with them or to hook me up with chicks. It's like I'm the Spuds MacKenzie of humans.

—Pauly Shore

If nothing else, showbiz extracts a price on your eyes, your eyesight, from all those flashbulbs. That is, if you're successful enough to be photographed that often. —Mildred Natwick

I can't control what's going on on the set if suddenly people are coming around with cameras and taking pictures. They're taking pictures of me and suddenly it's more about me than the film. So you do the best you can to avoid it or hide from it. —Robert Redford

★

I think our business beats pretty hard on us when they want us—and when they don't want us, man, they kick us right out the door. There's not much in between. —Shelley Long

★

You always think you're never going to work again. The function of this kind of life is every time you finish a job you're unemployed. You face that kind of fear. Even though people tell you not to worry about it, you worry about it. —Mary Stuart Masterson

★

In this business you do a part. You get your reviews. You win awards. Then five minutes later you go in and you're interviewed by someone who's never done anything in the business before and knows nobody's credits. You're a piece of meat, being examined from all angles. But perhaps Van Gogh or some of them felt the same way about their art. —Diane Ladd

★

Casting people have little or no imagination. They cast from your looks...and even admit that they make their decisions within five seconds of your walking in the door. They don't want you to have a personality, just to be a physical type. [Casting directors] are the least creative people in town, yet they hold the keys to the kingdom, damn it.
—Fernando Lamas

★

People see me and they think two things: he's funny and he's cheap.
—Jack Benny

★

I did make a pretty fair amount of money with the Monkees. Not much by today's standards, but a pretty fair amount. But I let it all go because I didn't understand value then. I didn't understand value in myself. What I've learned since then is you can't handle money well if you don't have an appropriate sense of self-value. —Peter Tork

★

If you're confident before you attain fame, then you're okay. Don't care *too* much what people think....If you're not happy or not confident before you're known, then no amount of fame or money will bestow instant happiness or self-confidence.   —Eve Arden

★

I spent a lot of my life blaming acting for how my life turned out. Until it dawned on me that most of what has happened is self-motivated. Not everything; there's a lot of good luck and bad luck for any actor. There's exploiting [sic] people in any profession...and how you deal with being an actor—and with fame in general—has more to do with your own personality than with the profession of acting.   —Tommy Rettig (*Lassie*)

★

New York is like a disco, but without the music.   —Elaine Stritch

★

I don't think Barbra Streisand's rendition of "Memory" was that good.
                              —Barry Manilow (think about it...)

★

The English are *so* good at accents. I think that's so facile, don't you?
                    —Paulette Goddard, who lost the role of southern belle
                       Scarlett O'Hara to Englishwoman Vivien Leigh

★

Jon Voight's a good actor. But he won the Oscar because he played a guy in a wheelchair. The Academy loves stuff like that.
  —Burt Reynolds, who for some reason declined the role in *Coming Home*

★

Jim Carrey isn't worth $20 million a film. Not if he plays a normal guy. Which I can do any day of the week....   —Tom Arnold

★

I haven't got a chance [to win the Best Supporting Actor Oscar]. I'm up against two Orientals, one of them an amateur, and one black guy, and Sir Ralph Richardson, who's dead.
          —John Malkovich (the so-called amateur, Dr. Haing S. Ngor, won)

★

Horror is knowing that you won't find anyone to give you a hand when you are down. A down-and-out actor is already a ghost haunting the corridors where he once walked a star.   —Bela Lugosi

★

I detest acting because it is sheer drudgery.   —Tallulah Bankhead

★

A painter paints, a musician plays, a writer writes—but a movie actor waits.
—Mary Astor

★

The really frightening thing about middle age is the knowledge that you'll grow out of it.
—Doris Day

★

I have to straighten out my karma. I've become a sex symbol, which is an absurd thing for me.
—Sharon Stone

★

It's hard to act in the morning. The muse isn't even awake.
—Keanu Reeves

★

I am a humble survivor of many regimes and development hell...of hostile hairdressers and breakfast burritos...of princesses and pin cushions...of breakfast, lunch, and dinner meetings....I've eaten enough salad to landscape a back yard.
—Bette Midler

★

I grew up when the good things about being gay were you didn't have to get married and you didn't have to go in the army. Now, we have to fight for both of those things....
—John Waters

★

My only complaint about having a dad in fashion is that every time I'm about to go to bed with a guy, I have to look at my father's name all over his underwear.
—Marci Klein, daughter of Calvin

★

Cocaine is God's way of letting you know you make too much money.
—Robin Williams

★

I think I was born an alcoholic. The story is that I got drunk at my christening.
—John Larroquette

★

Sometimes when I'm flying over the Alps I think, That's like all the cocaine I sniffed.
—Elton John

★

It's like a gypsy's curse, it's terrible. The more famous an actress becomes, the less she's allowed to eat. Unless she wants to play people's mothers. And in bad clothes, yet.
—Lana Turner

★

You know what the worst thing about fame is? The worst thing is, it lasts forever....
—Tony Curtis

★

When you become famous, you don't change, but everyone around you does.
—Cary Grant

★

What happens is I get attacked for my honesty. I once said I smoked pot with my kids. What a furor that caused! I suppose they'd rather I did it secretly and my kids did it without my knowledge. How would that be an improvement? You can't open your mouth without getting crucified in this country.
—Peter Lawford

★

[Since our breakup] I have been required to live in an environment in which Elizabeth would never reside.
—ex–truck driver and ex–Mr. Elizabeth Taylor Larry Fortensky

★

When someone is beautiful, that gives people an excuse to go out of their way to be mean, as if someone who's beautiful isn't really deep, doesn't really hurt, and isn't really a human being.
—Cybill Shepherd

★

My whole humor is based on the loneliness and hurt of being left out, of being thrown over—which I always fear and dread.
—Joan Rivers

★

You only have so much free time if you're successful, and I'd love to have more friends, but that takes a lot of time and also so much effort!
—actor-director Ray Danton

★

I'm frightened of eggs. Worse than frightened—they revolt me. That white round thing without any holes....Have you ever seen anything more revolting than an egg yolk breaking and spilling its yellow liquid? Blood is jolly...red. But egg yolk is yellow, revolting. I've never tasted it.
—Alfred Hitchcock (cholesterol champ?)

★

Sydney Pollack earned $14 million from his share in the profits in [*Tootsie*]. He said to me that if he could get back the eighteen months of his life which were total misery making it, he would gladly give back the money. He said it was the worst experience of his life.
—fellow director John Boorman

★

I have just come from the Actors Studio where I saw Marilyn Monroe. She had no girdle on, her ass was hanging out. She is a disgrace to the industry.
—Joan Crawford, in 1955

★

The trouble with nude dancing is that not everything stops when the music does.
—dancer-actor Sir Robert Helpmann

★

Education is when you read the fine print. Experience is what you get if you don't.
—musician Pete Seeger

★

Deep down, I'm pretty superficial.
—Ava Gardner

★

An optimist is someone who's never worked or socialized in Hollywood.
—Gloria Grahame

★

A pessimist is someone who, if he is in the bath, will not get out to answer the telephone.
—Quentin Crisp

★

For the first time in my life I envied my feet. They were asleep.
—Hedda Hopper, after viewing a dull movie

★

My father was a proctologist, my mother an abstract artist. That's how I see the world.
—Sandra Bernhard

★

My family wasn't the Brady Bunch. They were the Broody Bunch.
—Sandra Bernhard

★

I admit flying on airplanes can be scarier for a celebrity, since if you crash, let's face it, it makes more of an impact.
—Tom Snyder

★

I don't want to be difficult, and I'm *not* difficult. I'm only difficult with stupid, incompetent people.
—Val Kilmer

★

I'm hated for being too rich or too handsome or too liberal.
—Alec Baldwin

★

If I was a petite, brunette, ethnic lawyer, then my behavior would be totally acceptable. But we Barbie dolls are not supposed to behave the way I do.
—Sharon Stone

By the time I was thirteen I realized I'd be more successful at something physical than mental.   —Arnold Schwarzenegger

★

I got the worst criticism for doing comedy. It really hurt. But if people don't want me to make them laugh, that's cool.   —Sylvester Stallone

★

A few people see my movies and then they want to assassinate me.

—director Oliver Stone

★

People try to confuse me by urging me to repeat my past successes. That's so depressing.   —Barbra Streisand

★

I used to be the most famous Diana, [before] the princess. When your first name is almost a trademark, you don't get to keep it to yourself for very long.   —Diana Ross

★

First, the problem with beauty is it almost convinces people you've little talent. Later, the problem is people being disappointed that you have less of it—beauty, that is. There's *more* talent, but it doesn't photograph.

—Diana Rigg

★

Just standing around looking beautiful is so boring, really boring, so boring.   —Michelle Pfeiffer

★

Good-looking people turn me off. Myself included.   —Patrick Swayze

★

Women have no shame.... You really wouldn't believe what I have to put up with. Women come right up to [Brad Pitt] and press their bodies against him from behind. And I'm right there!   —Gwyneth Paltrow

★

I now have more paternity suits [seventeen in 1990] than leisure suits.

—Engelbert Humperdinck

★

Sometimes I go nights without sleeping because I'm up doing my homework because I had a premiere to go to the night before. It's the price you have to pay.   —teen star Natalie Portman

★

Being the son of a famous father makes an acting career very difficult at
first.   —Michael Douglas

Having two famous parents is really an ongoing ordeal.   —Desi Arnaz Jr.

Would I do a nude scene? Sure. What it would come down to is my saying,
"I hope I don't get a hard-on." It would be distracting to the crew and I'd be
embarrassed because, shit, maybe it's not as big as I want it to be.
                                                            —Robert Downey Jr.

I was under pressure from my agent to [audition] for James Bond, and I
subsequently left that agent....I just don't think I'd be very good for Bond
and I don't think Bond would be very good for me.   —Sam Neill

I never had fabulous sexual interludes as a child. At all my AA meetings and
when I saw my shrink in Atlanta, people were always asking me if I was ever
molested as a child. I told my shrink, "I was dying to be molested."
                                                                —Elton John

Every once in a while I'd scrape bottom. I remember signing an autograph
once, and wanting to ask the person for 30 cents to ride the subway.
                                                              —Esai Morales

Yes, my relationship with [cinematographer] Daniel Gillham has lasted
longer than any of my [four] marriages....What I learned about marriage is
don't marry everyone you fall in love with.   —Stockard Channing

★

I would *not* want to get stereotyped as a Latina.
                                        —Madeline Stowe, who is half Hispanic

★

You guys don't want to know about this crap. You guys just want to know
about the drugs and the whores.
    —Charlie Sheen, when asked by the press about his latest screen character

★

I just don't want to be stuck in a stereotype, playing only Hispanic
characters.   —Jimmy Smits

★

I want to play all sorts of roles, not just usual things.

—Charlie Sheen

★

It means you can read in your trailer, waiting for the next setup.

—Stockard Channing, when asked what a good
education (Radcliffe) means to her

★

I did not think that was at all funny.

—Tom Cruise, who *Movieline* magazine said "managed
to elude serial killer Andrew Cunanan"

★

I do tend to get typecast....

—Elle Macpherson, who has enacted models in four of her seven films

★

Sure! It's a big reason why we moved to the [San Francisco] Bay area.

—Sean Penn, whose wife got carjacked in Los Angeles

★

It's like some people are just learning I can actually act.

—Peter Fonda, fifty-eight, on rave reviews for *Ulee's Gold*

★

He is a distant acquaintance motivated solely by greed and sour grapes.

—Jodie Foster, on brother Buddy, who outed her in his memoirs

★

Ed Sullivan tried to hog the credit for everything. *I* put Elvis Presley on televison before he did. *I* introduced him on my *Stage Show* starring the Dorsey Brothers. I always had a great eye for talent....In the end all [Sullivan] was doing was recycling.   —Jackie Gleason

★

Shortly after [*Batman*] went on the air [in 1966], the Catholic Legion of Decency decided they didn't like the way [Burt Ward as Robin] filled his tights, so to speak. There was too much of him, too much bulge....A doctor at Fox gave him pills that reduced his problem for three hours at a "stretch," according to Burt. Burt complained to anyone who'd listen....I confess I was somewhat upset because the doctor didn't come to *me* with the pills too.   —Adam West, the small-screen Batman

★

The worst thing I saw not only this year but in my lifetime was *Sunset Boulevard* in Los Angeles with Glenn Close.   —Tony Randall

They all think they can do talk shows, like it's so easy. But movie stars read *other* people's lines....Chevy Chase did terribly with his talk show. It ran, what, one week? Then the ax. And then all those movie offers, regardless.
—Bill Maher

Now, the stars are doing what I used to do....I used to write about them, but in their own books they're telling every one of their own secrets.
—former author Rex Reed

A producer is just a dog with a script in his mouth.
—producer Peter Guber (later head of Sony Pictures)

Producing is the worst job in the world. When you're an actor, you get to play. When you're the writer, you get to stay home a lot. When you're the director, you're the boss and everybody has to talk to you. When you're the producer, everybody thinks you are a scum pimp who is not creative. It's terrible, and in the end you get blamed for everything.
—producer and prostitute basher Don Simpson, who died of a drug overdose, as did the doctor treating him for drug addiction

They exploit the rich by overtaxing us!　　　　　—Brigitte Bardot

I may have been tops for a time, but we didn't get the same super-salaries or the same perks as today's supermodels. I think they've gotten a bit spoiled....I've heard people say that Cindy Crawford travels with her own toilet seat.　　　　　—Twiggy

Whenever I talk about my success, I talk about retribution for my success, that you must pay for it. I guess in some sort of deep-rooted way I feel I haven't. I don't agree with that. Maybe I'm paying tribute in irony. It's the sort of thing that can make you bitter.　　　　　—Keanu Reeves

★

My biggest sacrifice has been college. Sometimes I just want to be a person having fun, going crazy over midterms. I feel guilty about not going to college. I went to UCLA for two days before I got *Smooth Talk* and to USC for two months before I got *Blue Velvet.*　　　　　—Laura Dern

★

Mediocrity is my biggest fear. I'm not afraid of total failure, because I don't think that will happen. I'm not afraid of success, because that beats the hell out of failure. It's being in the middle that scares me.

—Robert Downey Jr., who hit bottom in 1997 with a six-month jail sentence

Mia Farrow says she's tired of talking about herself and her former life with Woody Allen, and he says he resents the world's cameras intruding on him. I wonder if these two realize how tiresomely tired *I* am of having to listen to her and look at him.   —William Hickey (*Prizzi's Honor*)

I do...I feel personally persecuted.

—Woody Allen, on press reaction to his cheating on companion Mia Farrow with her daughter

It's such a feat that I actually married someone who is heterosexual.

—Ricki Lake

I've been outed and re-outed needlessly. I never came out of the closet because I was never in it.   —Quentin Crisp

I didn't take up jogging to be trendy *or* political. I just wanted to hear the sound of heavy breathing again!   —Phyllis Diller

It's too bad if some people imagine a woman cannot be funny and attractive at the same time.   —plastic surgery fan Phyllis Diller

It really was a relief to hear them call Liz Taylor's name. At my age, while it was an honor to be nominated [for an Oscar], the burden of winning would have been too much.   —Lynn Redgrave

★

He breaks my heart, he just does, you know...and when he got up there and gave his little speech, he broke my heart again.

—John Travolta, after listening to Oscar winner
Tom Hanks's acceptance speech

★

Actually, you know, anywhere where they speak Spanish that's not my mom's house would be cool.

—actor Wilson Cruz, when asked where he'd like to travel

You can take all the sincerity in Hollywood, place it in the navel of a fruit fly, and still have room enough for three caraway seeds and a producer's heart. —Fred Allen

★

A husband is what's left of a sweetheart after the nerve has been killed. —Lou Costello

★

I belong to Bridegrooms Anonymous. Whenever I feel like getting married, they send over a lady in a housecoat and hair curlers to burn my toast for me. —Dick Martin (*Rowan and Martin's Laugh-In*)

★

I love Mickey Mouse more than any woman I've ever known. —Walt Disney

★

If it weren't for pickpockets, I'd have no sex life at all. —Rodney Dangerfield

★

It's really hard to get into Australia sometimes. I had to get a work-related visa once, and the guy at the consulate was so snotty, he goes, "Do you have a prison record?" and I was so annoyed I said, "Yeah, but I didn't know you still needed one to get in." —stand-up comic Lea DeLaria

★

Secrets—No More

Older guys like to receive head but they don't like to give it. Even today [the mid-'70s], a man who's in his thirties or forties will immediately go to bed with you, but it will be weeks, maybe months, before he'll consider giving you head. —Victoria Principal (*Dallas*)

★

[After the service for his father John Carradine] we carted the coffin over to our house and opened it up. I looked down at him, and the undertaker had put a demonic, artificial grin on his face—like nothing I had ever seen him do in real life, except in a horror film. I reached out and, using the sculptural skills I had learned from him, I remodeled his face to be more naturally him. Then I poured half a bottle of J&B Scotch, his favorite, down his throat, and we had a wake. —David Carradine [*Kung Fu*]

Dear 338171, May I call you 338?
        —Noel Coward, trying to unlock the deep closet of Lawrence of Arabia,
                who used numerals in his personal correspondence

It's ill-becoming for an old broad to sing about how bad she wants it. But occasionally we do. —Lena Horne

When I was growing up in Kansas, I couldn't wait until I grew up so I could say the word "fuck." Now it's become my favorite word. —Kirstie Alley

I have had [sexual] relationships with women when I was younger. Not a lot of them. It just wasn't something that kept my interest. —Cher

I've never had sex with a woman, but I've been on dates with a woman.
                                              —Sharon Stone

I think organized religions are silly. Sartre, who was an atheist, had more religion than a lot of clergymen, who are just protecting a lifestyle and business. I'd love to be genuinely religious, not coerced. But like Ingmar Bergman told me, "Thoughts get in the way." —Woody Allen

If someone is very special to you, is it really that important if every now and then he takes off and has a liaison with someone else? I mean, is it really catastrophic? —Susan Sarandon

Fidelity is possible. Anything is possible if you're stubborn and strong. But it's not that important. Traditional marriage is very outdated. I don't think people should live together the rest of their lives suppressing frustrations.
                                              —Michelle Pfeiffer

There are no Ten Commandments when it comes to love. There is only one: unconditional love. —Marlene Dietrich

There are no Ten Commandments when it comes to love. There is only one:

People think I'm gay or bisexual. Well...maybe I am.
                              —Dennis Rodman, basketball star

I admitted it, I did make [oral] love to Sarah Miles, but not on the set [of *The Sailor Who Fell from Grace With the Sea,* 1976]. During a photo layout, pardon the expression, for *Playboy.* I don't know if it makes any difference, and I later felt embarrassed about it. I'm not sure if she did.

—Kris Kristofferson

★

It's stupid and unfair. They'll talk about "loose women." What about loose men? *Some* women may be loose, a very judgmental term, but I'd say easily 90 percent of men are loose. So why talk about or judge just one sex that way?

—novelist Patricia Highsmith (*Strangers on a Train, The Price of Salt*)

I've been attracted to every single person I've done a love scene with.

—Jennifer Tilly (*Bound,* co-starring Gina Gershon)

Most men are not good at cunnilingus! —Jennifer Tilly

★

I've always been embarrassed about sex in some strange way. No one would ever think Tina Turner is shy. But I am shy about some things.

—Tina Turner

The cure for starvation in India *and* the cure for overpopulation—both in one big swallow.... —novelist Erica Jong (*Fear of Flying*)

Dahling, any husband of yours is a husband of mine.

—Tallulah Bankhead, to Ginger Rogers (who was not amused)

I'm your basic flasher. I've always loved exposing myself.

—Michael Douglas

★

I'm not neurotic and have no obsessions or morbid fears. But I read something while researching a picture [*Bride of Vengeance*] set in Renaissance Italy, and it affected me for years....By the late 1400s, they had poisoned keys which were made for delicately worked coffers: the victim would have to force the key in slightly before the lock would be turned, and thus prick his finger on an ingeniously concealed sharp protuberance, and die....The Borgias would have felt right at home in Hollywood.

—director and designer Mitchell Leisen

We're not doing any harm to anyone else. We're not peppering the world with illegitimate children. The only people we could possible mess up are ourselves, and that's our lookout.

—Noel Coward's telltale line in his play *Design for Living*

I'm the American Princess Di!

—Sharon Stone, reportedly shrieking at her limo driver in Manhattan in 1998 (she briefly dated Dodi Fayed in the mid-'80s and she's a blonde)

I will try to protect the animals no matter how much criticism I receive....One thing I protested was a Moslem ritual they have in Pakistan...their stock market was low, so they decided to cut the throats of dozens of living sheep, as a sacrifice. To make the stock market go up, imagine! They killed the animals, and the stock market went down, down. What stupid, cruel men!　　　　　　　　　　—Brigitte Bardot

There's an unmistakable bias in reporting these things...because it's always something like "animal rights extremists," while the people who butcher or dissect or torture or even vivisect animals never get called extreme....If you don't give a damn for animals, you're called normal. If you care a lot, if you try to be vegetarian or you try to be a bit of an activist, then friends, relatives, news people, everyone's ready to label you a freak or an extremist. Well, I'm extremely pro-animal.　　　　　　　—Alicia Silverstone

He must have been a marvelous shot.

—Sir Noel Coward, on being informed that a dimwitted acquaintance had shot himself in the brain

Pornography is whatever gives a censor an erection.　　　—Pat Paulsen

Um, no. Not at this present time, no. But, I mean, I would be interested to hear some of the rumors.

—Mark Wahlberg (formerly Marky Mark), replying to the rumors that he's "available" to men

I just love the idea of being mean to a little girl!

—Roseanne, who post-*Roseanne* played the Wicked Witch of the West on stage in *The Wizard of Oz*

The other day she said, "I hate your shoes. Are they men's shoes?" And I said "Yes, they are, and okay, so you hate them." A few years ago, I would have been crushed. I'd never be caught dead in the stuff she wears, and it totally doesn't matter....I like men's clothing. And Mom says, "But you're so pretty."   —Chastity Bono, on mama Cher

I just want to suckle you....I want you to have my baby.
          —what George C. Scott allegedly said to twenty-six-year-old assistant
                    Julie Wright, who is suing him for sexual harassment

She is my favorite of my harem.
                    —operatic Luciano Pavarotti, on twenty-six-year-old
                                        secretary Nicoletta Mantovani

People are wrong when they say that the opera isn't what it used to be. It *is* what it used to be. That's what's wrong with it.   —Sir Noel Coward

I was coming out of the Dorchester [hotel] one time, and it started to rain. I stood there, under the canopy, and a colored gentleman in a fancy coat with epaulettes was standing next to me. I said to him, "My good man, could you get me a taxicab," and he turned to me and declared, "I am the ambassador of Nigeria." I was rather embarrassed, so I told him, "In that case, please don't bother with the taxi."   —Sir Robert Morley

As a Buddhist, I try to illumine my own life. I don't look to someone or something else to save me. That's not egotistic; it means you take responsibility for your own life. You march to the beat of your own drummer.   —Tina Turner

I'm not very religious. Religion has torn my country [Ireland] in two.
                                                    —Paul Hewson of U2

★

In the West, people kill each other over religion—history's full of that convert-or-die policy. But in the East, people say—especially the many Buddhists I have known—that different religions are merely different paths to the same Goal.   —Peter Finch

★

My mother said to me, "You're revolting. And on top of that, you're not even very feminine." Well, that led me to the stage, which is an accepting and comfortable place. So in a way I have my mother to thank....

—Carol Channing

What's better than roses on your piano? Tulips on your organ! —Liberace

My God, when I discovered sex! The first time...the embarrassment, the shame, the disillusionment, the guilt and remorse. And this was just masturbation.   —Woody Allen

I learned about sex the hard way....On my own. With my own. That was fun. Later, the hard part was learning to do it with somebody else in the same room.   —Andy Kaufman

Truly and guaranteed safe sex is masturbation. With the film star or model—or even neighbor—of your choice.

—Denholm Elliott (*A Room With a View*)

One must not mistake majority for truth.   —Jean Cocteau

I never felt guilty about a goddamned thing in my life. What the hell is there to feel guilty about? I never did a thing to hurt anyone. I never understood why anyone would feel guilty about sex. I never wanted any children. You know why people have children? Vanity, pure and simple: Look at what I created. But if I had any children, I would explain sex to them in simple, graphic terms. That it's a thing of pleasure. And if you don't want children, be sure you don't have any. And if you don't want a disease, be careful. No quoting from the Bible.   —Rudy Vallee

★

Custody of the children is pretty easy to figure out. You keep all the young children, and let their father have all those that are over eighteen or twenty. This is because of three reasons: (1) The older ones are never home anyway. (2) The older ones are a big headache to take care of. (3) They give away your age.   —Zsa Zsa Gabor

★

Most actors are dogs and predatory and will fuck up a relationship if given a chance.   —Eric Stoltz

JOAN FONTAINE

One might say I was surprised out of my virginity. I was twenty....The whole experience [via film star Conrad Nagel] was no more than a quick surgical violation conducted with considerable modesty and no conversation. It reminded me of the time when I had to stand up in class as a child and be vaccinated. This just wasn't as neat...and hurt more.

Conrad [revealed] that for the first year of his marriage he had slept with his bride in their double bed in total innocence. Only when they consulted a doctor about their childlessness were they enlightened on how to get the stork to visit them. Until that doctor's visit, neither the minister's son nor his wife had the slightest clue.

—Joan Fontaine in *No Bed of Roses*

★

Sure, yes, if I only had the time. As it is, I'm working so hard, I barely get in one good fuck a week.

—Shirley MacLaine, asked whether she'd have an affair with a woman

★

All of my sexual experiences when I was young were with girls. I mean, we didn't have those sleepover parties for nothing.   —Madonna

★

Sometimes I wonder if men and women really suit each other. Perhaps they should live next door and just visit now and then.   —Katharine Hepburn

★

My publicist told me that if I felt uncomfortable with a question, I should just say so.

> —Leonardo DiCaprio, asked by *Movieline* magazine,
> "Have you ever kissed a guy?"

★

One of the longest-running hot-gossip items in tinseltown history was when Frank Sinatra allegedly burst into a room in his Palm Springs house and found his love, Ava Gardner, in bed with her pal Lana Turner. And they were *not* asleep....Women often feel freer to experiment, and one tries most everything in show business. But none of those three stars will ever tell you what really happened. Stars don't.

> —actor Charles Farrell, co-founder of the Palm Springs
> Racquet Club and mayor of P.S.

★

Sammy [Davis, Jr.] was bisexual. He did ask me for lessons on giving head to a man, and he did practice on my manager. Sammy loved sex, is all, and he loved all kinds of sex.   —Linda Lovelace

★

One jealous trade paper columnist asked how a publicist got a Lamborghini six months after getting her job. "For eating Kim Basinger's c--t" was the answer.   —Paul Rosenfeld in *The Club Rules*

★

It's not true of all of them, but to me it seems that most men desire a girl's body or parts of it more than they desire the girl herself....Women usually love more than men.   —Pier Angeli

★

A man's mother might be his misfortune, but his wife is his own fault.

          —Groucho Marx

★

The only few times in my life I've felt even close to suicidal were because of the women in my life at the time....I agree with Dr. Joyce Brothers that divorce is the correcting of a mistake, it's not a moral dilemma. A bad marriage is unfair to the two people stuck in it—who don't need to be stuck in it—apart from any children caught in the middle of it....All the times I've divorced, I was trying to rectify something...a *mistake*.

—Henry Fonda

They say whoever decided to call it necking was a bad judge of anatomy. Right. But whoever chose to call it petting is more fond of animals than I am. —Jerry Colonna

Listen, I'm as much an equal opportunity enjoyer as anyone. Though I'm leery of producers; even when they have a contract in hand, the fountain pen's always in their hotel room....I'd advise women not to try a *ménage-à-trois* with two men. I was in a *ménage* like that once. I didn't like it. Because I was the baloney.... —Barbara Nichols

One more drink, and I'll be under the host. —Dorothy Parker

I learned some sad things about the later life of my friend and co-star Peter Lawford in his wife's book....But my mouth fell open starting on page fifty-six, not about Peter but Nancy Reagan and her past...and then the name Peter called her because of her alleged sexual specialty. I couldn't believe it—I mean I couldn't believe it got *published*. —Sammy Davis Jr.

★

Zsa Zsa Gabor is a cop-socker. —Debbie Reynolds

★

Eddie Murphy dropped his $5 million lawsuit against the *National Enquirer* on July 31 [1997] after deciding the tabloid did not maliciously publish a story about his encounter with a transvestite prostitute in West Hollywood on May 2. Murphy ended up paying all the magazine's legal costs in defending itself. Gosh, does this mean the story was true?

—columnist Harold Fairbanks

I'm not a big fan of religion when it gets to be like a corporation. I do believe we should tax the churches, and that they shouldn't own television stations and wide real estate holdings, and keep asking people to send in more and more money. —Rock Hudson

★

Censors are hypocrites. The movie ratings board is a bunch of parents from the San Fernando Valley...and if they disapprove of something, they give it a worse rating, which can kill a movie commercially. Two people of the same sex exchange a dry kiss, and it's an R rating; two people of the opposite sex stick their tongues down each other's throats, it's a PG....It all reminds me of a lady prude who congratulated Dr. Johnson because his dictionary didn't have any naughty words in it. The doctor thanked her but said, "And how do you know that, madam, unless you've read through it all looking for them?"   —director Bo Widerberg (*Elvira Madigan*)

★

I have very strong, negative feelings against what I would call "revealed religion."...I think one of the greatest accomplishments of the twentieth century is the movement away from these revealed religions....To me, the awful evil in our human history is the sacrificing of human life over and over again [for] religious reasons.   —novelist Anne Rice

★

All I know is, no one was ever killed in a war in the name of [the] Buddha.
                                                          —Elizabeth Ashley

★

Even before I became a Buddhist, I was more moved by the symbol of a man finding Enlightenment under a bodhi tree than a man being tortured on a cross....Buddhism is about 500 years older than Christianity, and preaches a surprising number of the same things...some scholars have theorized that the similarities might be explained by Jesus spending the "lost years" in India, where the Buddha taught....But the virtues that Christianity preaches, Buddhism practices....   —Peter Finch

★

I'm Catholic, or I was, and the one thing I learned from religion was that if you think you've sinned, then you've sinned. But if in your heart you don't believe it, then you should go by your heart. And that's what I did. I went by my heart.   —Cyndi Lauper

★

My feeling about the Judeo-Christian tradition is, you can't teach an old dogma new tricks.   —cinematographer Nestor Almendros

★

[On hearing her name read as winner of the Best Actress Academy Award:] I froze. I stared across the table, where Olivia [De Havilland] was sitting directly opposite me. "Get up there, get up there," she whispered commandingly. Now what had I done! All the animus we'd felt toward each other as children, the hair-pullings, the savage wrestling matches, the time Olivia fractured my collarbone, all came rushing back in kaleidoscopic imagery. My paralysis was total. I felt Olivia would spring across the table and grab me by the hair. I felt age four, being confronted by my older sister. Damn it, I'd incurred her wrath again!

—Joan Fontaine, who won an Oscar before her sister (who later won two)

★

When you think of AIDS and who's died from it in the USA, most of the time you think about Rock Hudson and Tony Perkins and other big white celebrities. But if you want to go into it, most of the celebrity deaths from AIDS have been black celebrities or their sons and brothers. But mostly that gets ignored, you know.   —Howard Rollins

★

I think I was twenty-five the first time I had sex. I stopped at twenty-six.
—Andy Warhol

★

Yes, I'm gay when I'm on that stage. If the role required me to suck off Horst, I'd do it.
—Richard Gere, who starred in *Bent* on Broadway (pre–Hollywood stardom)

★

I never touched my first wife at all. We got married in New York in 1920, on a Saturday morning. She made me marry her. She loved me so much that she just swept me off my feet. We would ride across town and she would stick her head out the window and yell, "I love Rudy Vallee!" We went together for a week and then got married, and on our wedding night I said, "Leona, I just can't go through with it."—avowed heterosexual Rudy Vallee

★

Once my mother—the only words she said to me about sex—came in and sat on the edge of my bed as I was lying down ready to go to sleep. I was around thirteen. And she said, "Do you ever play with your thing?"—or whatever she called it....And, lying, I said, "No. Why?" And she said, "Well, that's good, because it can make you crazy." The age-old bit. I didn't believe it. When she left the room, I remember saying to myself, "Oh, well, I'm going to go crazy and I'm going to have a ball."   —Jack Lemmon

★

It [having an abortion] serves me right for putting all my eggs in one bastard.
—Dorothy Parker

If we had had the benefit of psychiatry, then we would have seen how all that stuff about "nice girls don't" could really screw a person up, particularly if you think that nice girls don't and then you find out that your mother *does* it.   —Joseph Cotten, looking back

★

My mother thought double-dating would inhibit any kind of sexual exploration, but it worked in the reverse. We'd double with a couple who'd been together for a year or two and they'd be doing things in the front seat we had no intention of doing, but we'd feel, "Well, they're doing it so why aren't we?"   —Victoria Principal

★

One time [Fannie Flagg, Brown's longtime love] decided she was spending too much money at the beauty parlor. She'd wax herself. Well, that was tedious and boring, so she thought she'd singe the hair off her legs. However, she dropped the match, and I was treated to the spectacle of Fannie, her crotch in flames.   —writer Rita Mae Brown

★

I didn't have sex until I was about twenty-three. And then I didn't stop. Now, though, I'm very picket fence....I love promiscuity but why should I sabotage my life?...I never go to discos now. I'd feel like the Queen Mother if I went, I'm so old. I'd rather go to an antique show or read a book.

—Elton John, in 1997

★

Today, the word "theory" is a misnomer. In Darwin's time, it was "the theory of evolution." It [evolution] has since been proven time and again and beyond a doubt. Facts are facts. If people don't like reality, that's their business. But they have no right to try and ban reality from education.

—Morgan Fairchild, who studied to be an anthropologist

★

Most of the trouble on this planet is caused by people who must be right.

—William S. Burroughs

★

Yes, I have said that one should let some people be right, since they are nothing else. But even then I did not really believe it.   —André Gide

★

Hollywood runs scared of the general public. Fear is Hollywood's motivation; money is its goal....The Hollywood movers and shakers, most of whom should know better, go along with the pigeon-holing depictions. *We* know most Jews are not racially Semitic, as they were 2,000 and more years ago. We know most Jews don't have so-called Jewish noses. We know there are countless Jews with blue eyes. Hollywood knows this too. But they still cast Germans as blue-eyed blonds—go there, see for yourself....And Jews are inevitably played by brown-eyed, dark-haired people—most typically by Gentile actors.

—movie actor Sam Levene (*The Killers, Crossfire*)

★

The pope insists upon quantity. Quantity, not quality. Tunnel vision...no interest in the quality of life. Life here and now.

—Cesare Danova (*Cleopatra*)

★

Anyway, going against [secretly gay] Michael Bennett's stern advice—"Have a girl on your arm, even if it's [big boned] Pat Ast!"—Michel Stuart and I inched our way into the Shubert Theatre—the tall [Tony] nominee and his boyfriend. We were seated on the last row—me on the aisle, then a support column between us, then Michel's seat, so if the TV camera should need to land on me, you the viewer wouldn't see that I didn't have a girl date.

—Tony winner Tommy Tune

★

Men or women?   —Stella Stevens, laughingly replying to the question
"What stars did you date?"

★

I *adored* my ex-husband George Sanders's wife Benita [ex-actress Benita Hume], and she also adored me. She kept saying, "Come along and live with us, Zsa Zsa. I enjoy your company so much more than George's." She used to call me for dinner and say, "Come on over. We are so bored. You can pick us up a little." She used to call George "our husband," and she always said she wanted to adopt me.   —Zsa Zsa Gabor

★

When Ty [Power] died, he was forty-four but looked over fifty. His looks had coarsened due to the drinking that helped him ease his worries and fears about being exposed as queer [gay or bisexual]....Rock Hudson, for example, had an easier time of it...being younger and not spending most of his adult life with marriages or kids he didn't genuinely want.

—Twentieth Century–Fox publicist Harry Brand
(Hudson was godfather to Power's only son)

He picked me up once, when I was very young. It was the meanest fuck I think I've ever experienced. And every time I saw him after that, he pretended not to recognize me.

> —Arthur Laurents, on choreographer Jerome Robbins
> (co-director of the film *West Side Story*)

★

Desi [Arnaz, who was heterosexual] loved sex. He couldn't get enough....[But] an erection's an erection. It just wants satisfaction....Was it Gertrude Stein who said a mouth is a mouth is a mouth?...And to make a very pleasant story short, one day Desi said to me, "All right, we both know what you want. Let's get it over with." We did....Men aren't potato chips....

Desi said "One time only." For our friendship. Neither of us made a big deal out of it, excuse the pun, and we never referred to it again.

> —Cesar Romero, who admitted on tape to giving Arnaz oral sex,
> for the book *Hollywood Gays*

★

Believe me, I have no love for [Fidel] Castro. However, the U.S. censorship we had on TV in the 1950s was often ridiculous...and after Castro took over Cuba, CBS told Desi [Arnaz] his character Ricky Ricardo on the Lucy show had to switch nationality. CBS didn't want a show where the husband came from a country that was now communist! That's how paranoid things were, even in the late '50s after the [political] witch hunts were officially over....So [for] a few episodes there, Ricky Ricardo was officially Mexican.

> —Cesar Romero, a grandson of Cuba's liberator (from Spain), José Martí

★

If you were my husband, I'd put poison in your coffee.

> —Lady Astor, to Winston Churchill; his reply: If I were
> your husband, I'd drink it!

★

Well, there were three of us in this marriage, so it was a bit crowded.

> —Princess Diana on television, re her husband and his mistress.

★

I'm not conservative and I'm not liberal...I've never objected [to people seeing him as Dirty Harry or reactionary screen characters]. But it's an act, a part I'm playing.

> —Clint Eastwood

★

From images, people assume things. Understandably...and yet [the fact] that Bob Hope's two daughters are both openly lesbian only underlines that sexual and affectional orientation know no political boundaries.

—novelist Patricia Highsmith
★

[Meeting Garbo at a party:] I almost fainted. George [Sanders] informed Greta, "My wife has a wild crush on you." I blushed....Garbo responded, "She's very beautiful, your wife." [At another party:] Garbo spent most of the evening standing behind the bar flirting with me...Garbo was all over me. I nearly melted.

—Zsa Zsa Gabor
★

I think that due to his [conservative] politics, Howard Hughes would never have, as they now say, "come out." Anyway, he was only bisexual...he liked sex with women, but only certain ways. Hedy [Lamarr] said he offered her $10,000 to pose for a rubber dummy he wanted to make love to. "Why not sleep with me?" she wondered, but he declined, and she declined his offer....Howard did tell me that he preferred oral sex, and I explained that I had no interest in that. It didn't bother him, because then he'd just come to my house and sit and talk with me and my mother.

—Lana Turner
★

Don't talk about sex, or they'll think it's important to you. That was the gist of the advice all studios gave to actresses in my heyday as a Hollywood publicist.

—eventual novelist Richard Condon
★

"Never make public comments about religion—they might give offense to certain Christians." I did hear that comment made to a leading star of Jewish background...by a Jewish mogul.

—*Gone With the Wind* publicist Russell Birdwell
★

My counsel to actors would still be: Avoid talking politics—at most, say that you think the current president is doing a fine job, and then say no more.

—Fox publicist Harry Brand
★

If you want the opprobrium of the public, talk about sex, religion, and politics.

—MGM chief Louis B. Mayer
★

My way of joking is to tell the truth. It's the funniest joke in the world.

—George Bernard Shaw

Same-Sex Comments

I would rather drink latex paint than be in a movie with Steven Seagal.

—Henry Rollins

★

A triumph of the embalmer's art.   —Gore Vidal, on Ronald Reagan

★

I heard Michael Jackson is moving to France. For the first time my sympathies are with the French people.   —Boy George

★

I saw this empty taxicab drive up, and out stepped Sam Goldwyn.

—theater owner Sid Grauman

★

Those horrible things with those bold stripes and polka dots look like something that JonBenet [Ramsey]'s parents would pick out!

—drag queen Lypsinka, giving the *Wall Street Journal* his opinion of Princess Diana's auctioned-off dresses

★

My father, George Hamilton, was a boxer in college....Which college? Uh...the College of the Performing Tan.   —Ashley Hamilton

★

An overfat, flatulent, sixty-two-year-old windbag, a master of inconsequence now masquerading as a guru, passing off his vast limitations as pious virtues.   —Richard Harris, on Michael Caine

★

I am not thrilled by comparisons to Jim Carrey.   —Jerry Lewis

★

No, I *like* that. Let them say it [that Armani dresses the wife, while Versace dresses the mistress]. Giorgio [Armani] is a wonderful designer, but I think the mistress has more fun!   —Gianni Versace

★

Me with a guy? Never happen!...Well, maybe Brad Pitt.

—Rodney Dangerfield, on Jay Leno's show

TALLULAH BANKHEAD

Dahling, you're divine. I've had an affair with your husband. You'll be next.
—Tallulah Bankhead, to Joan Crawford, who was
married to Douglas Fairbanks Jr.

★

Darling, she's old enough to take care of herself. And him too.
—Zsa Zsa Gabor, on Elizabeth Taylor's latest divorce

★

I'll never put Tom Cruise down. He's already kinda short.
—producer Don Simpson

★

Crap floats too. It stays up there [until] decency or common sense sweeps it away.... Look at Rush Limbaugh. He rose without a trace.
—Al Franken, author of *Rush Limbaugh is s Big, Fat Idiot*

★

He is to acting what Liberace was to pumping iron.
—Rex Reed, on Sylvester Stallone

★

Whatever Francis [Ford Coppola] does for you always ends up benefiting Francis the most.
—George Lucas

Marlon Brando, who gave up acting shortly after [1954], is now [1971] simply a balding, middle-aged, pot-bellied man driven to undisciplined excesses that are clearly inexcusable on the screen. —Rex Reed

★

Speed seemed to be more of a concept and a style that [the director] created. I don't know if you can remember the characters' names from that movie. So you didn't need to see [him] in the new situation, although it would have been nice for you.
—Jason Patric, who became *him* when he replaced Keanu Reeves in *Speed 2*

★

I feel like Don Knotts every day of my life. Sometimes I pretend I'm him. If it's a slow day, I go in and out of being Don Knotts. When he was young, he was really my type. —director John Waters

★

Jack Nicholson is someone I'd like to work with. Not someone I'd want to socialize with. Not where women are involved. He treats them abominably...several of his shall we say girlfriends say he refuses to wear condoms. If that's not irresponsible and cruel, what is?
—director John Cassavetes

★

That's why John Wayne finally became a good actor in *True Grit*—he's got 150 [movies] behind him...he's developed...from mining that same vein over and over and over again. —Gregory Peck

★

I wasn't taken with [Mel Brooks's] *Young Frankenstein*. I thought we did better jokes in high school. I was with an audience, expecting to laugh. There wasn't one, and in the end they started to walk out.
—Jason Robards

★

Coppola is his own worst enemy. He has such dualities in his mind about success and artistry. He equates success with sellout and doesn't care to remember that nearly all the really good directors became successful.
—Peter Bogdanovich

★

Coppola couldn't piss in a pot. —Actor Bob Hoskins

★

Peter Boobdanovich [sic]? He began as a movie critic and I predict he'll end up writing. As a writer he's passable. As a director he's repetitive and unimaginative. As a man he has numerous insecurities which I legally don't dare elaborate on. And as a friend—he ain't.   —Sal Mineo

★

[Director Stanley Kubrick] is very meticulous and hates everything that he writes or has anything to do with. He's an incredibly, depressingly serious man...paranoid....He's a perfectionist and he's always unhappy with anything that's set.   —George C. Scott

★

Kubrick, like Hitchcock, is known to prefer preparing a film to actually making one. Once the camera is rolling, Hitchcock gets bored and Kubrick gets melancholy.   —Burt Lancaster

★

Kubrick isn't as daunting as his reputation, which is about complete control. He's kind and easygoing by comparison with a swine like Otto Preminger.   —Keir Dullea

★

One of the best actors alive. But my opinion of him as an actor is much higher than my opinion of him as a man.
                              —John Huston, on George C. Scott

★

I loathe and detest men who beat their wives or paramours. George C. Scott is one, on a long list. I knew first-hand, from Ava [Gardner]....Many actresses required expert makeup to camouflage the results of their husbands' or boyfriends' brutality.   —hairdresser Sydney Guilaroff

★

Talk about unprofessional rat finks.   —Billy Wilder, on Peter Sellers

★

English directors [are] the coldest, most heartless moviemakers I've ever seen—most of them. They're wonderfully proficient. The technical skill is out of this world. No one working in films, for instance, has as good an eye as Ridley Scott. But there's a coldness of temperament I can't get along with.   —writer John Milius

★

Bob Monkhouse, in his autobiography *Crying With Laughter,* has recently revealed that, at the opening night of Commercial TV's Birmingham studio, Tyrone Power tried to seduce him in the bathroom. Monkhouse resisted, and Power told him that he had "blown it." Silently, Monkhouse begged to differ.
                              —British TV host Ned Sherrin

She never says anything kind about anyone unless first you cross her tongue with silver.   —Joyce Haber, on fellow gossip columnist Rona Barrett

★

One thing you can say for O. J. Simpson. He never shed a drop of blood except in anger.   —Robert Mitchum

★

She was a friend of mine—a trying friend, but a friend.... She never really denied herself anything for me...she did what she wanted to do. And I have no right to change her fulfillment into my misery. I'm on my own broom now.   —Liza Minnelli, on her mother, Judy Garland

★

There is professional jealousy. However, there's also boredom with recycled plays. I once went with a playwright friend to see the latest Neil Simon [play]. Halfway through the first act, he asks me, "What's it about, really?" I said, "It's about all I can take." We didn't stay through the last act—didn't need to.   —playwright James Kirkwood

★

He's not a dancer. What he did in those dance scenes was very attractive but he is basically not a dancer. I was dancing like that years ago, you know. Disco is just jitterbug.   —Fred Astaire, on John Travolta

Roy Scheider

TOM CRUISE

[Carroll O'Connor's wife] came up to us and said, "Isn't this a wonderful party?" We all agreed. Then she said, "But you know, the one thing Carroll misses is his privacy." And Maureen [Stapleton] said, "Well, don't worry, he'll get it back."
—Roy Scheider

★

That German magazine said Tom Cruise's supposed to have a zero sperm count, and he sued. But since he claims all sorts of things but adopted two kids and had none with either wife, isn't it somewhat logical to at least wonder if Cruise is or is not sterile?...I think he overreacts. To everything!
—director Samuel Fuller

Wet, she's a star. Dry, she ain't.   —Fanny Brice, on Esther Williams

Jack [Benny] was extremely sharp, but he was also at times naïve....I once asked him what he thought about oral sex. He thought a while, then said, "I think talking about anything controversial is a good idea."

—George Burns

Some people don't come across well on stage....Barbra Streisand has the greatest voice in the business, but because she has been in a recording studio for so long, she's not a great performer.

—Lorna Luft, Judy Garland's other daughter

I'd really rather not discuss Marlon Brando....I do know that I'll never be nominated [for an Academy Award] until I scratch myself on screen— which will not happen any time soon.   —Cary Grant

Somebody criticized me for calling [LaToya] La Toilet, but that [Jackson] family is weird! I swear, this is true: When Janet travels on tour and goes to a new hotel, she demands that they install a brand-new toilet for her! And they talk about Howard Hughes! At least he achieved something in the real world...without an unreal brother paving the way.   —Judy Tenuta

I spent hours counting the freckles on Julie Andrews's face on the back album cover of *The Sound of Music*.

—Tony winner Cherry Jones, on knowing early that she was gay

One of her former clients told me Sandra Bernhard used to be a manicurist. I suppose that's as good a place as any to meet women.   —Alexis Smith

I don't belong to any political party, and certainly not the Republicans. I'm more liberal than Kristin's old man.

—Ron Reagan, in 1997, about his new TV show with Kristin Gore,
                                 daughter of Vice President Al Gore
★
Marilyn Monroe was smart for only ten minutes in her entire life. And that was the time it took her to sign with Twentieth Century–Fox.

—Anne Baxter
★

Tom Tryon keeps complaining that I drove him from the picture business! Doesn't he care about the motion picture–goers I have benefited? Besides, he is a big success in novels, so he should thank me!...It proves the point that those who can't act, write—they either remain critics or they become novelists. —Otto Preminger

★

I was at the Ivy restaurant in Los Angeles one night when I spotted Rupert Murdoch waiting for his car. I introduced myself, and he started fumbling through his pockets for a ticket. He thought I was with valet parking. I told him, "No, Mr. Murdoch. I do your show," and he mumbled, "Nice to meet you." —Arsenio Hall

★

Celine Dion filled in for Barbra Streisand on the Oscars. She sang Streisand's Oscar-nominated song. Barbra was there that night, but she didn't feel like singing, I guess....While Celine was singing—beautifully— Barbra just happened to be taking a bathroom break. —Fran Drescher

★

Miss [Elizabeth] Taylor is a spoiled, indulgent child, a blemish on public decency. —Joan Crawford, in 1962

★

My idea of a movie star is Joan Crawford, who can chew up two directors and three producers before lunch. —Shelley Winters

★

I saw Shelley Winters in *A Place in the Sun*. She gave a very moving performance, which surprised me, because Shelley is not a sensitive girl socially. —Joan Crawford

★

Who the hell hasn't Shelley Winters slept with?
—Bette Davis, after reading Winters's memoirs

★

Bette Davis says, "My name goes above the title. I am a star." Yes, she is a star, and a great one. But is it worth playing all those demented old ladies to maintain that status? —Myrna Loy

★

Given the things I said about Reagan—that he's a criminal who used the Constitution for toilet paper—it wouldn't surprise me if my phone was tapped. —John Cusack

★

Patrick Stewart and I are often mistaken for one another. I have a little more hair than he has, and I'm rather darker-complected, but those *Star Trek* fans become so excited they don't notice such details. Sometimes I sign Patrick's autograph, and he does the same for my fans. It's a matter of practicality. —Ben Kingsley

This American fan once came up to me, gushing and on the verge of tears. Totally tongue-tied, she was. Finally she managed to say, "You're my favorite actor. You would be even if you hadn't won the Oscar for *Gandhi*." What could I say? I placed my palms together and said, "Bless you, my child." —Patrick Stewart

I was in a department store in Beverly Hills, and this little old lady came up to me and said, "You're Dolly Parton." I said, "No, Ma'am, I'm not. I'm Barbara Mandrell." She seemed puzzled, then looked at my chest as discreetly as she could and said, "I think you're right."

—Barbara Mandrell

The stupidest comparison I [ever] got was when some fan magazine wrote me up as "a brunet Kirk Douglas" and even compared the clefts in our chins. I wrote them an obscene letter...besides, why isn't he "a blond Bob Mitchum?" —Robert Mitchum

I have to be honest. The first time I saw Cher I thought she was a hooker.
—Ronnie Spector of the Ronettes

I can believe Charlie Sheen's a sex maniac...also very rude and loves to shock for the sake of it. He has problems....
—Eric Stoltz, after Sheen publicly said he'd like to have sex with Stoltz's girlfriend, Bridget Fonda

★

Somehow I am now [1977] being offered all the parts they used to offer to Michael York....I'm turning them down. They're all right for Michael, I suppose; he hasn't a very large range, after all.
—British actor Robert Powell

★

She's a sexy bombshell and those are the kinds of roles she does. I do all kinds of different things. It makes me laugh when she says she got offered

Selena, which was an outright lie. If that's what she does to get herself publicity, then that's her thing.
—Jennifer Lopez, on fellow Latina Salma Hayek

★

It must've been hell the way [Prince Charles] was brought up. He's out of time. A generation skipped him....I wonder if his ass will ever touch the red velvet? —Keith Richards, on the potential king

★

Faye Dunaway says she is being haunted by my mother's ghost. After her performance in *Mommie Dearest,* I can understand. —Christina Crawford

★

Ever since they found out that Lassie was a boy, the public has believed the worst about Hollywood. —Groucho Marx

★

He's like a junkie, an applause junkie. Instead of growing old gracefully or doing something with his money, be helpful, all he does is have an anniversary with the president looking on. He's a pathetic guy.
—Marlon Brando, on Bob Hope

★

I introduced myself to Tom Cruise at the Golden Globes party, and he didn't give me the freakin' time of day.
—Neil Patrick Harris (TV's former *Doogie Howser, M.D.)*

★

Very, very lucky.... —Neil Patrick Harris, on Leonardo DiCaprio

★

Excellent actor, very attractive, very charismatic. I don't mind losing parts to Matt. —Neil Patrick Harris, on Matt Damon

★

Yes, Leonardo [DiCaprio] came to my show....I think he would love to look like one of those handsome male models. And I know that—ah, but I shouldn't say any more. Even today, one cannot say everything.
—designer Gianni Versace

★

A face unclouded by thought. —writer Lillian Hellman, on Norma Shearer

★

[Before acting] I was a dress model at I. Magnin in L.A., and Marlene Dietrich was a good customer. Well, one day I went into Marlene's dressing room, and there she was, sitting on a stool, without a stitch on, in all her glory. She just cooed, "I vanted to be cool." Other models told me she was an exhibitionist, [that] she loved to show people her body.

—Esther Williams

Garbo will be forgotten in ten years, and as an actress her memory will be dead when Helen Hayes's, Lynne Fontanne's, and Katharine Cornell's are beginning to grow greener.

—Clare Boothe Luce (a.k.a. Clare Boothe Who?), in 1932

★

There we were [at MGM] in a row, Marlene Dietrich, Lucille Ball, and myself, with Sydney Guilaroff....Hairdressing took a long time then [no blowdryers or hot rollers], and Marlene was bored. So she would inch [off] the hair cloth that covered her, a little at a time, until she was completely nude. Sydney, being such a gentleman, and so grand, would patiently ask her to cover up. Marlene would say, "I don't vant to." She would sit there in her magnificence and then Sydney would tie the cloth abound her neck again and again. Lucille and I laughed our heads off.   —Esther Williams

Oh, Mr. Thalberg, I've just met that extraordinary wife of yours with the teensy-weensy little eyes!

—British stage star Mrs. Patrick Campbell, to MGM honcho Irving Thalberg

★

[Edgar Bergen, Candice's once-famous father] was one of the luckiest so-and-so's in the business. This was a ventriloquist whose lips regularly moved, but he was a star on *radio*...and he did motion pictures that did well thanks to such stars as W. C. Fields. And he lasted and lasted, on a minimum of looks, talent, or personality—and the corniest, dreariest dummies you ever "heard." Bergen's outstanding attributes were his lovely wife, his lovely daughter, and his lovely son, all blondes.

—Rudy Vallee

If you adopt a child, what happens when the marriage goes sour? When Burt Reynolds and Loni Anderson fought, they could always leave Quinton with Dom DeLuise. But what about the kids who aren't that lucky?

—Bill Maher

★

The [school] was trying to mold Robin [Williams] into a standardized Juilliard product—Kevin Kline is the perfect example of it—but Robin was too special, too original, to be that.　　　　　　　—Christopher Reeve

★

Then I thought to myself, Darn it, maybe I can't do what Vanessa Redgrave can. But can Vanessa Redgrave do what I can do? Who's kidding who here?
　　　　　　　　　　　　　　　　　　　　　　—Raquel Welch

★

If you had to worship something mortal on earth, I would go and bow twice a day to wherever [Laurence] Olivier was standing.　　　—Sammy Davis Jr.

★

There have been times when I've been ashamed to take the money. But then I think of some of the movies that have given Olivier cash for his old age, and I don't feel so bad.　　　　　　　　　　　　—Stewart Granger

TRUMAN CAPOTE

I was visiting Italy some time after Gore [Vidal] moved there, and eventually we connected on the telephone. He called me to say, "I passed by your hotel yesterday." I was perfectly candid and said, "Thank you so much."　　　　　　　　　　　　　　　　　　—Truman Capote

★

I read where O. J. Simpson said he wasn't going to lower himself to read any of the latest books about him. "Lower" himself? To do that, he'd have to *climb*.

—director-producer George Schaefer

[Marlon Brando] has preserved the mentality of an adolescent. It's a pity. When he doesn't try and someone's speaking to him it's like a blank wall. In fact it's even less interesting because behind a blank wall you can always suppose that there's something interesting there.   —Burt Reynolds

He's like all these drunks. Impossible when he's drunk and only half there when he's sober. Wooden as a board with his body, relies on doing all his acting with his voice.   —director John Boorman, on Richard Burton

I don't tamper with my drinking formula. No, siree. I got it on good authority that when Humphrey Bogart kicked the bucket, his last words were, "I never should have switched from Scotch to Martinis."

—Dean Martin

Jerry Lewis, who's very talented, aimed his humor too much for kids.

—Woody Allen

[Jerry] Lewis used to be one of my heroes....But through the years I've seen him turn into this arrogant, sour, ceremonial, piously chauvinistic egomaniac. I'm just amazed at his behavior.   —Elliott Gould

That silly horse, Jeanette MacDonald, yakking away at wooden-peg [Nelson] Eddy with all that glycerine running down her Max Factor.

—Judy Garland

[Shirley MacLaine] is as changeable as an opinion poll. She varies her statements and beliefs, she invents a new public face, according to what is currently fashionable or acceptable...and she is as tough as nails and just as spiky.   —Carolyn Jones

★

It was common knowledge among Hollywood folk like my wife Paulette [Goddard] about Gene Raymond [being gay]. Times being what they were, it was often suspected that a blond actor might be that way....Paulette didn't know whether Jeanette MacDonald [Raymond's wife] knew....Now it's all come out about Raymond and his honeymoon with Mary Pickford's last husband [Buddy Rogers], in a book. I guess no situation is journalistically protected nowadays.

—Burgess Meredith (the men's tryst reportedly occurred when MacDonald and Pickford went on concurrent honeymoons with their new husbands in Hawaii)

★

When I was growing up, my mother [Joan Crawford] often would say I reminded her of Norma Shearer [who had small eyes], and she'd get a strange look on her face. Only later did I realize she was pathologically jealous of Shearer. —Christina Crawford

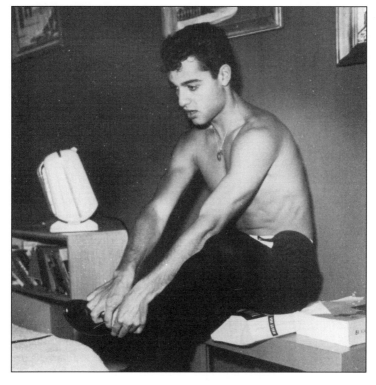

SAL MINEO

Back when Tab [Hunter] and Tony [Perkins] were real close, the story was that Tab told Tony, "Someday you'll make a fine actor." And Tony was supposed to have answered, "I already have. Several of them."

—Sal Mineo

They talk about Richard Gere, but the champ where male nudity [on the screen] is concerned is without question Malcolm McDowell. Well, he's English, so....But now, well, in a few years he aged almost a decade—the hair, the face, jowls...so his nudity days are behind him. Excuse the expression.
—Jeremy Brett (TV's *Sherlock Holmes*)

Merv Griffin does claim to have invented *Jeopardy!* In truth, his wife invented it but he got credit and the rewards....He's a better businessman than he lets on, with his seemingly jolly, light, and airy persona. However, he's less of a singer or a creative mind than he likes people to believe.
—sidekick Arthur Treacher

Most talk show hosts are failed actors—men too generic to be as individual as a film star is required to be....Game show hosts are the bottom rung; these are men with even less talent or personality, and fast-fading looks that never were much to begin with. Boy-men with names like Doug or Chip or Wink...and pompous, lackluster bores like Alex Trebek.
—Bert Convy, actor and eventual game show host

★

I was never a stripper. —Madonna, as opposed to Courtney Love (Madonna did work at a Dunkin' Donuts)

★

Goldwyn was a monster....Once I went to like twenty-four cities in twenty days. The publicity man with me had a nervous breakdown in Kansas City—the white coats just came and took him away!...You're like a broken record. You say, "Yes, Sam Goldwyn is *such* a great producer, he's like a *daddy* to me." All this bullshit that you had to say! I used to feel so guilty about it. And I didn't think the films were that great! Why was I telling other people to see them? I used to have great conflicts about that. But it was what one had to do. You really were a *property*. As a piece of script was.
—Farley Granger

When he got older and I was older and times had changed, my father [comedian Ed Wynn] started to talk about sex more freely....I was always anxious that he might tell me about his own sex life. But I think the most shocking thing you could learn about your parents' sex life would be that they still had one.
—Keenan Wynn

★

MAE WEST and friends

Mae West always insisted that she was sexually active, through her eighties. The man who lived with her for the last quarter-century secretly told me otherwise....For Mae, it was very important that everyone think she was sexual, to the end. She equated sex with youth, and for her the worst insult was the word "old."...Publicly she didn't acknowledge her relationship with Paul Novak. He was her husband in all but name....She wished the public to think she still went from man to man.

—columnist and West friend Joyce Haber

[In post–World War II Hollywood] at the studio, I ran into Gore Vidal....He said to me, "They have the most wonderful hustlers in this town. They're all straight, and they'll do anything, and they're only $25." So I said, "Well, actually, Gore, that's not my scene, but thank you." So I went back to the Chateau Marmont [hotel], and there was a costume designer named Miles White. He said to me, "Oh, they have the most wonderful hustlers in this town...they're gorgeous, they'll do anything, and they're $50." I said,

"Gore said they were $25." He said, "That's because he has them before six o'clock."   —Arthur Laurents

For a producer, the most important commodities are money and sex. Both signify power.... Which reminds me: I admired Joe E. Brown's talent, and I wanted him for *A Midsummer Night's Dream*. Not a giant role, but a plum nonetheless. I contacted his agent, Ivan Kahn, said I was prepared to offer his client a Cadillac for the role. Kahn snaps back at me, "What do I get for my commission—a bicycle?"   —producer Hal Wallis

Anyone who remembers the good times at Studio 54 wasn't there.... Steve Rubell and Ian Schraeger [the owners] were fakes and cynical opportunists ready to try and make a fortune at the expense of anyone's health or happiness.   —singer-composer Peter Allen

They are victims of laughter...they get nervous and resort to an insult or a four-letter word for a quick, cheap laugh. That goes on night after night until the whole act is cheapened. But that doesn't last. Usually, a couple of years later, they are remembered only as the old what's-his-name who used all the dirty words.
—Red Skelton, on Andrew Dice Clay, Eddie Murphy, Sam Kinison, et al.

I don't understand. [Antonio Banderas] said no to Madonna and yes to Melanie Griffith? She makes Madonna look intelligent. Not to mention attractive and thin. But he's Hispanic, isn't he?...
—Howard Rollins, on the Spanish actor

Madonna gives good voice. But she's too old to portray Evita Peron, who died at [thirty-two]. Madonna's in her late thirties but looks about forty. So much partying and sex will do that to a face.
—former actor Connie Clausen

I wonder how many Chinese had to go bald to supply Elton John with his latest hair?   —Peter Cook

You don't see many actors nude in the movies, but by now probably everyone's seen the nude photos of [Arnold] Schwarzenegger and [Sylvester] Stallone...not too impressive. Big muscles, is all.... They say

little pitchers have big ears. Seems to me big stars have little...you-know-whats. —director Don Siegel (*Dirty Harry*)

★

When movie stars fade and they're brainy, they write books. Take Lilli Palmer or Dirk Bogarde. When dumb movie stars fade, they paint—Tony Curtis, Anthony Quinn, [Sylvester] Stallone.... —Peter Cook

★

They said I was "too British" to work in Hollywood pictures. But Hal Roach, the famous comedy producer, once expressed cautious interest. He asked me several unusual questions...one of the usual ones was what had I worked at before performing? Among other things, I mentioned I'd been a cartographer at Stanfords [map shop] in Long Acre....The upshot was that, among other misinformation, the elderly producer reported back to his associates that I was a graduate of Stanford University, I loved to hike in the country, and I could turn cartwheels to order. I never did work in California. —British comedian Kenneth Williams

★

Darling, she's *so* distasteful! —Zsa Zsa Gabor, on Barbra Streisand

★

Lauren Bacall is the terror of Manhattan waiters. The woman is beyond demanding...when she displays her sense of humor, it's like you're witnessing a solar eclipse or some rare event....Not too long ago at some posh New York eatery she was all upset with her baked potato and the waiter. She placed the spud in his hand and yelled, "Can't you see this is a bad potato?!" The waiter saved the evening. With his other hand he spanked the spud and said, "Bad potato! *Bad* potato!" Miss Bacall laughed, so did everyone else, and there were no more serious complaints.

—Sally Blane, former actress and Loretta Young's sister

★

Come on, don't ask me to talk about other big funny men! I'm not competing with them...I'm not trying to outgross anyone....John Belushi [also from *Saturday Night Live*] was someone I really admired, and in a different way, the fat guy from The Three Stooges...yeah, Curly. I heard he had some problems in self-appreciation. But it never showed in his work. He was cool, man. —Chris Farley

★

Wallace Beery was about as big a star as anyone in the 1930s....He was uncouth. His table manners left, well, everything to be desired. I think it was Gloria Swanson who said Wallace got invited to every mansion in Los Angeles—*once*.   —'30s matinee idol Lyle Talbot

★

The bigger they are, the cheaper they are! Jodie Foster, trying to get a discount on her movie ticket by displaying and arguing about some VIP ID card she had. Even more astounding, one of my spies said Tom Cruise was going to one of the summer movies, in Westwood [Los Angeles]. He was on his own, and he was trying to get the theater to let him in for free. My spy didn't hang around to learn the outcome, but this is an actor who earns upward of $15 million a movie but balks at paying for one movie ticket.... These people are not normal in *any* sense.   —Connie Clausen

★

My voice and my attitude [were] there to provide the balance. That's what's missing from Van Halen when I ain't in it. I'm the fun in that band—always have been.... It's not something that you can fake or that you can hire anywhere else.... Classic Van Halen makes you wanna drink, dance, and screw, right? And the new Van Halen encourages you to drink milk, drive a Nissan, and have a relationship.   —singer David Lee Roth

★

I miss the old Woody Allen. The one who didn't look like your most boring or preoccupied uncle. The one who got involved with girls more or less his own age. The one who moved fast, not the one who shuffles.... One interview, they asked if he had any sexual kinks or secrets. He said yes, he liked to chew gum that's already been chewed by a midget.... Funny, he *was*.   —actor William Hickey

★

I just think Latrell [Sprewell] has a bad memory. He forgot a [basketball] player's supposed to keep his hands on the ball, not around the coach's neck.   —Dennis Rodman, after Sprewell allegedly tried to choke his coach

★

One might say that Tom Cruise is to hunks what Velveeta is to cheese. It *is* cheese, but not true cheese.... Normally, directors don't dish movie stars— we may want to work with them someday. I have no need or wish to work with Tom Cruise, though. And I'm not going to say why....
                    —director Emile Ardolino (*Sister Act*)

★

It is difficult to envisage Tom Cruise as Anne Rice's vampire [LeStat in *Interview With the Vampire*]. Not because of the ambi-sexuality...her vampire is sleek, sinister and sexy. I predict Cruise will come across like a case of fallen archness.   —director Lindsay Anderson

★

Victoria Principal married a plastic surgeon. Isn't that convenient...and *free*.   —Joan Rivers

BRAD DAVIS in *Querelle*

Michael Jackson is afraid to ever give the impression he might be gay. Maybe he's not...there are so-called gay-acting heterosexuals, besides straight-acting gays. What I think he really is, is a pedophile. Why else would he spend most of his time away from the paparazzi with little boys? The guy's thirty or something!...I'm just surprised he hasn't engineered a fake marriage, if only for his bizarre image.

—Brad Davis (who camouflaged his own bisexuality), before Jackson contracted marriage with Elvis Presley's daughter

★

I think Mel Gibson's father had eleven or twelve kids...if you want to know what he's like, they used to call him the Catholic Jerry Falwell. He took his brood from America [to Australia]—thought [America] was getting "too liberal."...Most people say Gibson is very like his father. Though I believe he has only six or seven children.

—Patrick White, Australia's Nobel Prize–winning writer

Alec Baldwin keeps saying he wants to go into politics. So *go*. He might be a good one....What's he waiting for—an engraved people's mandate?

—Don Rickles

One thing is sure. I'm not going to go in the role [of Dracula] forever...and end like [Bela] Lugosi, a morphine addict playing in tasteless parodies.

—Christopher Lee

I find him frightening...off-putting. Where some men are self-contained, he's vacuum-packed! —Anthony Perkins, on Steven Seagal

...a bunch of nuts.

—Disney chief Michael Eisner, about the Southern Baptists boycotting Disney, which owns ABC, which airs *Ellen*

Melissa Etheridge and k. d. lang haven't had their careers hurt by being [openly] gay, but I was the first star to discuss being bisexual...it doesn't pay to be ahead of your time. If I had a girlfriend today, my career might be in better shape! —Judy "Sock It to Me" Carne

Somebody was asking me. Said he thought Richard Nixon was obviously homosexual. I said, "Why do you think that?" He said, "You know, that funny, uncoordinated way he moves." I said, "Yeah, like Nureyev."

—Gore Vidal

They call Ronald Reagan the great communicator. Well, any man that can call a nuclear missile "Peacemaker" is free to call his son "Butch."

—gay comedian–turned–San Francisco politician Tom Ammiano

★

I have, a few times, been mistaken for [Meryl Streep]. Except at the Oscars.

—talented but un-Oscared Glenn Close

Mamie—what's her last name? It begins with V.D....I don't see her as a rival, no. Of course, she's blonde. So many are. But—if you know what I mean—she does seem rather small for her size....

—Jayne Mansfield, on Mamie Van Doren

★

I wouldn't throw Mick Jagger out of bed.

—Andy Warhol star Joe Dallesandro, in the 1960s

★

He's so fucking ugly now.

—Joe Dallesandro in 1993, on why he changed his mind about Mick

★

MICK JAGGER and DAVID BOWIE (DANA GILLESPIE)

Of course.   —Mick Jagger's reply at a 1994 press conference to the question "Did you really sleep with David Bowie?"

★

Lana [Turner] and Johnny Stompanato. Together, they were dynamite, in a totally negative sense. Something dreadful was bound to happen....I don't think they ever loved each other...it was closer to hate, but hating each other with lust. They had a great love life—*sex* life....The lust was stronger than their mutual dislike.

—Ava Gardner, on her friend and her friend's ill-fated lover

I attempted to [impersonate] Madonna, but it didn't work. She's not a singer-entertainer.

—female impersonator Jim Bailey, on why he no longer imitates Madonna

[Joan Fontaine] always acted [roles] younger than she was. Once she was no longer young, it completely caught up with her. Bette Davis was smarter. She began doing older parts while young, thus assuring a greater diversity and longevity to her career. —columnist Sheilah Graham

A good man but a bad boy. —Dan Aykroyd, on John Belushi

I like Don Rickles. But that's because I have no taste. —Frank Sinatra

True, Bob earns a lot—don't we all. Top of his profession? That's an opinion. To me, Bob's work indicates that he believes the old saying that imagination is the eccentric of the family.

—Stirling Silliphant, on fellow screenwriter Robert Towne

★

I remember Sandy Dennis—she was so wonderful—said something to me when I left to come to California. She said, "You're an actress, Brenda, and that's all you're ever going to be," and I said, "I'm going to be a movie star," and she said, "You're an actress, Brenda, and that's all you're ever going to be," and those words ring clear in my mind years later, because she was right. —Brenda Vaccaro

★

I once mentioned to Bing Crosby that Sinatra was a singer who comes along once in a lifetime. "Yeah," commented Bing, "but why does he have to come [along] in my lifetime?" —columnist James Bacon

★

Leonard Bernstein uses music as an accompaniment to his conducting.

—Oscar Levant, pianist

Someday I'll record an album titled *Music to Listen to Neil Diamond By*.

—Frank Zappa

★

I wondered what motivated Michelle Pfeiffer to do [*Wolf*]? It was a completely nothing role. It's the kind of movie I'd have to do because I needed the job.

—Mimi Rogers

★

If I come back in another life, I want to be Warren Beatty's fingertips.

—Woody Allen

★

Steve McQueen was notorious for orgies. Honest to God Roman-type sex orgies. The guy always needed an audience. Even sex...he had to make it into a party.

—Robert Mitchum

★

When I can't sleep, I read a book by Steve Allen

—Oscar Levant

★

Being with Gore [Vidal] depresses me...because Gore really exudes despair and cynical misery and a grudge against a society which is really based on his own lack of talent and creative joy.

—Christopher Isherwood, in his diary

★

There have always been mixed emotions about Howard Cosell. Some people hate him like poison and some people just hate him regular.

—Buddy Hackett

★

Better as a woman. If I were him, I'd never get out of drag.

—designer Mr. Blackwell, on Dustin Hoffman in *Tootsie*

★

Ed Sullivan will be around as long as someone else has talent.

—Fred Allen

★

Elvis is too popular, almost, for his own good. People have compared us. But they treat him like an idol, and that's not very healthy.

—Ricky Nelson, in 1964

★

Elvis died because his insane fame drove him to it...then he became a legend and a martyr.

—Rick Nelson, in 1978

I introduced Elvis Presley on my television show. I never thought of him as controversial. Everyone else did. But me, a guy who wore dresses? The only guy in America who wore a dress in public? And *only* in public. I didn't get shook up over the trivial stuff. —Milton Berle

★

Rick [Nelson] could definitely have been a bigger star, possibly as big as Elvis, if he'd been looser. He was rather stiff in performance....He was upper middle class; Elvis was from poverty. [Elvis] had his mom; Rick had two famous, very proper parents [Ozzie and Harriet]. He was quite withdrawn on stage. —singer Johnnie Ray

★

It's great to see what happened to Jughead after the "Archie" comic books, isn't it? —John Larroquette, on Quentin Tarantino

★

Sometimes I think I'm a reincarnation of [Rudolph] Valentino. But I don't envy him. He didn't have a period of not being popular, which makes you appreciate your more successful moments. —John Travolta

★

How difficult can it be to fly an airplane? I mean, John Travolta learned how.... —Graham Chapman of Monty Python

★

It means he didn't cry when Princess Di was killed, and he walks more like John Wayne than John Travolta.
　　　—openly gay actor Michael Kearns, on the term "straight acting"

★

[Producer] Allan Carr's license plate reads GREASE. He was responsible for that putrid movie and its totally unsuccessful sequel. Isn't it surprising what some people choose to advertise about themselves? —Rex Reed

★

No, I don't believe Katharine Hepburn ever said that [that she divorced Ludlow Ogden Smith so she wouldn't be known as Kate Smith]. That marriage lasted only a few weeks. There were other, extremely personal reasons....Two of her close friends have said she prefers friendships with men to marriage with them. —Frances Dee (*Little Women*)

★

I regret that I remember not one act of kindness from her all through my childhood. —Joan Fontaine, on sister Olivia De Havilland

★

ELVIS PRESLEY

It's a hell of a move. Makes the guy look pretty crass or desperate, whichever way you look at it.
—John Denver, on David Bowie's issuing bonds supported by the anticipated worth of future royalties from his songs, in 1997

To those who have sold or purchased the stolen video of my wife and I [sic], which by the way is against the law, our lawyers have been told to take the necessary actions!!! I seriously look forward to your visit to JAIL. Maybe I'll come to visit you there and film you getting [screwed] by *Bubba*, the inmate on Death Row!!! Now, that would be sweet revenge. Bend over, bitch!!!
—web site message from Tommy Lee (husband of Pamela Anderson, ex-husband of Heather Locklear), re unauthorized distribution of his homemade sex videotape

Stop whining, bitch!!! You're the luckiest guy in the world...(You know, you're not exactly Kurt Cobain, you're a lousy rock drummer for God's sake!!!) If not for your marriage to two of the hottest TV babes in Hollywood, you would be just another anemic-looking metal moron whose name nobody can remember. Wake up and smell the heroin, Tom—the tape's been the best thing that's happened to your tuckered-out career since your latest marriage to a bottled-blond bombshell.
—*New Times* columnist Rick Barrs's open letter to Tommy Lee

He was a no-good son of a bitch. But he was the greatest entertainer I've ever seen.   —George Jessel, on Al Jolson

★

Tommy Tune is such a dear. A nice guy, a wonderful talent....No, I don't think he'll ever come out of the closet—so you can't print this. But it's not like everyone hasn't guessed.
—choreographer Michael Bennett (Tune came out in his '97 memoirs, titled *Foot Notes*)

★

When Rosie O'Donnell...recently called for a one-year boycott of the tabloids by readers who want to honor [Princess] Diana, I was so outraged that I immediately bought copies of the *Enquirer* and *Star* in protest. O'Donnell was hypocritically using Diana's tragic death to grind her own axes: Omitted from her histrionic appeal was the inconvenient fact that the prior week's splashy *Enquirer* cover story...was about the motorcycle-straddling O'Donnell's alleged affairs with two lesbian lovers. Sugar-sweet, all-American Miss Rosie has a shadowy closet the size of Greenland. And folks, backstage she bites. —author Camille Paglia

★

I used to [worry] more before I did concerts, and I thought, Well, they hear me on record, where you perfect everything. When you go out and sing live...you could have flaws and imperfections, [but] in time I said, You know what? I love the flaw. I love the imperfections....
—hugely paid concert singer Barbra Streisand, on Rosie O'Donnell's hugely profitable TV talk show

★

When Sharon [Stone] was introduced to me she looked straight at my husband the director. When introduced to him, she declared, "We know each other, don't we...?" —columnist Holly Palance (daughter of Jack)

★

I know who you are! You don't live here, you *rent!*
—Shannen Doherty, unwelcomingly yelling at new neighbor Molly Ringwald in 1996

★

It's simple. Don Johnson asked me to have a drink with him. I didn't want to. So I said no. So he started a fight. And we fought, sort of. I don't like him. In fact, less than I did before. —Gary Oldman

★

Mel Gibson, pillar of the establishment. In the 1980s he was arrested for drunk driving in Canada and smashing into another car. Now he's Mr. Holier Than Thou. —British actor Harry Andrews

★

They should let the pigeons see Jackie Mason's picture. That would scare them away.
—Henny Youngman, on how to keep the San Francisco subways clean

★

Not hard to believe, but Jack Nicholson's being sued by two call girls for allegedly refusing to pay them for services rendered, plus he treated them roughly. The hard part to believe is why such an overpaid actor wouldn't pay these working girls. —Burgess Meredith

★

You know Roseanne's latest love match, Tom Arnold? He keeps saying he's a reformed cokehead. He doesn't say if he no longer pees publicly at McDonald's. He got arrested for that, you know. Just thought I'd tell ya.

—Sam Kinison

I joked with Hugh Grant after he got arrested [with a prostitute in his car]. All that publicity. It helped our movie [*Nine Months*], but I know Hugh's sort of a refined gentleman and...well, it was just humongous publicity! I said to him, "Hugh, you must really *shrink* from all that publicity...." Get it?

—Tom Arnold

I've had a few *sakes,* driven down Sunset [Boulevard], had wild fantasies—but I didn't pull over and say, "Give me a blow job!"

—Pierce Brosnan, on Hugh Grant

When I was in Los Angeles, I took a drive down the coast with a mutual friend and Charles Laughton. To somewhere called Palos Verdes where Laughton owned or had owned a cottage. His getaway. A place to be away from his wife [Elsa Lanchester], where he could paint, visit his boyfriend, and so on. A lush, green area, not dissimilar to England....I was struck by the shape of the terra cotta tiles on the roof of the cottage. I commented on them, and he smirked and explained that he'd had a boyfriend who was a potter and a sculptor, and he'd molded the clay tiles on his thighs. That detail has stayed in my mind....

—Laurence Olivier

I met Brad Pitt....He came up to me and said, "Oh, my God, it's Tom Arnold! I can't believe it! I can't believe I'm meeting Tom Arnold! It's just great to meet you!" I don't know what was happening. Was Brad being serious? Was he being sarcastic? Or what?

—Tom Arnold

John Wayne drank a quart a day for three decades, minimum. If cancer hadn't gotten him, booze would have.

—Robert Mitchum

Mel Gibson in *Hamlet*? Now I've seen everything. Except Mel Gibson's *Hamlet*.

—Robert Mitchum

And who can forget Mel Gibson in *Hamlet*? Though many have tried.

—Harry Andrews

I don't know if it's true Mama Cass died eating a ham sandwich. I've heard different versions of that. But if it is, then you got to wonder...those two fine singers might still be alive—this sounds like a bad joke, but it could be true—they might both be alive today if Mama Cass had given her sandwich to [anorexic] Karen Carpenter.... —singer Carmen McRae

★

Don't ask me why [gay or lesbian] black singers don't say it if they are. Johnny Mathis did...no, none of the girls I know about. Don't ask me. Ask Whitney [Houston] or her aunt [Dionne Warwick]. I'm too old to change; younger people can say anything they want. God bless 'em.

—Carmen McRae

★

David Hasselhoff is opening up a chain of *Baywatch* restaurants. In fact the sign on the door says No shoes, no silicone, no service.   —Jay Leno

★

Yeah, but I don't talk about it. It's sort of embarrassing for each of us....I had to sue [director] Peter Bogdanovich for a loan I made him in 1993 that he never repaid. He wouldn't take a hint. Or pay up.   —Richard Pryor

★

I get mistaken for my brothers all the time. I have a lot of fun with it. They say, "You were great in *Sliver,* can I have your autograph?" And I say, "Go to hell, you bastard." Then they walk away going, "That Billy Baldwin, he's such a prick." He does it to Alec too.   —Stephen Baldwin

★

A celebrity endorsement doesn't change any votes....I don't think that any American much cares to plumb the shallows of Charlton Heston's mind and follow his advice.   —Gore Vidal

★

A lot of the actors are so full of crap. They don't want to be bothered with the autographs. They want to hide. I remember telling Al [Pacino], "What are you doing? God forbid somebody doesn't recognize you. You'd have a heart attack." It's such bullshit.   —James Caan

★

Michael [Jackson] asked for my autograph and I asked for his. We trade them like baseball cards.   —Macaulay Culkin

★

Poor Kiefer [Sutherland] and what he had to go through [after Julia Roberts canceled their wedding]. I worked with him on *Article 99,* and I think that's why I've stayed away from going out with actresses.

—Ray Liotta

I felt that it was debilitating for me to always feel that I was being compared....You can understand debilitating when you're eighteen and they're expecting you to be as good as Jane Fonda. It's not like they're expecting you to be as good as somebody else who's eighteen, which is hard enough as it is. But to be as good as somebody who's already done *Coming Home* or *Klute,* I mean, *please!*

—Bridget Fonda, on her aunt's Oscar-winning roles

Pamela Mason only became famous, I mean rather famous, because she married a man who became a famous movie star [James Mason]. I never had to marry any man to become famous, darling. And I never married a big movie star, though I did marry a very good actor, George Sanders, who won his Academy Award.

—Zsa Zsa Gabor

My dear friend Alan Bates played in support of Mel Gibson in the latest [film] *Hamlet.* I doubt whether Gibson's read it, although it's possible. He was recently asked what makes *Hamlet* a great play. Gibson replied, and I quote, "It's got some great stuff in it." He then explained what he meant: It's got nine violent deaths in it.

—Jeremy Brett

Jerry Lewis can be a doll. When he wants to. He doesn't want to very much any more....He takes criticism much too personally. I can shrug it off after a few expletives. He explodes, then he stews, then he explodes again. It's as if to criticize him is treason.

—Dean Martin

★

His given Hebrew name was Schmuel. Through my mother, who had an accent, it became Shemp....He was my older brother. I looked up to him...we were very proud when he was chosen "The Ugliest Man in Hollywood," that was real recognition....Shemp went solo in 1930, but he rejoined us in 1946 (replacing their ailing brother Curly). We were together until he passed away in 1955. But he died happy—that day he went to the races, and he died telling a joke. *After* the big punchline.

—Moe Howard of The Three Stooges

HOWARD ROLLINS

I don't go with that. [Spike Lee] made a movie, it didn't get the big audience he wanted, so he kept yelling "racism." What kind of example is that? —Howard Rollins

★

W. C. Fields and Lou Costello, they [were] both jealous of Shemp, he was so funny. When he'd get in their movies, they'd cut his scenes way down. There was a story that Costello paid him not to work. Untrue.... Shemp was fearless in his comedy, he'd try anything. In real life, it was different. He was a scaredy-cat. He never learned to drive; and it was just one of his fears. His wife, Babe, once said Shemp was afraid of everything.... I miss him. I miss him every day. —Moe Howard

★

The reason so many people turned up at his funeral is that they wanted to make sure he was dead. —Samuel Goldwyn, on Louis B. Mayer

★

In some of his last movies, Errol Flynn had to play himself instead of Robin Hood or Custer, etc. Unfortunately, the role was beyond his acting abilities.

—Jack L. Warner

★

The grapevine has it Boy George was pissed that Mick Jagger's playing a drag queen [in the movie *Bent*]. Named Greta, I think. George thinks he's a better singer than Mick. And he *knows* he can do better drag. He's what, half Mick's age?   —British singer Jimmy Somerville

★

I was glad to hear Paul Reubens [a.k.a. Pee-Wee Herman] is making a comeback on *Murphy Brown*. He needs the exposure. Oops!

—Samson DeBrier

★

Mr. Harris, your fly is open.

—playwright George S. Kaufman, on visiting the office of theater
producer Jed Harris, who received him completely in the nude

★

I went to visit my friend Alec Woollcott at his country home one time, and I arrived in my Model-T [Ford], which was not in the best condition, to put it mildly. "What do you call that?" asked Alec. I said, "This is my town car." "What was the town?" he asked. "Pompeii?"   —Harpo Marx

★

George [S. Kaufman] has a very competitive streak. A friend of his once remarked that he was fourteen before he realized he was a Jew. George immediately said, "That's nothing. I was sixteen before I knew I was a boy."

—Alexander Woollcott

★

Frank [Sinatra] loves this one, though he's a very married man. Frank once asked an associate his marital status. The guy says, "Married, I've been. Now I simply rent."   —Dean Martin

★

I admired [the producer] Hal Wallis. As a man and an executive....An executive: That's a man who can always take refuge in his office after a long, hard day or night at home.   —Dean Martin

★

Before I got married my father warned me about not expecting too much. He said that marriage *can* be like a long, dull meal, with the tasty dessert at the beginning.   —Dean Paul Martin

I remember Pat Boone once told me—least I *think* it was Pat Boone...or some other guy in white shoes—he said to me, "Don't you know drinking is slow poison?" I had to laugh. I said to him, "Who's in a hurry?"

—Dean Martin

I married before my older sister [Olivia De Havilland] did, but before I wed she passed along to me some advice I'd once heard my mother tell a friend. She said that the *other* biggest cause of divorce, besides sex or money disagreements, was bad table manners—*his*.　　　　—Joan Fontaine

Artie used to tell a joke that Ava hated. "What do you call it when a man hates the woman he loves?...His wife."

—Lana Turner, who like Ava Gardner was married to bandleader Artie Shaw

I met Lee [Liberace] in Las Vegas one time when he was doing particularly well, which rankled a bit....We got to reminiscing, or he did. He loved to talk shop, but he was telling me what a child prodigy he supposedly was. How he was a virtuoso as a teen and playing the Waldorf at twenty....I wanted to cut it short, so when he bragged, "I played with the Chicago Symphony when I was nineteen," I asked, "All of them?" He was stunned. Finally he said, "Just the ones with major instruments."

—Johnnie Ray

When I was in London I worked at the same studio as Tom Jones, and the word around the studio was that he pads his pants. So people kept saying to me, "You have the same dresser, ask him, ask him if Tom Jones pads his pants." So finally I said, "Keith, tell me the truth, does he pad his pants?" and he said, "Yeah." So I said, "Great. He's smart. He's found out what the people like and he gives it to them." So he uses padding in his pants. Why not? Girls use silicone in their boobs.　　　　—Liberace

Your last album sold 2.5 million copies. How come I don't know anybody who owns one?　　—*Daily Show* host Craig Kilborn, to guest Joey Lawrence

In the mid-1970s I was at a party in Monte Carlo....Michael Douglas was there. He kisses his father on the lips in public, and they say he has a gay younger brother. But at that time, he was very...like a Neanderthal. I gave him a hug and a kiss, not on the lips of course, which we all do in Europe.

But he almost hit me, he became so angry. And they wonder why we speak of The Ugly American.... —Austrian actor Helmut Berger

★

Someone reportedly asked the super-dedicated, highly loyal Lowe, "Charles, do you ever sleep with Carol?" Lowe answered, "Why? Would it be good for her career?" —Liz Smith, on Carol Channing's manager-husband

★

It's not impossible...we could work together....All those years he was out of work and out of the limelight. I think now, with several movies a year, [John] Travolta's trying to make up for that. In quantity anyway.

· —director Samuel Fuller

★

I write for an adult market. Period. I've never censored myself, been a hypocrite....Today, marketing is everything, and everyone marketable can write a book or have one written for him....An alleged singer [rapper] named LL Cool J has an autobiography due...in two versions. One for kids, the other for adults. The latter covers his young life and includes his experiences as a random street mugger, his drug usage, his obsession with pornography, ad nauseam. So with the help of a publisher, this type of celebrity will be not only a millionaire and a role model to American youth, but an alleged author as well—in two versions, so as not to exclude any potential book buyer....Today the publishing and other media celebrate people who did such things—drugs, muggings, sexual addiction quote-unquote. In the past, we celebrated people who *never* did such things.

—author Harold Robbins

★

I don't know anything about her except the common gossip I heard. When it comes to men, I heard she never turns anything down except the bedcovers. —Mae West, on younger blonde sexpot Jayne Mansfield

★

Mae West was a natural exhibitionist, and very proud of her breasts. She would just nonchalantly take one out and show it to you, expecting you to admire its size and firmness. But I was informed that if a woman showed anything more than admiration, Mae West would turn to ice. You see, she didn't believe in lesbians. —Alexis Smith

★

Occasionally funny, usually superficial, always pompous.

—singer Bobby Darin, on Bob Hope

KURT COBAIN and Nirvana bandmembers

It's a tragedy, but it [Kurt Cobain's suicide] also demonstrates how damaged a lot of our youth are now. There's almost a need for violence...and their comfort with violence, that can cut both ways.... —John Denver

★

I worked all through the 1930s, '40s, and '50s...eventually I intuited that my [good] looks were something of a drawback. I wasn't taken as seriously as some of the more plain or brooding fellows. My name was also not an asset...the next Lyle to create a stir was that handsome chap on Carol Burnett's show [Lyle Waggoner], and he was a supporting player, then he was *Playgirl* magazine's [first] celebrity centerfold—I didn't see that, nor have I seen him since. —Lyle Talbot

★

I wouldn't put anything past Hollywood, and most ambitious actors will go along....Hugh Grant's arrest, the prostitute, the tremendous brouhaha, and then his nationally aired contrition and the resultant, expected surge in the box office of his Hollywood studio film...I wouldn't doubt the entire thing was pre-planned.   —Jeremy Brett

Red Skelton sort of stole my career. I'm not sure he knew he was committing this act, but they brought him to Hollywood to redo my silent movies in sound and in color, so I guess at some point it must have dawned on him who was being, ahem, screwed.   —Buster Keaton

Louis B. Mayer is the most written-about mogul in Hollywood history. That's because happy reigns have no history.

—producer David Lewis (*Camille*)

It's very telling how we keep hearing about [President Bill] Clinton evading the draft. But this all goes way back. My dad used to tell me how Jack Dempsey the fighter was almost ruined by bad publicity over his getting out of serving in World War I....In World War II, which was a hell of a lot more crucial and unambiguous than Vietnam, [Ronald] Reagan and John Wayne didn't serve. They got out of it. But you don't hear that about *them....*   —Raul Julia

So much of it [success] is luck. Not to pick on anybody needlessly, but Jeff Daniels, now he's extremely lucky. How else could you explain such a dull-looking and dull-acting personality—so to speak—starring or co-starring in big-budgeted motion pictures?   —Cesar Romero

A venerated, self-satisfied boob.   —actor Charles Bickford, on Bob Hope

In movies, Bob Hope was often funny. But on TV, often not. Which I think has as much to do with TV, and his age, as with Hope himself.

—Phyllis Seaton, former acting coach and mayor of Beverly Hills

★

All that money, mind you, and two things Howard Hughes never bought himself were a good wardrobe and a personality. —columnist Lee Graham

★

The first time I saw Winona Ryder and Jodie Foster, I thought they were actors—*boys*. One hears that Miss Ryder is heterosexual....

—Alexis Smith

I had a cousin who had an old photo of Mae West when she was still brunette—before her film career. And my cousin dearly wanted to get the photo autographed. To make a long story short, a good friend fixed it for my cousin to meet Mae, and my cousin asked for the autograph, but Mae said the photo wasn't *her*. Which it was. But Mae insisted, "That's not me." Then she offered to buy the photo, which alarmed my cousin...so in the end, no one got an autograph, and Mae was very upset. She obviously hated not being able to change her distant past to match her Hollywood image.

—Patsy Kelly

Talk about Streisand, Dunaway, etc. They can be witchy and all, but no one ever out-ego-ed Mae West. When she was in London to do her play *Diamond Lil,* she made all the other actresses darken their teeth so hers would appear the whitest and brightest. She also hired corpulent actresses for the few feminine roles, whose primary function—as in all her vehicles, stage or screen, American or British—was to demonstrate that Mae West was the fairest of them all.... —British actress Evelyn Laye

I remember way back when, Jerry Lee Lewis the singer married his little cousin. She was thirteen. Big backlash. Later on, Don Johnson, the *Miami Vice* guy, he was dating Melanie Griffith when she was fourteen, I think....Now it's Jerry Seinfeld and his teenage fiancée. The young guys now, they can get away with anything. Unless the girl's a guy!

—Morey Amsterdam

I'm not cynical. Maybe he loves her. But it's a smart move—he caught a prize fish! It's certainly one way for an aging TV star to get back in the spotlight, and it beats the route O.J. took....

—Morey Amsterdam, on James Brolin and Barbra Streisand

[Success] has nothing to do with intelligence. Look at Conrad Hilton. He's hardly the brightest man in the world—when he married Zsa Zsa [Gabor, as Sanders later did], he thought he was marrying Eva, and he seems to spend

most of his time dancing with sixteen-year-old girls. But he's a huge success as a hotel man....   —George Sanders

★

I heard Brando sold his island in Tahiti because he kept getting food poisoning. or maybe he just ate too much—you know, the Great White Whale....Either way, he developed a severe case of Poly-nausea.

—Jesse White

★

Nothing to it. I was out of town making a movie, and Barbra is cheap. She hates to buy her own meals. Sharif was just somebody to pick up the tabs.

—Elliott Gould, on Omar Sharif's dining with Gould's then-wife Streisand (most of the dinners were consumed in Sharif's suite in the Beverly Wilshire Hotel)

ROBERT DOWNEY JR.

There are the George Hamiltons—the sun worshippers—and there are people like Robert Downey Jr. He avoids tanning. Which makes sense: People with wax brains should stay out of the sun.

—former juvenile star (*Lassie*) Tommy Rettig

★

We all know how the Reagans have downplayed the fact that Nancy's godmother was the famous actress Alla Nazimova, who was a Russian lesbian. But [editor] Michael Korda has revealed that in Reagan's memoir he originally made no mention at all of his first, more successful wife [actress Jane Wyman]. Korda had to persuade him to finally include any reference to that whole chunk of his life....The question is, did Reagan omit her because she was a bigger star than he or because Nancy didn't want her acknowledged? You know, Eva Peron tried to pretend she was [Juan] Peron's first wife....   —Harold Robbins

★

I wouldn't even mention it if Mrs. Reagan and her husband weren't setting themselves up as such arbiters of public morality. But the record shows that when Nancy and Ron got married, she was already pregnant with their [daughter]. And at that time, that was a very serious thing. About which people were ready to be extremely judgmental—as the Reagans themselves now are.   —screen star Myrna Loy

★

In showbiz, sometimes the most amazing things do come true....Back in the early '70s I was receiving an award, and I had a chauffeur, who told me he wasn't really a chauffeur. Said he wanted to be a professional comic, and he said to me, "Mr. Lemmon, if I'm successful, I want to be your neighbor in Beverly Hills." As a matter of fact, he does live on the same street I do, and his name is Jay Leno.   —Jack Lemmon

★

Not while I'm alive!
                    —impresario Rudolf Bing's comment when told that conductor
                    George Szell was his own worst enemy

★

They've said [Louis B.] Mayer's his own worst enemy. Well, not really. Not while I'm around.   —fellow mogul Jack L. Warner

★

I don't *get* his clothes. I just don't get it. I don't get the pushed-up sleeves, the luminescent ties.   —David Letterman, on Jay Leno's wardrobe

★

Those ties look like they were made in summer camp, like fabric ashtrays he's wearing around his neck.   —Dennis Miller, on Jay Leno

★

Zsa Zsa Gabor is a cat...*not* a compliment. She began as a brownhead named Sari...and changed everything about herself except her tendency toward plumpness, and became a publicity hound....Initially she disliked all beautiful rivals, then women who became beautiful, then all actresses, then all women. That woman hates women—and try saying that five times, fast! Her mother and sisters are the only exceptions, and even *then*.

—talk show host Pamela Mason

It used to be said that a lady had to choose between silence about herself or self-deprecation. That was before actresses became very public figures. Most actresses cannot choose between those two ideals....Mae West has taken it to a new extreme...she is a braggart and constant press agent for herself. She seems to enjoy it so, as [does] her coterie of fanatics. I don't envy her at all [because] the result is *so* unladylike.   —Mary Pickford

I preferred [Michael Jackson] when he was black.   —Gianni Versace

All of a sudden I'm the celebrity of yesteryear—even on my own network. I'm not David Duchovny, I'm not Scott Wolf...I might as well be George Hamilton.   —Jason Priestly (*Beverly Hills 90210*)

I think I slugged some respect into the guy.
   —director Quentin Tarantino, who fought with producer Don Murphy in a
      Hollywood restaurant (Miramax boss Harvey Weinstein broke it up)

The D A...has decided not to press charges against Michael Jackson....He can stop pretending to be married to Lisa Marie [Presley] now!

—Jay Leno, in 1994

[Michael Jackson] is the best friend you could ever have. He's gentle, not rough like the other guys.   —Emmanuel Lewis (*Webster*), in 1984

The subject of girlfriends is off limits. So is his friendship with Michael Jackson.   —*People* magazine, on Emmanuel Lewis in 1994, when he was
      twenty-three and still living with his mother

...that cunning little linguist.   —Dame Edna Everage, on Jodie Foster

I have to live my life being who I am. You know, secrets kill. They really do—just ask Michael Jackson. If you go around hiding your true self, then you create a monster. —Boy George

★

Marilyn [Monroe] was a very lucky young lady. If she hadn't died tragically and young, her lack of real acting talent would have shown up by forty. Until you're forty, you can coast on your looks. After that, as I've had to find out, you'd better develop your acting muscles! —Lana Turner

★

She's cruel...shrill...and common...she's grammatically challenged... she's whining all the way to the bank.
—movie columnists Marilyn Beck and Stacy Jenel Smith on controversial talk show shrink Laura Schlessinger

★

[My critics are] against family, principles, morals, religion, ethics, and God.
—Laura Schlessinger, on Marilyn Beck and Stacy Jenel Smith, among others

★

Mike Tyson, Marv Albert, and Laura Schlessinger....
—Beck and Smith's *readers'* nominees for 1998's Tacky Taste Award

★

Ray Milland was a heterosexual Cary Grant. But I still didn't like him.
—producer and RKO bigwig Pandro S. Berman

★

He writes songs for dead blondes.
—Rolling Stone Keith Richards, opining that Elton John's sole claim to fame is the Marilyn Monroe tribute "Candle in the Wind" and its record-breaking reworking as a tribute to Princess Diana

★

I am glad I have given up drugs and alcohol. It would be awful to look like [Keith] Richards. He's pathetic, poor thing. It's like a monkey with arthritis trying to go on stage and look young. —Elton John, now Sir Elton John

Co-star Warring

I hated working with that bitch. She was the biggest bitch in the business. Thank God I'll never have to work with her again!
—Tom Bosley (*Happy Days*), on Lucille Ball

Ricardo Montalban, compared to me, is proof that quantity is not quality.... —Hervé Villechaize, on his taller *Fantasy Island* co-star

★

I could have shot Fred [Astaire], but didn't. Fred had no feeling at all....Fred was impatient....Fred yelled at Audrey [Hepburn in *Funny Face*]....Fred was irritating...a most disconsolate person....He was just somebody who was frightened.   —Kay Thompson

★

That was a negative experience [the 1982 TV movie *Honey Boy*]....Erik Estrada didn't care for competition, and the producers made me look less than beautiful so I wouldn't detract from him.   —Morgan Fairchild

★

The least couth actresses I've ever worked with?...Bette Davis and Jodie Foster.   —Helen Hayes

★

Actually, before we were dating, my wife, Phoebe [Cates, later a co-star], said she saw me in *Sophie's Choice* and assumed I was gay. I said, "Hmm, really? Why is that?" She said, "Well, because you moved your hands so much in that movie. And you seem so, uh, clean."   —Kevin Kline

★

[Clark Gable had] a magnificent array of dazzling teeth. These originated with a dentist named Wallace and were known as the Wallace Collection. They were easily detachable, and Clark occasionally liked to shock people by taking them out, thus letting his face collapse into unrecognizability.

—Lilli Palmer

★

Uma Thurman has a horrifyingly great brain.   —John Malkovich

★

I used to write for Lucy. She would say to me, "Garry, funny is not enough, you've go to *do* things." She also used to say that no woman could possibly ever dream about [directing] a movie that would gross over $100 million. Well, my sister Penny has—twice.   —writer-director Garry Marshall

★

I'm #10 [at the box office]. Right under Barbra Streisand. Can you imagine being *under* Barbra Streisand? Get me a bag. I may throw up.

—Walter Matthau, nonhunk

★

Streisand kept insisting I should be thin, I should look good. . . . Sometimes I wondered, Who's the leading lady here?
—Nick Nolte, on his *Prince of Tides* co-star and director

★

She is good with the singing, but she could not pass for a Latin American except in Hollywood. —Antonio Banderas, on Madonna in *Evita*

★

In my scenes with Bo Derek I had to imagine I was not there as her acting coach. —Richard Harris [Derek's dad in *Tarzan*]

★

I worked one day with her and I quit.
—director Henry Hathaway, on Kim Novak

★

I don't usually get into battles, but dressing Kim Novak for her role in Mr. Hitchcock's *Vertigo* put to the test all my training in psychology.
—costume designer Edith Head

★

He was in love with both of us at the same time.
—Lauren Hutton, on writer-director Paul Schrader, during *American Gigolo,* which co-starred Richard Gere

★

I guess she decided to keep the faith, instead of the face.
—Jim Hutton, on Dolores Hart (*Where the Boys Are*), who became a nun

★

All my women friends think [Laurence Fishburne] is suave and smoldering, but off-camera he's a goof. —Alfre Woodard

★

Sweetie, did you floss?
—Clint Eastwood's ritual pre-sex question to Sondra Locke

★

There's no getting around that William Hurt is a nut. You don't realize that it isn't appropriate to walk up to him and go, "Hi, Mr. Hurt, nice to meet you," until he snaps at you. . . . He treated the director [Lesli Linka Glatter] like shit. —Neil Patrick Harris (*Doogie Howser, M.D.*)

★

William [Hurt], in his soul, is a truly conflicted, turbulent human being. . . . He wants his work to be art, in a world where that's becoming

increasingly difficult....And he has a rage in him that is really scary to a lot
of people.   —Madeleine Stowe
★

Diana [Ross]'s attitude has earned her the nickname Miss Cute....I noticed
Diana standing in the wings watching us [a young Gladys Knight and the
Pips]....I knew trouble was brewing....The next day the word came down
from Motown that we were yanked from the tour. —singer Gladys Knight
★

[After she and her brother Bubba heard Michael Jackson and his brothers
sing for them:] I got on the phone to our manager at Motown. When it
became apparent that the Jackson 5 were going to be superstars, [Motown
boss] Berry Gordy decided their discovery should be credited to another
one of his biggest stars...none other than Miss Cute, Miss Diana Ross.
                                          —Gladys Knight
★

I was told that Truman Capote didn't want me at all for *Breakfast at
Tiffany's*. He wanted Marilyn Monroe. Thank goodness I didn't know that
before we made the picture, or I never would have been able to do it.
                                          —Audrey Hepburn
★

Even though I had a boyfriend at the time, [Wesley Snipes] went full court
press. He was flirting with me—you always flirt with your co-stars; it's
harmless. Then he started getting a little more serious. He would invite us
all out together and then at the end of the night he'd drop me off last and
try to kiss me. I'd be like, "Wesley, please. I'm not interested in you like
that." He got really upset about it. His ego was totally bruised. He wouldn't
talk to me for two months. I was like, What an ass----. Actors are used to
getting their way and to treating women like objects. They're so used to
hearing the word "yes."   —Jennifer Lopez (*Anaconda*)
★

Have you seen *Boogie Nights*? Some of the cocaine scenes they did took me
back to the '70s, and I don't ever, ever want to be back in that. Rick [Nelson]
got into it quite a bit. He got more and more withdrawn, more and more
where he wouldn't go out, blackout shades on the windows, he was scared.
That's what happens...it really becomes a way of life.
            —Kristin Harmon Nelson Tinker, on her former husband and
                                          Ozzie & Harriet co-star

She looked as though butter wouldn't melt in her mouth—or anywhere else. —Elsa Lanchester, on Maureen O'Hara

★

Anthony Quinn is, yes, he is rather a good actor. Not nearly as good as he thinks....He's in somewhat of a rut. How many peasants of every nationality can one actor play? Or wish to.

—James Franciscus (*The Greek Tycoon*)

★

Well, [Charlton] Heston *is* good at portraying arrogance and ambition. But in the same way that a dwarf is good at being short. —Rex Harrison

★

A vacuum with nipples. —director Otto Preminger, on Marilyn Monroe

★

How can they tell?

—Mary Wickes (*White Christmas*), on hearing that Bing Crosby had died

★

No, they were very coarse...foul-mouthed. I won't sign autographs on [photos] of the three of us. —Mary Wickes, on Abbott and Costello

★

Bud wore a toupee and Lou used to blacken his scalp because his hair was very thin—unlike the rest of him.

—Sheldon Leonard, on Abbott and Costello

★

I worked with that trio of blonde bombshells....Marilyn Monroe was a class act, yet insecure....Jayne Mansfield was desperate; she knew she had nothing much that would last....Mamie Van Doren was in the same spot as Jayne, basically, but she was a lot harder than Jayne. I mean, both would try or say anything for publicity.

—Tommy Noonan (*Gentlemen Prefer Blondes*)

★

Of course I do. I'm paid to—otherwise it would be appalling. Have you never heard the expression, "Whose bread I eat, his song I sing?"

—sidekick Arthur Treacher, on being told he "fawned"
over talk show host Merv Griffin

★

That, I don't understand...I never had looks to lose [but] Brando was a looker, and then he let himself gain so much weight.

—Stubby Kaye (*Guys and Dolls*)

Well, [Brando] is getting a bit thick, in our [British] sense of the word. I hear he believes in cue cards now, in place of memorizing his lines....And a friend who lunched with him recently said he didn't mumble very much during their meal, and afterward he sat staring into his empty mug of coffee as if the next thing he [was] going to say [were] written down there.

—Michael Rennie

I remember when Warner Bros. was threatening to sue the Marx Brothers because they used the film title *A Night in Casablanca*. The Warners felt that would compete with their film titled *Casablanca*....But Groucho wasn't intimidated, and I heard he sent a cable to Jack Warner threatening him back, "And I'll sue you for using the word 'Brothers!'"   —Eve Arden

Burt Lancaster is impossible and Kirk [Douglas] a pain in the neck, but when they argue their aim is to make a better picture, and I'm for that. Sinatra, on the other hand, only argues about how to shoot the scene quicker so he can get away.   —director Robert Aldrich (*Four for Texas*)

Sinatra's behavior was unbelievable. There was an old lady playing the slot machines nearby, and this annoyed him. He kicked a couple of bottles of champagne toward her and said, "Get away, you're bothering me."...We weren't given any choice. He chose wieners and sauerkraut for everyone. And there was more trouble. Sinatra decided he didn't like the pianist. So he tossed a handful of coins at him and told him to take off. That did it. My friend and I got up and left.   —Valerie Perrine

We never got on. The trouble is with [Charlton Heston] he doesn't think he's just a hired actor, like the rest of us. He thinks he's the *entire* production. He used to sit there in the mornings and clock us in with a stopwatch.   —Richard Harris

There was a lot of creative tension. Well, I don't know how creative it was.

—Katie Couric, on Bryant Gumbel

★

All I can say is that when I'm trying to play serious love scenes with her, she's positioning her bottom for the best-angle shots.

—Stephen Boyd, on Brigitte Bardot

★

ROBERT MITCHUM

Elvis Presley did say I was his favorite actor....We never worked together, of course. The grapevine had it that he lacked confidence around nonsinging, dramatically oriented actors...I don't know if it's true he imitated me; I keep hearing he did the sleepy eyelids, whatever that means....I did create a project [*Thunder Road*] that was meant to star him; I tailored it for him. But his greedy old manager, Colonel [Tom] Parker, pulled him out of it, shoved him into another crummy musical. Old fool never had any taste...and ran Elvis's movie career into the ground later.

—Robert Mitchum

★

She thinks she doesn't get old. She told me once it was her cameraman who was getting older. She wanted me to fire him.

—producer Joe Pasternak, on Doris Day

You knew where you were with Errol [Flynn]—he always let you down.

—David Niven

I was fed up because Peter Fonda was a star and I wasn't. And Peter couldn't act....He never bothered to sit and learn. He never studied....I don't begrudge the fact that he has talent. But he's not an actor, by any stretch of the imagination.   —Bruce Dern (Laura's father)

When I first saw [Erich Von Stroheim] at the wardrobe tests for his role as [Erwin] Rommel [in *Five Graves to Cairo*], I clicked my heels and said, "Isn't it ridiculous, little me, directing you? You were always ten years ahead of your time." And he replied, "Twenty."

—Billy Wilder, on the former director

Jon agonizes his way toward every decision: what his next movie should be, whether to go out to lunch. He's a good, tortured person.

—Jane Fonda, on Jon Voight

[Jeanette MacDonald] had a reputation for being prudish. She would always object to someone telling a risque story....I don't know if she really liked sex. I don't think her husband [actor Gene Raymond] did either. Or so they said.

—Maurice Chevalier

His relationship with Ismail is more than a marriage.

—Shashi Kapoor, on director James Ivory and producer Ismail Merchant

[Elizabeth Taylor] has a double chin and an overdeveloped chest, and she's rather short in the leg. So I can hardly describe her as the most beautiful creature I've ever seen.   —Richard Burton

Mario Lanza had a little problem about being fat. You had to record his songs when he was fat. Then you had to close down the show while he reduced. You would then make the picture. His ability as an actor was somewhat less than zero.   —Leonard Spigelgass

She's one of the reasons I left show business....We'd give her a new scene, and she couldn't remember the lines. She couldn't sing and, surprisingly, she couldn't do the dances. And all through the horror of it all she was smiling and grinning and unreal...she almost smiled me into bankruptcy.
—stage producer Paul Gregory, on Ginger Rogers
★

Ginger Rogers was one of the worst, red-baiting, terrifying reactionaries in Hollywood. —director Joseph Losey
★

[Carole Lombard] was married to [Clark] Gable...I did a whole series of shows with her, and I said, "How are you and Gable getting along?" and she said, "He's the lousiest lay I ever had."...Very sexy dame. She was also a hell of an actress. —Groucho Marx
★

I think she decided to go into show business when she was an embryo, she kicked so much! —Judy Garland, on daughter Liza Minnelli
★

You don't have to hold an inquest to find out who killed Marilyn Monroe. Those bastards in the big executive chairs killed her.
—director Henry Hathaway
★

There wasn't a thing that gal couldn't do—except look after herself.
—Bing Crosby, on Judy Garland
★

I liked Deanna Durbin all right [but] it was her *voice*. Her and all those other sopranos: They sound as if they live on seaweed.
—Robert Cummings
★

I can't imagine Rhett Butler chasing you for ten years.
—producer David O. Selznick, declining to cast Katharine Hepburn as Scarlett O'Hara
★

It intrigues me and dismays me that when Americans write of their parsimonious film performers, it is always and solely about male actors....We know the names of those gentlemen who have been branded as cheapskates, skinflints, and so on...I could add a few female names to the list, chief among them Katharine Hepburn. I doubt in her entire life she's ever bought lunch for herself or anyone else. Which is the sole detail I care to offer.   —Sir Ralph Richardson

★

Age cannot wither her nor custom stale her endless uniformity.
                    —Sir Max Beerbohm, on the legendary Eleonora Duse

★

[Marlon Brando] always likes to talk about how much he hates acting. I think he uses that. That's a great way to protect yourself. If everybody believes that you're only doing it for the money, you can never fail. They can't say to you, "You gave it your best and it didn't work." But the reality is, he is so invested in acting.
                    —Jeremy Leven, director of *Don Juan DeMarco*

★

We were shooting a scene and I had nothing to do, just stand around. I happened to be standing in the wrong place or something, and he looked and said, "Who the fuck do you think is the star of this picture?" I said, "Oh, Spence, come on." ...That's the other side of Tracy. He could be very petty and egomaniacal.   —Richard Widmark

★

[Spencer] Tracy as a man had many personal and emotional problems, but that is not what came through on the screen. This is a paradox I won't attempt to explain here....I do know that actors who have some sort of emotional problem going on underneath seem to give a more interesting performance on top.   —director King Vidor

★

We discovered we each needed a wife to take care of us. That role is not for me, and it is certainly not for Shirley [MacLaine]. She is a very strong woman. She is Warren Beatty's older brother, not his sister....We just couldn't live together.   —Russian director Andrei Konchalovsky

★

She just behaved badly, like she was competing with me. I understand that Shirley grew up in a different era, when women had flesh under their fingernails from competing with one another, but I'm not like that.
                    —Debra Winger (*Terms of Endearment*), on Shirley MacLaine

★

My opinion, and it's not mine alone, is that [Shirley] MacLaine's books are, to quite an extent, semi-fiction...and I don't necessarily mean the out-of-body experiences and all that.   —Dack Rambo

Yes, Steve McQueen was the most difficult actor I unfortunately worked with. —director Norman Jewison

It was like being in a blender with an alligator.
—director Peter Bogdanovich, on working with Cher

I'd rather stick needles in my eyes.
—director Danny Cannon, on working again with Sylvester Stallone

[Eddie Murphy] once came to me and said, "Jeez, I'd love to do some of those small films you do." I told him, "We make those films for less than your salary," and he said, "Oh, well, I can't cut my salary." —Nick Nolte

"I am the biggest c--t in the world."
—sign that Charlie Sheen reportedly hung on the back of actress Sean Young, on the set of *Wall Street*

Roger Moore made it solely on his face, and after *The Saint* his face went to his head. James Bond has made him a star again, but the face is slipping, and after Bond I think he, unlike his face, will disappear from the screen.
—Anthony Perkins

Of course I've heard about [Robert Downey Jr.'s] drug habits and jail sentence—quite a surprisingly long sentence for a celebrity. But I don't wish to make comment. Thank you. —Hugh Grant

When Mia [Farrow] first wanted to adopt, I was against it because I felt she had seven children already at the time. But once she adopted [daughter] Dylan [now named Eliza], I fell madly in love with her....
—Woody Allen

★

Go ahead, Lou. Tell the man all you know. It won't take long.
—Bud Abbott, to Costello

★

Bud loves his wife and he's got three dogs. I don't love mine and I've got two children. You figure it out. —Lou Costello

★

ERIC ROBERTS

I haven't talked to my mother since I was fourteen, except once. I went through all those years without a mother. But when I met Lee Grant...we really bonded. And now she's what I call my surrogate mother. What's wonderful about it is, I got to choose her, which doesn't happen often with mothers.   —Eric Roberts (Julia's brother; they too reportedly are estranged)

★

Cary [Grant] was so wonderful with dialogue...not so good with kissing scenes. He didn't like them very much.   —Ingrid Bergman

★

Well, we were two Stooges [including Shemp Howard] when we joined with Ted Healy in 1922. He was a vaudevillian, popular, and he was the straight man....In Chicago, we met Larry [Fine]. He was a violinist. He wasn't a comedian. But we wanted him for our stooging...but Larry didn't want to leave his job at the café where he worked. What happened was, the day after we made Larry the offer, the café's owner killed himself, so Larry joined us—and he's been one of The Three Stooges ever since.

—Moe Howard (Shemp left the act in 1930, replaced for several years by brother Curly)

★

No, everyone got along great. It wasn't like with Abbott & Costello....I came in late; it was The Three Stooges from 1935 [sans Ted Healy] to 1965, and I enjoyed my years with them...nothing dramatic behind the scenes....What most people didn't know with Bud and Lou is, Bud suffered from epilepsy. And that put a bigger and bigger strain on their relationship. Especially at night, when Lou wanted to have them perform in nightclubs for big fees. But Bud, after all day at the studio or making our TV series (*The Abbott and Costello Show*), just wanted to go home, relax, and have a few drinks. —Joe Besser, one of the latter Three Stooges

★

Mick [Jagger] and I have had our differences. We still do. It's sort of like a marriage—the differences get more aggravating over the years. It's gotten to where it's hard to be in the same recording studio together. I don't look forward to touring together, but we'll see....Money isn't quite everything.

—Keith Richards, 1997

★

The fans are so young! Their parents could hardly have been born when Bette started out.

—Olivia De Havilland, at the New York premiere of *Hush, Hush, Sweet Charlotte* with Bette Davis

★

People keep asking what it was like kissing Keanu Reeves? They want intimate details where it would really be technical details. They want me to compare him with kissing other actors. I don't go into any of it, that's a smarter policy. —Sandra Bullock (*Speed*)

★

Julie [Newmar, a.k.a. Catwoman] can be unexpectedly aggressive. I remember Adam [West, a.k.a. Batman] flirting with her on the set...testing the waters through seemingly innocent conversation. Julie listened to a couple of shovelfuls, then stood up and walked over to him. Looking down into his eyes, she said something I could not hear. Whatever it was, it left Adam red in the face and at a loss for words. That doesn't happen often. It was a rare treat. —Burt Ward

People think it's romantic or sexy, and it's not....When I had to kiss Jim Carrey, I didn't know him well, and we were shy about it. We were like kids, we kept laughing and giggling and talking about using Binaca. We did it, got through with it...that was that.   —Cameron Diaz, actress

★

Lillian Gish did confide that one of the advantages of being old was not having to do love scenes anymore. If I'm not mistaken, she lived to be ninety-nine, although *The Whales of August* was, as everyone knows, her last picture....At one point, Bette Davis asked me if I'd found out anything about the rumors about Lillian [being lesbian]. "Is she or isn't she?" she hissed. I whispered to her, "Don't ask me, Bette. Ask her longtime girlfriend."   —director Lindsay Anderson

★

Our love scenes in *The Prince of Tides* did get rather hot. But whenever that happened, Barbra [Streisand, actor-director] would *cut*....She would get very self-conscious, and I know a lot of that was because all these men were around us—the crew—watching. That can often intimidate an actress, you know.   —Nick Nolte

★

He has the memory of an elephant and the hide of an elephant. The only difference is that elephants are vegetarians, and [Louis B.] Mayer's diet is his fellow man.   —screenwriter Herman J. Mankiewicz

★

Mayer was a prime hypocrite. In the Depression he was giving himself raises while asking contract players and crew members at MGM to take pay cuts, all the while emoting that "We're one big, happy family, and we're all in this together." Another charming habit was Mayer and his cronies trying to get every MGM employee to vote against the Democrats. Illegal...but at the time, no one made a fuss, and who dared oppose him? He hated Franklin Roosevelt with a passion.

—two-time Oscar–winner Melvyn Douglas

★

The thing about so many older stars from the studio system, when image was everything, is that at some point they stop acting. Somewhere in middle age. They don't even try anymore....Loretta Young, John Wayne, Joan Fontaine, etc., etc. It's no longer acting; it's maintaining an image, holding to a comfortable and positive stereotype, year after year, decade after decade...[until], in the women's case, they get laughed off the screen. Or [until] the men die. —Brian Keith

How would you feel about a co-star who earns so much more than you, for no discernible reason, and feels he's worth it? No, we are *not* close, except when the camera's running and we're doing our job. That's when I like him—'cause that's when I'm acting.

—Gillian Anderson, on David Duchovny (*The X-Files*)

Jackie Gleason stole my material. When he was real young, working in Newark. At a dump so lousy, the rats went next door to eat. So I got the tip-off and went from Broadway to Newark, and it was awful. Not only was he doing my act, he was funny doing it. I confronted him, [and] he didn't bat an eye. He was arrogant as hell, and a nobody, but I could see some of myself in him. So I didn't prosecute. I just warned him it was one thing for him to do *my* act in Newark, but if he ever went big-time, he'd better steal from someone else—Henny Youngman....We became friends. He admired me, what can I say?

He had a reputation for never rehearsing. But when I guest starred on his [TV] show, he rehearsed. That was a tribute to me. —Milton Berle

Sometimes you have to settle, and it turns out to be much nicer than you thought. Burt [Reynolds] and I have formed a company, we're Burt and Bert, and *Win, Lose or Draw* is our first show. I host it, it's great fun, very colorful, very animated—unlike most such [game or quiz] shows. And it has an *inside* feel because so many of our celebrity guests are Burt's or my friends from the stage, movies, and TV. Burt's lovely wife Loni [Anderson] is a frequent guest....I'm going to be hosting another show for us, and our TV ambitions are mammoth: There's hundreds of millions of dollars to be made in this game! —Bert Convy

★

Stars will say anything, depending on the situation. Before we shot the interrogation scene in *Basic Instinct,* Sharon [Stone] handed me her undergarments. She said the scene wouldn't require them. After the news reached her handlers and filtered through the industry, she claimed I tricked her into doing the scene that way! Then the film comes out, the scene becomes world famous, and she claims it was her idea all along.

—director Paul Verhoeven

JOEL SCHUMACHER

The Batman outfit that Val Kilmer and Michael Keaton wore will fit George [Clooney] everywhere except for the codpiece, which will have to be dramatically enlarged.   —director Joel Schumacher (*Batman & Robin*)

★

I'd rather, frankly, have a director who has a crush on me, like George Cukor—who never let that interfere with the work—than some hard-hearted SOB who's supposed to be guiding me through a performance but sees me as some kind of adversary.   —Aldo Ray

★

Hedda Hopper was ready to be anyone's enemy. She relished it; her whole outlook was adversarial....When it came to herself, self-worship was her approach. Her living room had a shrine centered on a magazine cover of Hedda, framed in real gold, she said. The cover was blown up to worship-size, and there were even votive candles flanking the holy likeness of St. Hedda, whose favorite pastimes were her cocktail bar, going to the races, and trying to crucify anyone who crossed her or she didn't like.

—Lew Ayres

★

Bill never really wanted to hurt anybody. He just felt an obligation.

—director Gregory La Cava, on W. C. Fields

★

Howard Hughes bought RKO as a tax deduction, and, looking back, I think he fully expected to run it into the ground. Though he had fun doing it....His taste was nil, his pictures [were] lousy, he treated employees like serfs....After his plane crash, he got much worse, more paranoid and fearful. Food: Every day he had one steak and twelve—no more, no less— peas. He might wear gloves while eating, or during a summer heat wave, because of his germ phobia....And meanwhile he'd run background checks on actors and other employees. As he put it, "I don't want no pinko nuts around here." —Burt Lancaster

★

The good old days at MGM were anything but that. Louis B. Mayer was the meanest sonofabitch in Hollywood and that really is saying something.

—Michael Wilding

★

Sophia [Loren] was marvelous to work with, a real joy....One inconsistency: She did tell us during a card game that she'd longed to have an affair with Cary Grant...and in her book it says she did have a big affair with him. I later heard Grant had privately denied anything beyond a working friendship. Publicly, of course, he wasn't about to deny it....

—John Cassavetes (*Brass Target*)

★

How do you bond with Madonna? What do you say to her? "Hello, I have a vibrator." —Rosie O'Donnell (they became bosom buddies)

★

In England, we have an all-girl entertainment group called Cunning Stunts. But of course in Hollywood, you have....Never mind: I'm dyslexic at times! —John Cleese (*Monty Python*)

★

No, Quentin [Tarantino] did not suck my feet....I hear Cameron Diaz said he's pretty good at it. —Bridget Fonda, on her *Jackie Brown* director

[Woody Allen in *Mighty Aphrodite*] didn't just keep his clothes on under the sheet. He kept his shoes on too. When I asked him why, he said it was in case there was a fire. —Helena Bonham Carter

The very first day on *Plenty,* we had to go to bed and do a sex scene. She, frankly, insisted we be clothed, so I still had on my overcoat or something, and there I am rogering her on the bed, so very nervous, thinking to myself, I'm on top of Meryl Streep! I'm on top of Merrryl Strrreep! I was so shy about pelvic contact with Meryl Streep, I was sort of sliding on top of her. It looks completely and utterly unconvincing.

—Sam Neill, Down Under actor

I was engaged when we were shooting *U-Turn,* and one day Sean Penn said, "If I weren't married and you weren't engaged, would this have been a very different movie?" and I go, "Yeah! Very different." —Jennifer Lopez

Marilyn Monroe was never on time, never knew her lines. I have an old aunt in Vienna. She would be on the set every morning at six and would know her lines backward. But who would go to see her? —Billy Wilder

The movies are about magic. *Not* about lowering everything to a child's level, nor squeezing every last penny of profit from classic pictures! Jimmy Stewart and I are firmly opposed to this horrid colorizing of our or anybody else's black-and-white pictures. *Adamantly.* It is a terrible thing Mr. [Ted] Turner is doing. —Bette Davis

Glenda Jackson had the bad taste to appear on television and criticize her performance [as Lady Hamilton in *The Nelson Affair*—titled *A Bequest to the Nation* in England]. This never used to be done....Perhaps it is the new fashion to knock the film you're in. But she has not, so far as I know, returned her cheque....She played Emma as a mean-spirited bitch instead of a great-hearted whore, but I suppose that is her range.

—screenwriter Terence Rattigan

I acted opposite Keir Dullea, a merely visually talented performer. I was later informed that he'd worked in the States as a carpenter, which did much to explain his wooden performance. —Sir Noel Coward

I wrote a play partially based on events in Rex Harrison's life.... He agreed to star in it but refused to play the man as a louse who later transforms into a kind and caring man. Which entirely robbed the play, while he was in it, of its emotional and developmental power.... Rex kept saying, "I don't want to seem like a shit," so I finally said, "Why stop now?"   —Terence Rattigan

★

The week has been hell, made so entirely by Lilli [Palmer]... with untiring energy.... I have made a truce with her because I have to play with her. But I have never—with the possible exception of Claudette Colbert—worked with such a stupid bitch.   —playwright Noel Coward

★

As a writer, one meets and works with many strange and outrageous personalities. One of the worst has been [director] Franco Zeffirelli, a most capricious, dictatorial, and unhappy man. He loathes Hollywood but I think he longs to become successful enough, again, to be invited back.... Zeffirelli, possibly the most soured man I know, has been eaten up by jealousy and hate.   —Anthony Burgess

★

A legend in his own time and in his own mind—like the rest of us are peons.   —Jennifer Lopez, on Jack Nicholson

★

Not since Attila the Hun swept across Europe leaving 500 years of total blackness has there been a man like Lee Marvin. —director Joshua Logan

★

I remember *Pocket Money*.... At the beginning, it was understood that [Paul] Newman and I would earn the same amount and have roles of equal importance.... Well, I've never seen a situation so much reversed. It was Newman's company who produced the film, and when they came to show it, Newman had become the sole star and I was nowhere.   —Lee Marvin

★

I've never thought that Paul was a particularly good actor. He's one of the sweet people of the world, an excellent producer. But I've never been a Paul Newman fan as far as acting goes.   —George C. Scott

★

[Robert] Redford does not want to be an actor; he wants to be a movie star.
                    —screenwriter Arthur Laurents (*The Way We Were*)

★

JOAN RIVERS

A few stars [in Las Vegas] treated me as a threat, hard to follow. Paul Anka must be about three-foot-two, and when I came offstage filled with excitement, there would be this little man screaming into my chest, "Too long! Too long!" I never saw anything but the top of his head.

—Joan Rivers

"Probably the very worst actress that ever made it to the top."

—director John Cromwell, on Lana Turner

You know how he was so ugly there was a certain beauty about him. But he had his nose altered, wore contact lenses instead of his thick glasses, had his hair straightened, and no one wanted him. He became so morose that he walked out into the middle of the road and killed himself.

—Joseph Cotten, on Everett Sloane (*Citizen Kane*)

Shirley Temple was difficult. I used to have to go down to Palm Beach to coach her, and she'd get involved in a badminton game with me, and her father would call her and she'd say, "I'm not ready, and *I'll* tell you when I'm ready. *I* earn all the money in this household." Of course she's a different type of person now.

—composer Jule Styne

I can now admit that [Charlton] Heston was miscast. His English accent came and went; mostly, it went. And he conveyed little of his character's inner conflicts... I found he'd done minimal research on the character, the period, or the place [*Khartoum*]. When he saw my dark makeup, he suggested it might not be dark enough. He'd thought that because the site was in Africa, anyone from there would be black....However, with me he was civil, which I understand is an exception in his behavior.

—Laurence Olivier

★

I fear Anthony Quinn has given a distorted impression of our working relationship. He has informed the press that I was cold or unfriendly. I was merely professional, and not unfriendly....I've never been overfond of fellow players who wish or feign to fall at my feet.   —Laurence Olivier

★

I found out with Tony Quinn, who's inclined to be dreadfully flamboyant and overdo things terribly if you let him, that the way to get a good performance is to goad him to the point of tears, be nasty to him. If you let him take over, you're dead.   —director Edward Dmytryk

★

[John M.] Stahl was a real son of a bitch. He was the kind of director who would do it over and over again as if to say, "I have to do it again because they gave me lousy actors." We were all downbeat, and everybody hated him. I finally chewed his ass out on the set, and my co-workers gave me a silver cigarette box with all their initials engraved on it.   —Henry Fonda

★

He brutalizes actors....How the hell is he going to direct a film if one day all the actors walk off the set? He has no respect for actors at all.

—Anthony Hopkins, on Tony Richardson

★

I'm sorry...not actually. I'm sorry he died that way [of AIDS], but Tony Richardson was a terrible person. Not because he had AIDS, not because he was bisexual, not because he was hypocritical [closeted] about it. Because he was a terrible person. Not a terrible director, just a terrible human being.   —Anthony Burgess

Some communist! She travels by Rolls-Royce.

—Robert Duvall, on Vanessa Redgrave (ex-wife of Tony Richardson)

★

If things ever get real bad, I can live off her.
                    —Ryan O'Neal, on Tatum O'Neal, his Oscar-winning daughter

I have never met a man like my father. He is so mad, terrible and vehement at the same time. Because of him, I never knew anything other than [anger]. When I began to meet other people I saw that it wasn't normal.
                    —Nastassja Kinski, on Klaus Kinski

She says she's fifty-two. That would make her twelve years old when we made *The Private Life of Henry VIII* together.
                    —Binnie Barnes in 1973, on Merle Oberon

★

James Dean was not straight, was not gay, he was bisexual. That seems to confuse people, or they just ignore the facts. Some—most—will say he was heterosexual, and there's some proof for that, apart from the usual dating of actresses his age. Others will say no, he was gay, and there's some proof for that too, keeping in mind that it's always tougher to get *that* kind of proof. But Jimmy himself said more than once that he swung both ways, so why all the mystery or confusion?
                    —*Rebel Without a Cause* director Nicholas Ray

To quote Emerson's opinion of Daniel Webster, "The word *liberty* in the mouth of Mr. Webster sounds like the word *love* in the mouth of a courtesan." I can say the same of Mr. [Buddy] Ebsen when he uses, or misuses, the words *freedom* and *justice* in his malicious attempt to swing the congressional election to my opponent.
                    —Nancy Kulp, on her Republican *Beverly Hillbillies* co-star, who chose to
                        aid her opponent in a Pennsylvania political race

★

I couldn't stand Chris O'Donnell when we met on the set of *Batman Forever.* He was such a jock, such a frat boy, the kind of guy who expects you to be impressed by the labels on his clothes. I think he resented that I'd been in Hollywood so long....We did become kind of friends later on.
                    —Drew Barrymore

A hit TV series is always a joy and a rarity. By the time I did *Moonlighting,* I was no stranger to success. I hit all that, fame and fortune, when I was twenty....Bruce [Willis] had never had such a success, and it went to his

head, and he made us all pay in so many ways, big and little....Success goes to men's heads more. Especially if they're relatively young.
—Cybill Shepherd

Chris Reeve was a sweetheart, I loved him. But doing that movie [*Switching Channels*] was a killer. I cried. I did. Kathleen Turner was so rotten, so vicious, so mean. She thought she was at the summit, so she could get away with anything. I never had that ongoing meanness....*Now* where is she? She's not young and she's not a movie star. Isn't that sad?
—Burt Reynolds

The thing is, despite our success and privileges, one still ought to treat others well. Otherwise what are we, really, as actors *or* as people? That extends to the press, even. Just kidding. But some of my colleagues, like Sean Connery and Alan Bates, have expressed what I think is excessive contempt for journalists, who are, after all, people. People with jobs which hopefully they'll try to do well and ethically....An actor I won't name says that whenever an interviewer asks him what has been the low point of his life, he likes to answer, "This interview."   —Peter Finch

Filming with [Barbra] Streisand is an experience which may have cured me of movies.   —Kris Kristofferson in 1981 (he's still uncured)

She's a real kvetch [Barbra Streisand]...always moaning about something or other, a really hard-to-please lady. But when she's kvetching I just say, "Shut up and give me a little kiss, will ya, huh?" or "Stick out your boobs, they're beautiful." And after that she's fine for the next ten minutes.
—director Peter Bogdanovich

Alec [Guinness's] passions run more to things and animals than people....On location[for *Dr. Zhivago*], Alec had a pet parrot named Percy. It would whistle Scottish tunes to Alec, who said he loved the bird deeply. But I recall that one day Percy, who was rather temperamental for a bird, became annoyed with Alec for not giving him enough attention. So he flew away. Gone for days, and Alec was beside himself, so sad and feeling very guilty. Then one night, there was a whistle from a branch in a tree, and Alec looked up to see Percy. Alec said their eyes met and he knew Percy had forgiven him. Then Percy flew onto Alec's outstretched arm...and fainted. Alec says he almost did too.   —director David Lean

★

Everyone thinks he can write a motion picture....Long ago, a relative of [John] Wayne sent me a screenplay he'd written in his spare time. A purported thriller. I read it. Finally he called; I didn't call him. He apologized: "I know. I should put more fire in my script, right?" "No," I said. "Vice versa."   —John Huston

★

His success on television is no reason for me to cast him in a picture....He has no voice, the face is temporarily prettier than average, and I see no great progress since his bit in *Myra Breckinridge*.

—John Huston, on Tom Selleck

★

I've read that [Dirk] Bogarde's cruel streak can be attributed to his fight for acceptance as an actor, as a homosexual man, and as a writer. And all the time I thought it was just because he's quite an unpleasant fellow.

—British actor Michael Hordern

★

[Director Alain] Resnais screwed me. Put Johnny G. [Gielgud] in and, well, you can forget about me. No one, and I mean no one, upstages Johnny G. So I was a bit pissed off. But [*Providence*] was a good movie.

—Dirk Bogarde

★

[I] hated that bastard. —William Holden, on Humphrey Bogart in *Sabrina*

★

I hated working with Marlon Brando. Because he was not there. He was somewhere else. There was nothing to reach on to.   —Joanne Woodward

★

Montgomery Clift was an exceptionally bright man who liked to pretend he wasn't. Unlike [Marlon] Brando, who likes to pretend he's bright, whereas in fact he isn't really.   —director Edward Dmytryk

★

She worked with a full-length mirror beside the camera. I didn't know which Loretta to play to—the one in the mirror or the one that was with me.   —Robert Preston, on Loretta Young

★

[Loretta Young] was and is the only actress I really dislike. She was sickeningly sweet, a pure phony. Her two faces sent me home angry and crying several times. —Virginia Field

★

Once I had a terrible fight with Jack Warner, who asked me what I thought of a picture I had done with Humphrey Bogart. I told him I didn't go to see it. Mr. Warner was furious. I said that I only get paid for making pictures. If he wanted me to see them, he'd have to pay me extra. —Peter Lorre

★

She's a monster. If you think she's not strong, you'd better pay attention. —Robert Mitchum, on Sarah Miles [*Ryan's Daughter*]

★

I've been guilty of some high-handed or temperamental behavior in my time. But as an exception, not as the rule. I did a TV movie with Loretta Young, and I can see why certain stars of that old-time era died out, or their careers did. Like dinosaurs. Everything me-me-me. That just doesn't go, today....Miss Young thinks she's still right up there with the queen of England. Sad, really. —Brian Keith

★

Johnny [Carson], you're my favorite straight man, and I've known my share of straight men.... —Bette Midler

★

Mr. [David] Letterman is rather difficult to work for [as a guest] because he expects you to be funny, and frequently, but not quite as funny as he is. —author and wit Quentin Crisp

★

The most romantic thing I've ever heard is something said to me by my co-star, Robert Davi: "You're a hell of a guy, for a girl." —Ally Walker [*Profiler*]

★

I feel that part of the success of *White Christmas* is that the cast was excellent and we were individually well cast. Rosie [Rosemary Clooney] and I hit it off; we've worked together since then....Danny Kaye and Vera-Ellen did not quite hit it off or enjoy the same chemistry. Those two individuals are pretty much loners. Fine performers, but solitary...and somewhat moody. Still, Kaye and I had a certain chemistry, and I don't know anyone who's seen it that hasn't enjoyed that picture. —Bing Crosby

★

That face that [Doris Day] shows the world—smiling, only talking good, happy, tuned into God—as far as I'm concerned that's just a mask. I haven't a clue as to what's underneath. Doris is just about the remotest person I know.   —Kirk Douglas

★

Kirk [Douglas] was civil to me and that's about all. But then Kirk never makes much of an effort toward anyone else. He's pretty wrapped up in himself. The film I made with Kirk, *Young Man With a Horn*, was one of the few utterly joyless experiences I had in films.   —Doris Day

★

Richard Gere has taken his shirt off in every movie he's made. He's falling out of his clothes.   —Christopher Reeve

CHRISTOPHER REEVE

Kirk [Douglas] would be the first to tell you he's a difficult man. I would be the second. —Burt Lancaster

★

I liked [Richard Gere] *before* we started [*An Officer and a Gentleman*], but that is the last time I can remember talking to him. —Debra Winger

★

[Richard] Gere plays the kind of guy who's saying, "I wanna get laid, and you're gonna get laid whether you like it or not." I'm the kind of guy who says "Please." —Christopher Reeve

★

His films are like the dreams of a country boy imagining what it's like to be in the big city. His greatest danger: to be a very great director with precious little to say. —Luchino Visconti, on fellow director Federico Fellini

★

It seems that boredom is one of the great discoveries of our time. If so, there's no question but that he must be considered a pioneer.
—Luchino Visconti, on director Michelangelo Antonioni

★

One of my unfavorite directors, if I may say so, is [Michelangelo] Antonioni, because he tells the same story all the time in the same style. To me he is like a fly that tries to go out of a window and doesn't realize there is glass, and keeps banging against it and never reaches the sky.
—director Franco Zeffirelli

★

One fault— he is inflexible. He's horrified if you give him ideas. He only appreciates his own.... That's his greatest fault. If he wasn't so inflexible he would be very great. —Charles Bronson, on director Robert Aldrich

★

Richard Jaeckel was a good friend of [Robert Aldrich]. He went to see him on his last stretch in the hospital. He was in a coma much of the time. And Jaeckel asks if there is anything he can get him. And Aldrich says, "Yeah, a good script." —Lee Marvin

★

I have never been a fan of Woody Allen's... many people say he's the funniest in the world, but I've never been able to appreciate his humor. I find him neurotic. —George C. Scott

★

It's quite disturbing that [Woody] Allen has, and has had for a long time, a thing for far younger girls. In his films, as well. He gets older and older, and if anything the girls get even younger. This is *not* funny. It's quite gross, and one *should* be disturbed by it.

—Maureen O'Sullivan (Mia Farrow's mother)

[Director John Farrow, Mia's father] gave me almost no direction at all. God forbid I should miss a cue! Then he would snarl, "You know your lines, don't you?" I resolved not to fight with him. It would only have made things worse. And he was not very pleased with the other actors either.

—Lana Turner

[John Farrow] was a really nasty man, not especially with me, but I have rarely seen a sadist of such magnitude....He was quite a good-looking man but the spirit of evil, looking to antagonize everybody.   —Michel Kelber

[Director] Otto Preminger started in on [Groucho Marx], giving him a hard time. And Groucho was old and feeble....Preminger also started berating Frankie Avalon...it was just terrible to see. So when that was over I said, "Otto, come here. If you ever talk to me like that, I will hit you over the head with a fucking chair." From then on, he was as gentle as rain with me.

—Jackie Gleason

O.P. [Otto Preminger] is only happy if everybody else is miserable. Still, if you can keep his paranoia from beating you down, you can learn a lot from the guy.   —Michael Caine

Mia Farrow looks slight, but she has the intensity and presence of a much larger person...a shrewd cookie.   —John Cassavetes

All turned in and vulnerable, a child with a highly energetic brain. From the neck up she's eighty.   —Shirley MacLaine, on Mia Farrow

Some guy's written that [director] Blake Edwards is a man of many talents, all of them minor. I don't know about that....Julie [Andrews, married to Edwards] has definite talent, but she's annoyingly aware of the fact. And she and Blake, together, are very hard to take, very smarmy together. Not a pleasant couple or whatever you want to label them....   —Rock Hudson

Claire Trevor once went back to see Judith Anderson after a performance of *Medea*. She had been truly bowled over and she said, "I simply can't find the words to tell you how superb you were." Judith Anderson just said, "Try."
—Rock Hudson

Fred Astaire wanted to be an English aristocrat....His biggest regret in life was that as an American he would never be able to become Sir Fred.
—Astaire's choreographer Hermes Pan

Six years of mutual aggression. From 1933 to 1939 [Fred Astaire and Ginger Rogers] did nine pictures for me. Overnight they became one of the hottest box office attractions in the industry. But I've never known two people who wanted to be further apart. It was a constant struggle. I'll never forget how horrified Fred was when I notified him that Ginger was going to play the part of a titled English lady in *The Gay Divorcee*.
—producer Pandro S. Berman

Of course I knew. I didn't talk much, but I *listened* attentively. By about the sixties, some people would talk about this on the [film] set, usually in whispers. But it was known. He was a TV star, so people asked, found out, others in the know had told....Oh, we *knew*.
—Joan Bennett, on Raymond Burr's homosexuality

I was very, very angry about Michael saying that. It was not true. [Errol] Flynn wasn't like that when I worked with him. He didn't even drink a lot in those days. He later became very unruly, but not when he was young, and he never took advantage of me.
—Olivia De Havilland, after Michael Caine said Flynn had
deflowered her at nineteen on the Warner lot

I did my first movie with Bette Davis. And you know what she said to me? Oh, it just haunts me. I wonder if it's true, maybe she's right. She said, "You can't have a relationship and a career. You can't have both."
—Rosanna Arquette

Well, I'd say he has a certain je ne sais queer....
—Orson Welles, on Anthony Perkins

★

Franco Zeffirelli is bigoted, vengeful, and angry most of the time. But other than that I like him. Sometimes.

—the Metropolitan Opera's Ruldolph Bing

★

The man insisted on enhancing his reputation as one of the meanest bastards who ever walked a soundstage. Otto [Preminger] was crude. Though most men have been guilty of looking on women as sex objects, ...Otto was the only man I ever met who did that on his *good* days. The rest of the time he treated them like dirt. He would swear at them, insult them, comment on their weight, the size of their nose (if it was too big) or their breasts (if they were too small), say anything that might hurt them.

—Adam West (*Batman*)

★

Ingrid [Bergman] loved me more than any woman in my life loved me. The day after the picture [*Saratoga Trunk*] ended, I couldn't even get her on the telephone.   —Gary Cooper

★

Men find it tougher to adjust to success gracefully. They throw their weight around...try and make everyone else feel less than successful. Bruce Willis, for instance....   —Cybill Shepherd

★

Lauren Bacall is a pro, but I found her a rather icy lady. Me, I could never get that way....Do you start out that way, or does life or our line of work make you that way? Obviously I didn't have the guts to ask her!

—Betty Grable

★

Very happy to be working with Mr. Victor Mature. I believe he was the first man to make that well-traveled transition from male model to male actor.

—Peter Sellers

★

Vic [Mature] can play good guy or bad guy. Only, he can overdo the emoting. One critic said he sneers and curls his upper lip so often, it gives the impression he had it permanently waved.   —Betty Grable

She [Mae West] was older than people thought. Probably the oldest actress to ever enter the movies and become a star. She was certainly older than she'd ever admit...and sensitive about her weight as well. She liked gowns that were skin-tight, so tight she couldn't move in them. I know this

because she had different, somewhat larger versions made of each gown for when movement was required....Edith Head claimed she invented the reclining board [which had armrests and was tilted at an angle] so Mae could lean against one and rest in between scenes in one of her nonmovable gowns.   —Cary Grant

★

Kirk's an old friend. We've worked together, and often. But we are *not* interchangeable!   —Burt Lancaster, on Kirk Douglas

★

She's sort of a Marilyn Monroe gone to seed. And I'm not a big fan of Marilyn's either.   —Dan Dailey, on Jayne Mansfield

★

As a director he was ten times more wonderful than as a lover.
                                        —Nastassja Kinski, on Roman Polanski

★

I don't feel envious [of] or competitive with Art Carney. I've been starring in pictures for a long time, and long ago I cottoned to the fact that I'm too big a star on television ever to get any kind of Academy Award, which I've never been seeking anyway. I think mostly it's a popularity contest.
                                —Jackie Gleason, after Carney was nominated for an Oscar

★

I'm happy for Art. In a million years it would never occur to me he could win an Academy Award....I still think of him as my [*Honeymooners*] sidekick—the best in the business. I can't think of him as a leading man, though maybe someday I will—I guess he's gonna make more pictures after this....   —Jackie Gleason, after Carney won

★

Oh, he's nice to look at. Good voice. But that's not enough. Robert Goulet isn't star material....They can put him in a few movies, but we'll wait and see if he remains a star, shall we?   —Keenan Wynn

★

We were filming a scene [*Jinxed* director Don Siegel] didn't want to do [with a song in it]. We started to fight over it. It got pretty ugly. He started calling me names, and he jumped out of his trailer and I followed him. His wife—she's very large, about six feet tall—grabbed me because I was getting ready to haul off and hit him. She held me from behind, and instead of me hitting him, he hauled off and hit me...*slugged* me. I was livid. It was terrible, just traumatic.   —Bette Midler

I worked with Dean [Martin] before he worked with Jerry Lewis....My nose job was an improvement—I broke it as a pro boxer—but not as big an improvement as Dean's, which Lou Costello bought for him. Dean's original nose, it looked like he was eating a banana. The nose job made him into a matinee idol.   —Alan King

I can't remember why we're not speaking.
—Rod Steiger, to Marlon Brando upon their chance meeting in a Montreal restaurant, thus ending a forty-four-year estrangement following *On The Waterfront*—for which Brando won an Oscar and Steiger didn't

Anyone who has come close to Warren [Beatty] has shed quite a few feathers. He tends to maul you.   —Leslie Caron

I think I'm in so many of his pictures because no other actress would work with him.   —Jill Ireland, on husband Charles Bronson

I'm a very good actor: I played all those love scenes with Phyllis Calvert and we didn't like each other very much.   —Stewart Granger

Monty [Clift] was the most sensitive man I've ever known. If somebody kicked a dog a mile away, he'd feel it.
—director Edward Dmytryk (*Raintree County*)

I had respect and admiration for him which touched him....At one point, he wanted to marry my mother so that I could become his son.
—Jean Marais, on his director and lover Jean Cocteau

Much more attractive without his wig on.
—Barbara Carrera, on Sean Connery

If Bette [Davis] has an emotional scene, she tackles it completely consciously, and when you say "Cut" she might ask, "Do you think that was a little too much this or a little too much that?" But when [Joan] Crawford plays an emotional scene, you have to wait twenty minutes until she comes out of it after you have said "Cut," because she is still crying or laughing or whatever; she's still going.   —director Curtis Bernhardt

★

Three times a week she'd sit down at a desk just to answer the fans' letters.
—writer-director Joseph L. Mankiewicz, on Joan Crawford

★

[Joan Crawford] even had a special outfit just for answering her fan mail.
—Anthony Perkins, who didn't work with Crawford and once said,
"I'd probably rather have a cannibal for a co-star"

★

[Joan] Crawford and [Bette] Davis were perfect pros on the set of *What Ever Happened to Baby Jane?* until 6 P.M. Then I'd get a call from Joan asking, "Did you see what that bitch did to me today?" A couple of minutes later Bette would call and ask, "What did that bitch call you about?" First one and then the other. I could count on it every night.
—director Robert Aldrich

★

[Bing Crosby] was a tough guy. Make one wrong move and he'd never speak to you again.
—Phil Harris

★

I made them [the movies]—Willy only directed them.
—producer Samuel Goldwyn, on William Wyler

★

Miss [Jane] Russell was a very strong character. Very good-humored when she wasn't being cranky.
—Robert Mitchum

★

Don't let her fool you. Tangle with her, and she'll shingle your attic.
—Bob Hope, on Jane Russell

★

[Bob] Hope? Hope is not a comedian. He just translates what others write for him.
—Groucho Marx

★

Acting with [Laurence] Harvey is like acting by yourself—only worse.
—Jane Fonda

★

The tales I can tell of working with him are too horrendous to repeat.
—Lee Remick, on Laurence Harvey

★

She was a gigantic pain in the ass. She demonstrated certifiable proof of insanity.
—*Chinatown* director Roman Polanski, on Faye Dunaway

★

When I got here I walked in thinking I was a star, and then I found I was supposed to do everything the way [Faye Dunaway] says. Listen, I'm not going to take temperamental whims from anyone...I just take a long walk and cool off. If I didn't do that, I know I'd wind up dumping her on her derriere.
—Robert Mitchum

★

Danny Kaye is an acquired taste. On the screen. In person, he wasn't the least bit funny. Rather, he was egotistical and one of those comedians who secretly envy dramatic actors. Add to that his ever-present and unpleasant wife, and his being as they say in the closet, and he was no picnic to work with!
—Elsa Lanchester

★

She's as beautiful as death, as seductive as sin, and as cold as virtue.
—director Luis Buñuel, on Catherine Deneuve

★

Part of aging gracefully is acceptance of the prominence of youth in our profession. In my final picture, *Parrish* [1961], I shared the screen with Troy Donahue and Connie Stevens and so on....I've never objected to youth, but I'm less happy about untalented actors and salacious storylines.
—Claudette Colbert

★

[*The Specialist*] is an action film, and the politics of the film were such that Sylvester [Stallone] and Sharon [Stone] had fifteen assistants and huge motor homes, and I'm in the back and I'm treated like I'm just one of the extras. I may not have the billing and get the attention from the producer and the director, but I know that this part could steal the picture, so I got in there whenever I could get in there....Alec Baldwin said, "Jimmy's an acting terrorist. He's got to win every scene." That kind of competition is healthy.
—James Woods

★

I did three pictures with [Abbott and Costello]. Costello was a clever little guy, but pushy. He was the star and wanted everybody to know it. Bud Abbott was a very sweet guy...didn't have all those Italian hangers-on like Costello. Bud invited me to his house. I didn't know him really....A nice guy. A lonely man.
—screen gangster Marc Lawrence

★

It took six days. [First] I said to Gary, "I'm a fan of yours. I hate doing this, Gary, putting my dirty finger into your beautiful nose, your lovely eyes...."

He was such a sweet, gentle guy.

—Marc Lawrence, on doing a fight scene with Gary Cooper

★

I was in Spain on the set of *Solomon and Sheba* [directed by King Vidor], standing resplendent in my costume, when some American tourists came marching up, stared at me, then broke into beatific smiles. I stared back, and one of them asked, "You're playing King Vidor from the Old Testament, aren't you?'

—George Sanders

GEORGE SANDERS

[Yul Brynner] had an entourage of seven. The function of one member of this retinue appeared to consist of placing already lighted cigarettes in Brynner's outstretched fingers. Another was permanently occupied in shaving his skull with an electric razor whenever the suspicion of a shadow darkened that noble head. While these services were being rendered unto him, Brynner sat in sphynx-like silence and splendor wearing black leather suits or white leather suits, of which he had half a dozen each, confected for him by the firm of Dior.

—George Sanders, on his *Solomon and Sheba* co-star

★

I can't act, but 90 percent of the actors and actresses now acting can't act. I've never said I *can* act....Jean-Claude Van Damme sure as hell can't act, though I don't know what he's said about it.   —Dennis Rodman

I was not so eager to direct John Travolta, but the deal was an attractive one....We did have a huge fight. There is no need for details. But it began when I dared to criticize his religion, or cult.

—Roman Polanski on Scientologist Travolta

I couldn't begin, and wouldn't try, to say things as vicious about Ken Wahl as he said about me during *Jinxed*....I can see why he became a TV star [in *Wiseguy*], but I can also understand why he sabotaged his career. He seems to hate everyone, including himself.   —Bette Midler

Charlton Heston has the same problem I do. He's not likable. Difference is, I am in real life. On the silver screen, we're both rather wooden. I can do accents—American, English—being Irish....Heston had to star in a huge hit and play some supposed kind of a saint to win an Oscar.

—Stephen Boyd, on his *Ben-Hur* co-star

Sometimes John [Huston] does stunt-type casting. Rather than hiring a lady to play a whore, he'll hire a whore. I'm not being vicious, I'm sure he'd confirm it, but that's most likely the reason he cast Zsa Zsa Gabor in a quality picture like *Moulin Rouge*.

—José Ferrer, who played Toulouse-Lautrec in it

Two things was always sure to get Eva [Gabor] riled up. One was when folks called her Zsa Zsa, 'cause a lot of 'em couldn't tell between her and her sister. And the other was when her makeup and hair-fixing people [weren't] around when she yelled for 'em....I remember the time when Judy Garland died over in New York [she died in London, then was flown to New York City], and her will said she wanted her makeup guy from all those movies at Metro to fix her face up one last time, for eternity. And the guy was working for Eva on our show [*Green Acres*]. Well, Eva said Judy could rot in hell before she'd let her makeup guy off the set.

You have to admit Eva was kind of decorative on the set, and she didn't look her age, though she had big ole massive legs....The one she did get along with, most of the time, was Eddie Albert, who played her husband....When it came to any acting ability, Eva was 'bout as useless as teats on a boar hog. —Pat "Mr. Haney" Buttram

★

The day before we read [*The People vs. Larry Flynt* script] together, [Courtney Love] called [director] Milos Forman and he handed me the phone. I said, "So you're the freaky rock star drug addict," and she said, "And you're that guy who's fucked every woman in Hollywood."
—Woody Harrelson

★

He's not aging well. The best thing to happen to his career is for him to die immediately. —director Werner Herzog, on actor Klaus Kinski

★

I'd scare her, I'd bribe her, I screamed at her....I had to feed her her lines one at a time. I couldn't believe it when she won the Oscar.
—Peter Bogdanovich, on directing Tatum O'Neal in *Paper Moon*

★

I'm tired of all that Pamela [Anderson Lee] crap...she attracts a very tacky press line. It was starting to turn off viewers.
—David Hasselhoff, *Baywatch* star and producer

★

In the old days, some people thought blonde bimbo types like Suzanne Somers and Farrah Fawcett were rather tacky. But compare them to the latest clones like Pamela Anderson and Anna Nicole Smith, and they seem so lady-like! —John Ritter of *Three's Company*

★

It's a sad gimmick. [Farrah Fawcett] looks great for fifty, but a lot of us look very good for our ages. That doesn't mean we degrade ourselves by posing naked in magazines and television announcing our real ages and pretending we're human paint brushes and that it's "art." That's bullshit, and you don't have to have played Van Gogh [1956] to know that. Back around 1980, we did a space movie [*Saturn* 3], she went topless in it, very nice, no big deal. And she didn't try to make some artsy production out of it or throw away her hard-won credentials after it. Like I say, it's sad.
—Kirk Douglas, in 1997

★

For a sex symbol, I found Omar Sharif almost sexless. So he is a good actor. But it is one thing to act, another to make false advertising....Recently I saw him on television doing a commercial for a copper bracelet. He mentioned his "ancient Egyptian ancestors." Only later did I remember he was born in Lebanon [as Michel Shalhoub], and he did not become Egyptian and Moslem until he married Egypt's biggest actress, which is the way he became a star originally.   —French actress Anouk Aimée

Bela Lugosi was a very bitter man. Before he became Dracula he was a romantic lead. But after, it was always the horrors. Then Boris Karloff came along, and he was more talented and much nicer, I worked with both, and Boris always called him "poor Bela." He refused to have the feud that Bela wanted to have....On the set of one picture, Bela was playing a deaf-mute. He kept telling the director, "I am a star, give me more lines!" The director said how could he, when the character had had his tongue ripped out. But Bela kept getting angry and saying, even though he had a small role, "I am a star! I am a star!" If I were the director, I would have told him, "*Was*, Bela, *was....*"   —Peter Lorre

I won't say she was dumb, but one time Jayne [Mansfield] squealed out loud on the set and said she had a terrific idea. The director stared at her, then said, 'Treat it gently, dear. It's in a strange place.'   —Tony Randall

Hell will freeze over before I speak to that drunken bum again.
                    —Frank Sinatra in 1988, after Dean Martin appeared drunk
                                              on stage with him

The most obnoxious actress I've ever worked with.
                    —Anthony Hopkins, on Shirley MacLaine

Childish and impossible.
                    —director Joel Schumacher [*Batman Forever*], on Val Kilmer

I don't like Val Kilmer, I don't like his [lack of] work ethic, and I don't want to be associated with him ever again.
                    —director John Frankenheimer (*The Island of Dr. Moreau*)

★

If you argue with [Dustin Hoffman], he wants his point and he wants his way. Finally if you say, "All right, we'll do it *your* way," he'll say, "No, I don't want to do it my way until *you* like doing it my way." It's not enough to give in to him; you have to *like* what he wants too!   —Terri Garr (*Tootsie*)

Let the Chips Fall

[Frank Sinatra] was married *and* having an affair with Ava Gardner. I think he decided if he also had an affair with me, he wouldn't get a divorce, but it would knock out the affair with Ava. I should have obliged.... It was stupid. I was crazy about him. But... it was not so much he wanted me as he did *not* want Ava....   —Shelley Winters

[A] skinny, no-talent, stupid Hoboken bastard.
         —Shelley Winters, on Frank Sinatra, who later wed Ava Gardner

Ken is so tired, his sperm are on crutches.
         —Emma Thompson, on then-husband Kenneth Branagh

I have no belief in the system. So Sonny's perfectly at home there. Politicians are one step below used-car salesmen.
         —Cher, upon Bono's election to Congress

I'd say nepotism has literally reached a new low where Pamela Lee's concerned.... Her baby boy was chosen to enact an abandoned baby on a beach in her series [*Baywatch*] and earned $60,000 for the assignment. True, he may be more talented than [she], but that is bald nepotism. It's also sexism: a male infant earning more than the average adult actress.
         —William Hickey (*Prizzi's Honor*)

I hope the next time she crosses a street four blind guys come along driving cars.   —Frank Sinatra, on his biographer Kitty Kelley

[Jackie Kennedy has a] voice that one hears on the radio late at night, dropped softly into the ear by girls who sell soft mattresses, depilatories, or creams to brighten the skin.   —writer Norman Mailer

[John F.] Kennedy's only complaint about Jackie in all the years I ever knew him was that she spent too much money.... "That Jackie," he'd yell. "She's unbelievable. She absolutely does not appreciate the value of money. Thinks she can keep on spending it forever. God, she's driving me crazy—

absolutely crazy. I tell you...George, she's run through all the government funds and is drawing on my personal account. If the taxpayers ever found out what she's spending, they'd drive me out of office."

—former U.S. Senator George Smathers

★

This [Dodi] al-Fayed guy, he's dated more than his share of models and actresses, and from what I've heard he's been bad news for most of the girls he went with. This latest one, the [model] represented by [attorney] Gloria Allred, he allegedly promised to marry her, then dumped her for Princess Di....Like I say, he's far from Prince Charming himself, but how tragic that for Diana he was fatal.

—Connie Clausen

★

Amusing, but small.

—Mamie Van Doren's description of alleged lover Burt Reynolds

★

A complete *nada* [*nothing* in Spanish].

—columnist Cindy Adams, on President Reagan's son Ron

★

[During] a trip under the aegis of a British War Relief campaign [in World War II] we were at the Mormon temple in Salt Lake City. It happened to be the anniversary of a college sorority and all the girls celebrated by coming to meet the handsome actor. Microphones were thrust in front of us. Brian [Aherne] was to deliver a message to the R.A.F. [Royal Air Force] pilots who would be listening to a shortwave rebroadcast. Did he have anything in particular to say to these brave airmen?

Brian said yes, indeed, he did. "Chaps, keep your peckers up!" Silence...the girls fled in embarrassment. The presiding minister blanched. Only when I got my English husband back to our hotel did I inform him that in America "pecker" did not mean "chin."

—Joan Fontaine

★

Did you hear? Heather Locklear of *Melrose Place* is taking four whole months off so she can be, she says, "a full-time mom." Isn't that *so* maternal of her?

—Chris Farley

★

When my son Sean was eight he wanted so much to meet Michael Jackson. He did, and they became friends. But it was rather difficult at times, and the press made so much of it. I think eventually the press just came between them.

—Yoko Ono

As they say, people's taste tends to reflect what they are...and in the 1970s they asked Bette Davis and Joan Crawford who their favorite newer actresses were. Bette said Glenda Jackson and Joan said Faye Dunaway. The first one chose substance and the second chose style.

—director Colin Higgins (*Nine to Five*)

★

Many stars sooner or later believe their fantasies....Bette Davis was by no means senile. Sharp as a tack. Feisty! But she was convinced that she'd been up for an Academy Award for her breakthrough role [in *Of Human Bondage,* 1934]. You could *not* convince her otherwise, and she *said* she was nominated, in interviews. I don't know if anyone ever dared show her a book recording that she was not in the Oscar derby that year....

—Richard Jaeckel

★

I was watching this very offbeat film, *The Little Girl Who Lives Down the Lane* [1976], and it starred Jodie Foster, but it also had Alexis Smith. And honestly, it was riveting—it was like Big Butch and Little Butch.

—Graham Chapman (Monty Python)

★

Carol Matthau once said that *nobody* marries beneath himself or herself. That could be debated, but really, these Hollywood women don't seem to profit from the experience of their mistakes. Has Liz Taylor well and truly sworn off marriage? Or is it just until the next beefy swain convinces her he loves her more than her bank account? Tune in next year...and Roseanne, who's married her bodyguard after two dreadful marital mishaps. How can that last?...People in England tend to marry within their own class. But actresses pick up and wed their hairdressers or bodyguards or a lorry [truck] driver. Such pretend-unions can't last.

—British writer Anthony Burgess (as of early 1998 Roseanne is filing for divorce)

★

Beauty and the beastie. Seems Brooke [Shields] is being influenced by her recent hubby [Andre Agassi], as she's finally back in the news, but for talking dirty at tennis matches. I thought by now she'd be old enough to know better than to take up new bad habits, if not bad boys.

—Eric Idle (Monty Python)

★

WHOOPI GOLDBERG

First off, I have dated black men. But a woman with power is a problem for any man but particularly for a black man because it's hard for them to get power. I understand that, but I have to have a life and that means dating the men who want to date me.

—Whoopi Goldberg, answering criticism of her friendship with actor Frank Langella

Les Enfants du Paradis! Maybe the best movie ever made. You know, that's the only time I ever fell in love with an actress. I was mad about Arletty....My first trip to Paris, the thing I did right away, I asked to meet Arletty...was that a mistake! What a disillusionment. She was a tough article.... —Marlon Brando

Once I asked him, "Why do you ride those motorcycles like that and maybe kill yourself?" and he said, "So I won't forget I'm a man and not just an actor." —Bette Davis, on Steve McQueen

It's embarrassing that wherever I go I am asked, "How is your nephew?" and I can't answer them because I have never seen him.
—Janet Jackson, who has sent word to her brother Michael that she'd like to visit him and the baby

★

Although they haven't spoken in over three years, Lorna Luft swears she is *not* feuding with sister Liza Minnelli. —columnist Jack Martin, in 1998

★

I remember after Elvis died, Marlon Brando did an interview, I think in *Playboy,* and he was so rude. But now I remember it because now it's so ironic. He called Elvis bloated and over the hill.... —Carmen McRae

★

President Kennedy, as usual, I love you.
—Carly Simon, performing for President Bill Clinton at a 1996 campaign rally

★

I thought it was very humanitarian of Sean Penn and Madonna to marry each other. That way, they make only two people miserable instead of four.
—Cesar Romero

★

Sean [Connery] can't console himself for not being a second Laurence Olivier. —Shelley Winters

★

As an emcee, Ed Sullivan has delusions of adequacy. —Sheilah Graham

★

Charlton Heston has made acting in period pictures an art. A minor art.
—Ava Gardner

★

Tom Cruise is so much less in person than on the screen. Mousy and vaguely hostile....Some people bring more life into a room when they enter it. Tom Cruise seems to do that when he *leaves a room.*
—Pamela Mason

★

Grace Kelly told enough white lies to ice a cake. —columnist Herb Caen

★

[MGM hairdresser Sydney Guilaroff] once told me [that] the night before the Johnny Stompanato murder, he ran into Lana Turner at Hughes Market in Hollywood, buying steak knives.... —Rex Reed

Helen confided in me that her son [actor] James MacArthur almost never spoke of Jack Lord [*Hawaii Five-O*], even though they've been together on that [TV] series for years. And Helen knew why. "Why?" I asked her. "He remembers what I taught him as a child: If you have nothing good to say about someone, say nothing at all."

—Anita Loos, Helen Hayes's friend and co-author

Jack Lord has made hairspray for men acceptable. Yes. That is his obsession. Wind-proof hair. He never worries about his face. His plastic surgeon in Beverly Hills does that—every five years.   —comedian Totie Fields

If Elizabeth Taylor wants to go around looking like a Goodyear blimp pumped full of Chasen's chili instead of butane gas, that is her own business.   —critic Rex Reed

My husband will never chase another woman. He's too fine, too decent, too old.   —Gracie Allen, on George Burns

Every politician should have been born an orphan and remain a bachelor.

—Lady Bird Johnson, widow of the thirty-sixth U.S. president

Behind every successful man is a surprised woman.

—Maryon Pearson, wife of a former Canadian prime minister

Two of the more trivial topics I never discuss are my marriage [of three weeks] to Wallace Beery and those frozen dinners which have become famous with my name on them.   —Gloria Swanson

I know a lot of people didn't expect our relationship to last, but we've just celebrated our two months' anniversary.

—Britt Ekland, then-wife of Peter Sellers

I left Sean Connery after he bashed my face in with his fists.

—Diane Cilento

Jill St. John...what a sack of shit!   —Tony Curtis

Oh. They consider him a star?
>—Roseanne, on being informed that ex-husband Tom Arnold
had been voted the most boring film star

The public wanted Bing Crosby as a grand old man, but everybody knew he was a drunk who screwed around and beat up his wife.... I am particularly disgusted that the public buys the hypocrisy of the men revered as national institutions. —Joan Rivers

Bob Hope is a barely funny, very selfish reactionary and user. He used patriotism and the troops overseas for publicity. —Myrna Loy

That awful Michael Jackson...from Los Angeles, with the smog. The nerve: he comes to [the French Riviera] and wears his stupid surgeon's mask outdoors, as if he is being polluted by our cleaner air! —Brigitte Bardot

You know, if anybody—any of my dancers—got their hair cut like yours, they couldn't be in my show. Because it's tired.... These couches have to go! When you drive down the street...and these couches are in the window, it always says "Half Off."
>—Madonna, to Arsenio Hall while guesting on his show

I told Mia Farrow to title her memoirs *Mama Mia*. Great title—catchy. You can remember it. Somebody said her book is wonderful, you should read it. But he couldn't remember its name. See? Stars don't want to listen.
>—Larry King

I did used to be a bouncer. So what? Roseanne, my ex-wife, *bounces*. Not her checks, of course. *Her.*

>—Tom Arnold

[Burt Reynolds] was a very macho man, and I got the show business break first. The more I did well, the more invalidated he felt as a man, and consequently the more destructive he became. It started with pushes and slaps. As things got worse, it was very painful. I was terrified of him.
>—Judy Carne, then-wife of the aspiring star

My mother was disowned by her father [playwright Eugene O'Neill] because she married my father [Charlie Chaplin]. He had a reputation for seducing

very young women...girls. She and her father never became reconciled, so
I never met my grandfather, and I wish I had.   —Geraldine Chaplin

Fernando Lamas said to me, "I really would like to marry you, but could
you stop being Esther Williams?" I said, "That's a really interesting
question. I've been Esther Williams since I was twelve, when I started
competitive swimming....Could you stop fooling around?" He said, "I don't
know."   —Esther Williams, who did wed the Latin Lover

What can I do? I'm hot.

—Jack Nicholson, when Angelica Huston discovered
he'd been having affairs with younger women

She's like that old joke about Philadelphia. First prize, four years with Joan.
Second prize, eight.   —Franchot Tone, Joan Crawford's second husband

She knew more days on which gifts could be given than appear on any
holiday calendar.   —Conrad Hilton, on wife Zsa Zsa Gabor

When I first met Hedy Lamarr...she was so beautiful that everybody would
stop talking when she came into a room. Wherever she went she was the
cynosure of all eyes....Of her conversation I can remember nothing; when
she spoke one did not listen, one just watched her mouth moving and
marveled at the exquisite shapes made by her lips. She was, in
consequence, rather frequently misunderstood.   —George Sanders

Excuse me. *Speed* was the movie Sandra Bullock did with me which made
her a star. I was already a star, thank you very much.

—Keanu Reeves, setting the stellar record straight

Mel Gibson is *no* Clark Gable! No, sir. Gable would never use the same foul
language or behave as poorly....I hear the excuse that Mr. Gibson is
unhappy because he's losing his looks. Yet he wasn't much better-behaved
when he still had them.   —actress Sally Blane

Carol Channing can be hilarious. She can be fun....Contrary to her image,
she is not eight years old mentally. In fact, she can be as tough as a nut. She
is a survivor, plus.   —playwright James Kirkwood

Yes, it's wonderful that [in 1997] Carol [Channing] is still touring. Even if it's still *Hello, Dolly!*...You know what they've nicknamed it? She's seventy-five, I believe, so some of them are calling it "the death tour."

—actor/coach Bobby Lewis

During the five years I was married to Zsa Zsa Gabor, I lived in her sumptuous Bel Air mansion as a sort of paying guest. My presence in the house was regarded by Zsa Zsa's press photographers, dressmakers, the household staff, and sundry visitors and friends with tolerant amusement. I was allotted a small room in which I was permitted to keep my personal effects until such time as more space was needed to store her ever-mounting stacks of press clippings and photographs.

I was accustomed to austerity and it was no great sacrifice for me to dispose from time to time of some of my belongings so as to empty drawers in my room and make them available for the more vital function of housing Zsa Zsa's memorabilia. All of the tables, walls, cupboards, and closets of various kinds were pressed into similar service.

—George Sanders, whose autobiography was titled
Memoirs of a Professional Cad

All the women in America are hating me! Matthew [McConaughey] and I are *not* dating, we're *not* married. I'm *not* with Matthew. He's a single man.

—Sandra Bullock

Misha [Mikhail Baryshnikov] was more like a friend, and there was a lot of distance. Monogamy wasn't in his book—he had a long-term girlfriend who, unbeknownst to me, got pregnant while we were going out. But I was in love with him. —Janine Turner

The man who owned [*sic*] Twentieth Century–Fox [Darryl F. Zanuck] tried to bring me to Hollywood. But he was a liar. He brought some women from Europe, but only to be in small parts and to be his mistresses. He did not want to have a strong woman or make her a big star. Not if she was from Europe, and especially not from France. All those men who owned Hollywood, all of them were scared of proud Frenchwomen!

—Brigitte Bardot

★

PAUL MCCARTNEY

Cute people do not age well. Look at Paul McCartney. It's hard to believe he was ever the cute one among the Beatles. Who would ever have believed that someday Ringo [Starr] would look better than Paul?

—British actress Beryl Reid

★

Call me naïve, innocent, whatever. But I did hang out with [madam to the stars] Heidi Fleiss three times before I caught on what her profession was. It's not like she handed out business cards or anything. —David Lee Roth

★

Most of the men who become Tinseltown bigwigs—the David Begelmans, the Balabans, the Ladds and Puttnams and Zanucks—they're monsters and narcissists. They lust for women but hate women....Attending a Hollywood board meeting, it's a circle of jerks. In more ways than one.

—Sandy Dennis

★

My first marriage was [to author] Thomas McGuane—I was cast in a movie he directed in 1975...he broke up with his wife [who later wed Peter Fonda] *and* his girlfriend [actress Elizabeth Ashley] to marry me, and we had a daughter. It lasted about three years...I married an actor [John Heard] for a few weeks, and the third time was to a director [Philippe de Broca] for about nine months. But none of this is so unusual, not these days or in this business....

—Margot Kidder

★

I think Cher looked a lot more natural with her pre-plastic Armenian nose, don't you?...Then there's the lips—I don't know *what* she had done to them....All these older women with the big collagened lips, it looks so *weird*. It wouldn't look good on young women, let alone people over fifty. Come to think of it, how come men never get collagened lips? I imagine it wouldn't look good on most white guys other than Mick Jagger.

—Broadway actor Larry Kert

★

Why pick on the fat man? It's not just me. Sometimes I eat or drink a lot, but I do it in public. I'm no recluse....If I get a little rowdy, I tend to do it in public...it doesn't mean anything. But I read how Rosie O'Donnell is so nice, so modest, and she's cool, man, okay? But she's also famous, behind the scenes, for firing people and using as much profanity as I do any day of the week. So why pick on *me*?

—Chris Farley

★

As to Anita's fear that she'll be assassinated? The only people who might shoot Anita Bryant are music lovers.

—Gore Vidal, on the homophobic singer and ex-activist

★

I guess you could call Judy [Garland, his former mother-in-law] a fag hag, though the term's old-fashioned....She did have a gay father, some gay husbands, a lesbian affair or two herself, and a few other assorted gay relatives and in-laws.

—openly gay singer-composer Peter Allen

★

He was AC/DC.
—Ann Miller, on Garland's husband Vincente Minnelli (the quote was
censored from a TV biography of Ann's friend Judy)

★

I first did Ed Sullivan in 1967 because of a mistake. Ed had agreed to book
Johnny Rivers, the folk singer. But by then in his career, Ed was getting
more and more confused from what I think now was early Alzheimer's.
"Next week we'll be having Joanie Rivers," he announced on the air. So they
had to let me in.... — Joan Rivers

★

During the last years before Ed had to give up the show, he became
increasingly dotty. Once Jane Morgan was singing "Bolero," and he walked
on the stage and said, "Everybody clap along." To a bolero beat? Sometimes
on the air he would ask questions that made no sense. He called Woody
Allen over after Woody's act and asked him for no discernible reason,
"How's your father? Is he better?" Woody, improvising, said, "He recognizes
me now and he's able to blink." — Joan Rivers

★

...like an illustration for a bird-seed commercial. Maybe those wide-eyed
one-liners and pregnant pauses work on television, but if Miss Hawn is to
have any kind of future in movies, she needs to learn something about the
rudimentary techniques necessary to sustain a comic scene without
putting the audience to sleep. — Rex Reed, on Goldie Hawn

★

She's a con artist and a freeloader, but she does have a warm, gay soul.
— Jack L. Warner, on professional hostess Elsa Maxwell

★

I don't like Josephine Baker because of her radical politics, that's all.
— columnist Walter Winchell

★

He [Walter Winchell] hates me because I am a colored woman who made
good...I left America to go to France, where I became famous and rich.
— Josephine Baker

★

Ellen [DeGeneres] came out—big surprise—but I predict she'll create an
even bigger splash when she reveals that she and Leonardo DiCaprio are the
same petite blond person. — Allen Ginsberg

★

The thing about Maggie Smith, who is a great performer, is that she never allows you to forget that she is performing. —Jeremy Brett

★

Hollywood likes old Englishmen. It doesn't have much use for old Englishwomen....No disrespect, but there was old Sir Cedric Hardwicke, who had a naughty nickname [Sir Seldom Hardprick]. Man had a thriving career in one Tinseltown production after another, yet he possessed no glamour or excitement. He had the personality and drive of an old tortoise hunting for lettuce. —Welsh actor Rachel Roberts

ANTHONY PERKINS

People ask me if I stuff things, like birds or animals, because of *Psycho*. They're almost disappointed when I say no.... If you think I'm strange, one friend told me that Sarah Miles wears her late Skye terrier as boots! —Anthony Perkins

★

It was so long ago...I slapped my wife [actress Katherine DeMille, Cecil's daughter] on our wedding night [because] she wasn't a virgin. I was so disappointed. But it was a very long time ago.   —Anthony Quinn

I got this doll that was a replica of my mother [Tippi Hedren] that was in a coffin from Alfred Hitchcock for my birthday. Nice, huh? I think he was very strange. That's a strange thing to send to anyone, much less a five-year-old little girl. I never played with it. I just put it away.

—Melanie Griffith

Another reason for feeling blue was that on the evening of the 26th I broke off my capped tooth and swallowed it as the result of biting violently into a piece of saltwater taffy—due to my indignation at having to watch *The Farmer's Daughter* and reflect that Loretta Young got an Oscar for it.

—from Christopher Isherwood's diary

I believe Miss Raquel Welch got her good looks from her father. He is a plastic surgeon, isn't he?   —Groucho Marx

Women do pay a price. I played a bitch and was constantly called one during *Dynasty*. However I never played a bitch on the set....I understand that women like Brett Butler, on her series [*Grace Under Fire*], behave in a manner I wouldn't dream of doing....I think bad behavior is more apt to occur when a series is built around *one* star....We kept hearing that Burt Reynolds hurled chairs regularly on the set of *his* series [*Evening Shade*]. Yet *I'm* the one some people think of as a bitch to this day!

—Joan Collins

I turned down *Kramer vs. Kramer*. I thought it was middle-class bourgeois horseshit. Later I heard [Meryl] Streep rewrote the courtroom scene herself! Even if it's only half true, I wouldn't have put up with it. She was hired to act, not write...no chick's ever gonna rewrite any scene I'm in!

—James Caan

Warren's conquests of women are not totally unsuccessful. His percentage is about 50-50.   —Lee Grant, on Warren Beatty

...a famous poet and a pansy.
>—Simone De Beauvoir (who was bisexual), on Jean Cocteau, who was gay

An inveterate liar who lived in a fantasy world.
>—ex-model Kelly LeBrock, on ex-husband Steven Seagal

What's Mick Jagger's girlfriend's name? I...did four parts [a four-part interview] with her. *You* try that sometime. It's like talking to a window.
>—Bryant Gumbel, on Jerry Hall

I won't use her. We have a no-assholes clause.
>—designer Todd Oldham, on supermodel Naomi Campbell

Don't just listen to me. Ask around. Jodie Foster is very, very, very bossy. And then some.
>—Robert Downey Jr.

Margot Kidder's acting daffy now. She couldn't handle it [fame] too good [*sic*]. Now she can't get a good grip when it's sort of over and done with.
>—Richard Pryor

Frankly, who in Hollywood hasn't made love with him? Not having sex with Warren Beatty is like going to Rome and not seeing the pope.
>—Sonia Braga

The Antichrist.   —Hart Bochner's nickname for ex-girlfriend Sharon Stone

An old man who loves to live vicariously through young people and suck up all their life because he has none of his own.
>—supermodel Stephanie Seymour describing ex-beau Warren Beatty

You're boring, stupid, and I don't have any fun with you. Goodbye.
>—Nicollette Sheridan's farewell note to Harry Hamlin

Smoking is not only not good for you, it's catastrophic for an actor. Wrinkles galore....A good example is Maggie Smith, a chain smoker. She used to have an excellent skin. Have you seen her face lately? In a few more years, they'll have to unfold it to find out who she used to be.
>—Jeremy Brett

SANDY DENNIS

Some actors are despicable people. We've all met and had to endure working with them.... One actor I would never work with is Jan-Michael Vincent. Apart from the usual vices and overindulgences, he's violent—to women and animals. One of his ex-wives or ex-girlfriends said he stomped her pet kitten to death. That's inexcusable.   —Sandy Dennis

Now it's Tim Allen all over the place—TV, a movie, a book. But I remember when if you had spent time in jail, or lots of time as he did, you kept very silent about it. These days, actors brag about their arrests and misdemeanors. Before, if you had a prison record like Tim Allen's, you never got the chance to become a star, never mind being a role model or hero.
                                                              —Art Carney

★

Richard Simmons has a personal license plate that says Y R U FATT. Look who's talking! Why doesn't he ask *himself* that?   —Roseanne

She's got this gold tooth in her mouth and all this shit around her eyes. She looked like Beetlejuice or something.

> —"Marky Mark" Wahlberg, on Madonna

★

I have seen her on many occasions, and she is quite simply in need of a shower or bath.

> —Donald Trump, on Daryl Hannah

★

Rosie Perez? I don't think I could spend eight or ten weeks on a movie set with her. Her voice would drive me back to heroin.

> —Charlie Sheen

★

Burt Lancaster got worse as he got older. The charm turned to hardness, and he began to drink in the late afternoon. Everyone would say if you worked with him at night he would be a terror, drunk and mean...and he became more and more suspicious.

> —Claudia Cardinale

★

Mel Gibson has to be the center of attention, otherwise he gets very unhappy and leaves. And it seems like he hates it if a woman is getting any attention when he's there.

> —Janeane Garofalo

★

Look what happened to Christopher Reeve....Do I believe [TV Superman] George Reeves was murdered [instead of the contested suicide verdict]? I don't know....But a curse of Superman? Yeah, sort of. Look at me....Just kidding.

> —Margot Kidder, ex–Lois Lane

★

What a hypocrite, Jodie Foster...a self-appointed anti-drugs spokesperson, and then she gets arrested with drugs in her luggage at the airport. I'm no hypocrite; I never said *I* was anti-drugs.

> —Anthony Perkins, also arrested for drugs

★

I think he was called Poison [Sean] Penn before Madonna married him. She knew what she was getting into, though a lot of people want to feel sorry for her. But after he allegedly tied her to the chair and did all those things to her, and then the police report, it was over. She'd finally had enough of him.

> —Sandra Bernhard

★

Man, I'll never forget that punch. It was when I fought with [wife] Robin [Givens]....She really offended me, and I went *bam,* and she flew

backward, hitting every fucking wall in the apartment. That was the best punch I've ever thrown in my fucking life.   —Mike Tyson
★
James Woods thinks he's the world's best actor and the smartest man since Einstein. When he's wrong, he's wrong all around.   —Sean Young
★
I hate hearing that I was in love with Brad Pitt! That's so embarrassing.
—Juliette Lewis
★
Tom Arnold's penis is three inches long. Okay, I'll say four, 'cause we're trying to settle.   —Roseanne
★
Even a 747 looks small when it lands in the Grand Canyon.
—Tom Arnold
★
I'm not upset about my divorce. I'm only upset I'm not a widow.
—Roseanne
★
When I call my ex-husband [Lex "Tarzan" Barker] anal, people think I'm being intellectual or Freudian. But merely I'm using a polite word for what he really is, deep down....   —Lana Turner
★
I scarcely knew [Clark] Gable, hardly worked with him, though I was in the last picture he made [*The Misfits*], as was Marilyn Monroe....I think Gable was anal-retentive...and not a profound man, nor a free spirit... suspicious, a worry-wart. One asked how he was; he had to ponder before replying—and in a *non*committal way....I felt even his mustache was clenched. He worried about people respecting him, about people's opinion of him...and I think he worried himself into an early grave.
—Estelle Winwood, on Gable (1901–60)
★
I was advised by my agent not to discuss the fact that I was Jewish.
—Lesley Ann Warren, re making her film bow for Walt Disney
★
I've been on every show...I think the girl talk show hosts have improved a lot, there's more substance....I'm less keen on Kathie Lee, in fact I'm underwhelmed by her...she gushes endlessly, she tends toward shallowness in a shallow field...and her fetish about her husband, her

kid....It's like the gal who says how much her husband loves her, [until] you have to remind her that a real Frenchman loves his bidet too.

—George Peppard

★

When Hitler's favorite director, Leni Riefenstahl, came to Hollywood during the Nazi era, every studio head refused to welcome her, including the Gentile Darryl F. Zanuck [of Fox], but not including the Gentile but very right-wing Walt Disney, who treated her most warmly.

—Gale Sondergaard

★

[Walt] Disney hated Democrats, he hated Jews, he hated unions, he hated sharing credit for his animators' creations....It's unusual that someone so successful was so full of bitterness and animosity. Most of the movies' cranks and arch-conservatives are people who didn't make it or who made it late. —Elsa Lanchester (*Mary Poppins*)

★

Kathie Lee Gifford just discovered what the whole country knows—that there is no Tuesday night football. —Norm Crosby

★

I gave her her first break. My sister got her first movie because I was right in the middle of it.... There's more competition as an actor, and she's pretty, so her career skyrocketed...you notice she hasn't asked me to be in any of her movies. Not that I'd necessarily accept, but she could ask.

—Eric Roberts, Julia's elder brother

★

I don't know if Warren Beatty resented that when he came out to Hollywood from Virginia, his older sister [Shirley MacLaine] was already a star yet she didn't go out of her way to push him along. There's no reason for real resentment between a brother and sister—they don't compete for roles. It can be different for two brothers or two sisters....

—Natalie Wood, whose younger sister Lana was also an actress

★

It became Barbra Streisand's *Yentl*....She should never have opened her mouth to sing in this picture. —Isaac Bashevis Singer, author of *Yentl*

★

I'm a New Yorker at heart...I'm also a singer—I have recorded, though only [record producer] Ben Bagley knows that....Like most New Yorkers, I love Barbra Streisand. Two things about her I don't like: her taste in clothes and her taste in men. I am glad she recovered her taste in hairstyle after she dumped the stud hairdresser—or he dumped her, whichever... her taste in studs seems close to masochism.

—William Hickey

★

Start with the finale, and go up from there!

—Carol Channing's advice to Tommy Tune on playing Las Vegas

★

Ellen DeGeneres and Anne Heche are talking about having a baby. They're worried, though, because if the baby is anything like Ellen, it's going to take much longer than nine months to come out. —Conan O'Brien

★

Brad [Pitt] is a good friend of ours, but he did *not* donate the sperm for our baby. —Melissa Etheridge, on her and Julie Cypher's child

★

I think Brad [Pitt]'s a good friend and he's awfully cute, but I think he's afraid of commitment.

—Juliette Lewis, after Pitt and Gwyneth Paltrow split up

★

Brad Pitt is handsome but not that talented. And he admits he goes through four cartons of cigarettes a week. Need I say less?

—Helena Bonham Carter

★

Many a successful actor has come from a deprived background. That used to give Americans incentive; nowadays it seems to give them an excuse for...self-indulgence and shifting blame. Look at so many, from O. J. Simpson to Robert Downey [Jr.] and Christian Slater...and it's shocking when women behave like hooligans. We've gone from New Age to new rage in the '90s. Of course, you always had the Raquels [Welch] and [Faye] Dunaways throwing combs or mirrors or hitting people and yet avoiding lawsuits, but Shannen Doherty's assorted behaviors and misdeeds seem to have hit a new low...the news that she's taking anger-control therapy isn't cause for congratulations; it's a sign of young people's increasing irresponsibility—it's unwillingness to be responsible for one's own emotions and actions.

All these actors and athletes solicit our pity or want an excuse when they explain or intimate that they're depraved because they were deprived.

—Jim Kepner, Hollywood archivist and historian

Hedda Hopper was a mental defective. She wore corrective hats.

—Stewart Granger

★

You'd retouch until you couldn't put any more lead on the emulsion. My God, she wanted her face ironed out.

—George Hurrell, Hollywood photographer, on Rosalind Russell

★

Errol Flynn is priapic! Don't ask me to explain....The man never stops! They should tell the birds and the bees about *him*.   —Anita Louise

★

Errol Flynn could have had any number of epitaphs, most of them rude. Let's just say that an apt one would be: He sleeps alone at last.

—Sheilah Graham

★

If Woody Allen ever married Soon-Yi [Previn], Mia Farrow would be his mother-in-law!   —columnist Cindy Adams

★

Americans *are* more puritanical....When Gloria Grahame, known as The Girl with the Novocained Lip, and an Oscar winner, married the son of a former husband of hers, it ended her film career. She was away from the screen for most of the '60s. It made her ex-husband her new father-in-law...in no way was it incestuous....The press portrayed it as incest, and the studios—anticipating possible audience reaction, I say *possible*—quit hiring her. A puritanical, hypocritical waste!   —columnist Arthur Bell

★

She had perfect posture, but it was rather intimidating. She looked as if she'd swallowed a yardstick.   —Glenn Ford, on Joan Crawford

★

I was in Joan Crawford's last two pictures...made in England. She was still a star here; she still commanded respect and leading roles. Miss Crawford was every inch a star, yet despite the dozens and dozens of motion pictures she'd headlined, she still retained a vulnerability [and] a desire to please.... In this country, we don't have, or at least didn't used to have [in the late 1960s], the tendency to make jokes of older women or relegate them to the dustbin once they pass fifty.

—British actor Michael Gough (the butler in the *Batman* films)

No matter how much housewives want to believe in them, novels are fiction....Robert Waller became a multimillionaire from *The Bridges of Madison County,* about a middle-aged marriage that outlasts passion and temptation. He wrote it so convincingly, he moved so many housewives... [but] now he's divorced from his wife of thirty-five years and is living with a woman who's twenty-three years younger than his ex-wife.

—actress–turned–literary agent Connie Clausen

Man, you gotta see Lily Tomlin as a horny straight housewife to disbelieve it!   —Sammy Davis Jr., on *Moment by Moment,* directed by

Tomlin's life partner Jane Wagner

I never wanted to put down my thoughts, dreams, and whatnot on paper and make dough out of them, book after book....

—Frank Sinatra, discussing former friend Shirley MacLaine

My father is too extreme to live with. He treats most everyone badly. If you stick with him, it only reflects on your own psychological problem.

—Nastassja Kinski, on her estranged father, actor Klaus Kinski

The answer is still no. I have no reason to change it.

—Rebecca De Mornay, still estranged from her father, Wally George, an ultra-right-wing "shock TV" host

I think Marv Albert should make a New Year's resolution to shop at Victoria's Secret for other people too.   —Rita Rudner

There is no denying [Helen] Hunt's talent on screen, but I wish she were more tolerant off screen. Hunt is one of those who [do] not suffer fools well, which makes her particularly ill suited to participate in press junkets. Colleagues tell me that Helen was not in the best of moods as she faced likely silly question after silly question [which] is par for the course. If there is an Oscar campaign in Helen's future, she is simply going to have to learn to better play along.   —columnist Sam Rubin

I don't blame Christina Crawford at all. Just because someone is your parent, biological or adopted, they're not sacred or immune to criticism if it's earned....A parent can't just treat a kid any old way and abuse

you...and if there is abuse, you have the right to report it. Even an obligation, if it helps stop it for other kids too....I haven't written a book, but [brother] Gary has [*Going My Own Way*]. I just carry my bad memories of my father around with me—I don't dwell on them, I did *not* create them, but they are there.
—Dennis Crosby, one of two sons of Bing's first four who committed suicide

I've been badgering him for more than a year to marry me. My heart leaped with joy when he agreed—but sank when he listed all the conditions.
—Soon-Yi Previn, on the eve of her marriage to Woody Allen [the conditions, according to *Time Out* magazine, included that she dwell in her own home, visit Allen just twice a week, sign away all rights to his money, and not speak to her mother, Mia Farrow, without the director's permission)

Just ignore what I'm placing between you. She's very beautiful. Very stupid. She's just arrived from England, so Jack will want to have first crack at it.
—Gore Vidal, reportedly quoting Jackie Kennedy as she seated him near JFK at a White House dinner

★

Jack [Nicholson] was so angry when I let it be known that our son was ours [conceived while the parents made *Five Easy Pieces*, 1970]...but we're on good terms now.
—Susan Anspach, who made the revelation in the mid-1990s

★

The more she talks, the more you begin to respect [Greta] Garbo. When she had nothing more to say, she got the hell out of town. But [Marlene] Dietrich plunged on, sewing herself into tortuous gowns and singing the same old songs....Now she's bored, humorless, and cranky.   —Rex Reed

★

It's amusing but gratifying to watch the old Hollywood films where the actresses try to sound as English as they can. They were rigorously coached for vowel sounds....From my *aural* point of view, it was more pleasing than listening now to English actresses like Angela Lansbury or Kate Nelligan, and sometimes even Julie Andrews, trying to sound American. Or mid-Atlantic—a nonexistent entity. It's somewhat depressing, because now the motivation is either monetary or fitting in with the majority.
—Donald Pleasence

[Greta Garbo] turned one day to the director and she said, "Is it necessary for that man to be here?" It was the cameraman! She didn't even recognize him—it was just a man standing there, looking at her.

—director Henry Hathaway

★

I told [Mae West] she was one of the three greatest talents ever to come out of the movies, the other two being W. C. Fields and Chaplin. She said, "Mmmn, well, I don't know about Fields."   —Tennessee Williams

★

You could say it's been the year of the blonde on television this year [1997]. The two biggest TV events were the death of Diana and the rebirth of Ellen [DeGeneres].   —Harold Robbins

★

They are trying to show he's a great lover, but they'll never prove it to me.

—Zsa Zsa Gabor, on Cary Grant

★

When I'm feeling lousy or jaded, I try and get in touch with my inner child star. Then I feel even more jaded and depressed, so I stop thinking of Lassie and all the late child stars I knew, and I come back to my previous mood and I feel lots better!

—Tommy Rettig (*Lassie*)

★

She is a sheep in sheep's clothing, and I don't mean wool!

—Peter Allen, on Olivia Newton-John

★

How's this for a rumor? You can't confirm anything; Stanley Kubrick's keeping a completely closed set [on *Eyes Wide Shut*]. But it's been reported that Kubrick has hired a sex therapist to counsel Tom Cruise and Nicole [Kidman] on enacting the relationship between their characters, who are married....   —Jim Kepner

★

It's that old showbiz thing: an actor and an actress who join up, sincerely or not, get more than double the publicity together they could ever get solo....An example was [Alfred] Lunt and [Lynn] Fontanne. Neither was even close to movie star material. Neither a flaming talent...but together, as a husband–wife team, they were a Broadway box office attraction for a very long time. People wondered why they never had or even adopted a child, but they loved that Lunt never looked at another woman and

Fontanne never looked at another man. People were naïve—they didn't guess. —Broderick Crawford (*Born Yesterday*)

★

Hal Wallis the producer told me that [playwright] Lillian Hellman had invited him to the opening night of her latest play. She would send two tickets for him. "Bring a friend," she added. "If you have one." Hal said he couldn't make it that night. Instead he requested tickets for the second night, and added, "If there is one." —Paul Henreid

★

Kids today are out of control. E.T. told Drew Barrymore at the end of the movie to be a good girl. Boy, is he going to be surprised when he comes back! —Bill Maher

★

My crush on [Tom Cruise] has nothing to do with anything that is adult. It's a pre-pubescent girl's desire to have his picture thumbtacked to my bedroom wall. It doesn't have to do with a thirty-five-year-old woman's adult desire. —Rosie O'Donnell, partly explaining her desire

★

Elvis rented an entire cinema for us, for our first date. The movie was *Goodbye, Columbus*...and we dated for about a month. He was sweet...he was vulnerable, and very sexy. He was sensual, and I liked that his face was soft and even feminine, with his full lips. I found him terribly attractive...but there were the, uh, bodyguards and hangers-on, also the drugs. So that helped end it. —Memphis belle Cybill Shepherd

★

One of the media's worst failings is the time and buildup it gives to people who do wrong. And then patting them on the back for not doing it anymore....Carol Burnett had three daughters. One of them became a drug addict, and it was hell for her parents. And that is the one whose name became known, who got so much coverage, who went on talk shows, then got a chance at an acting career...and meantime the two other daughters, who either didn't do drugs or didn't become addicts, well, who's ever heard of them? There's something wrong with such a system, with only rewarding the ones who get out of line to begin with. —Cleavon Little

★

Robert Downey Jr. is doing interviews saying he's insured for his next film even if he's found to be on drugs. And that his smoking heroin during *Home for the Holidays* was why he feels it's such a "wonderfully relaxed

performance." How could [*Home* director] Jodie Foster not have known? If she didn't, how irresponsible. If she did, how even *more* irresponsible! Downey's a loser, but you expect optimum working conditions from Ms. Foster.
                                                              —director Samuel Fuller

★

I'm not sure these guys deserve to be movie stars.... Robert [Downey Jr.]'s record with drugs is frightening, and now Christian [Slater]...the violent behavior and the drugs and alcohol....It's a very worrisome trend that substance abuse and violent behavior—particularly against wives and girlfriends—seem to go together, increasingly so.   —Dawn Steel

★

[Ronald Reagan] is really the only man I've ever known who loved dancing.
                                                                    —Doris Day

★

Hugh [Grant] was very gracious, in his behavior and apology [after the incident with the hooker on Sunset Boulevard]....Marv Albert hasn't really apologized for assaulting a woman. He just keeps defending himself! Using *other* words for justification....Nobody really cares if he's attracted to women's clothes or underwear or the people in them, but it's repulsive how easily woman battering is swept under the carpet....Albert even defended his toupee, by calling it a "weave." We already knew that toupees and wigs are woven! And *so?*   —Dawn Steel

★

Epilogue

Th...Th...Th...That's all, folks!   —Porky Pig

★

Index